Missing
Believed Killed

For those who never came back
and all those who went to
look for them

Missing
Believed Killed

The Royal Air Force and the
Search for Missing Aircrew 1939–1952

Stuart Hadaway

Pen & Sword
AVIATION

First Published in Great Britain in 2008 by
Pen & Sword Aviation
an imprint of
Pen & Sword Books Ltd
47 Church Street, Barnsley, South Yorkshire S70 2AS

ISBN 978-1-84415-734-1

A CIP catalogue record for this book is
available from the British Library.

Typeset in 10/12pt Palatino by
Concept, Huddersfield

Printed and bound in England by
Biddles Ltd

Pen & Sword Books Ltd incorporates the Imprints of Pen & Sword Aviation,
Pen & Sword Maritime, Pen & Sword Military, Wharncliffe Local History,
Pen & Sword Select, Pen & Sword Military Classics and Leo Cooper.

For a complete list of Pen & Sword titles please contact
PEN & SWORD BOOKS LIMITED
47 Church Street, Barnsley, South Yorkshire, S70 2AS, England
E-mail: enquiries@pen-and-sword.co.uk
Website: www.pen-and-sword.co.uk

Contents

Acknowledgements

This book has not been the easiest to write, and there are many people without whom it simply would not have been possible. My father, David Hadaway, to whom this book is most respectfully dedicated, has been tireless in providing encouragement, information and advice at every turn. Kathleen Navarro de Paz has been a constant supporter and sounding board. David 'Bulldog' Buttery, one of the best historians I know, who's endless advice and support has been invaluable, and Peter Devitt has aided me more than I can say.

Dr Lories Charlesworth provided encouragement and ideas beyond measure. Linzee Druce was instrumental in providing the leads needed to get this project off the ground. Ellen Soall provided moral support and proof reading. Doug Radcliffe of the Bomber Command Association-helped to trace so many veterans. The staff of the Air Historical Branch, especially Clive Richards and Graham Day, who provided some quite extraordinary sources. Matt Poole, who opened up the Far East for me, and Peter Hart of the Imperial War Museum for his help.

A special thanks must go to all of the staff of the RAF Museum, especially Peter Elliott, Nina Burls, Gordon Leith, Guy Revell, Daniel Scott-Davies and Ian Thirsk for all their practical and moral support and leads.

None of this would have been possible without all the veterans who have so very kindly allowed me access to their memories and papers of their most astonishing work:

Mrs Ann-Marie Archer
LACW Iris Catlin
Cpl Douglas Hague
Sgt David Harrap
WO James Kingham
Sqdn Ldr Bill Lott
Wg Cdr Bernard Moorcroft
Flt Lt Ronald Myhill
Wg Cdr Ray Sheppard
LACW Lillian Taylor
Sqdn Ldr Tommy Thompson

Flt Lt Roger St Vincent
Flt Lt Harry Wilson
And the MRES [Missing, Research and Enquiry Service] officer who asked
to remain anonymous.

A further thank you must go to the various families who facilitated my
contacts, most especially John Archer, who went 'above and beyond' to
provide access to the collection of his extraordinary father.

Introduction

MRES was the greatest detective job in the world.

Cpl Douglas Hague[1]

Investigation Report

From: No. 3 M.R.E.U., B.A.F.O.

To: Air Ministry, P.4 (Cas), 73/77 Oxford Street, London.

Copy to:

Date: 28 January 1947 **Investigation Officer:** F/Lt. J.L.N. Canham
Section: 17

A.M. File Reference: P.431826/45   **A.M. Cas. Enquiry No:** G 126

Unit Reference: **Section Reference:** 17MRES/G126

Aircraft type & number: Halifax MZ467

                              Date & Time: 16/17 April 1945

Position of crash: In woods near Ahlingen **Map Reference:** T2402

Crew: **Particulars of burial:**

AUS 426118 F/O Lodder   As under in report
       161430 F/S Naylor
      1601854 F/S Windus
AUS 434183 F/S Foster
      1694825 Sgt Casterton
      1572467 Sgt McGarvie
      1595698 Sgt Gray
AUS 432388 F/S Tisdell

Cemetery & Map Reference: Ehingen T2504 Westendorf T2801

Articles found: Nil

Any further action: Identification of those buried and registration of graves.

* * *

Flying Officer Lodder's crew were both statistically normal and very unusual. Firstly, as can be seen below, Lodder himself escaped, whereas pilots were more likely than most crew members to be killed. They were also from a specialised unit, 462 Squadron, flying what was known as Bomber Support operations. These were a mix of what would today be called electronic counter measures (Flight Sergeant Tisdell was the specialist equipment operator) and simple diversions. The main Bomber Command effort that night was over 200 Lancasters of No. 5 Group against Pilsen and over 160 Lancasters from Nos 6 and 8 Groups against Schwandorf. Both were against marshalling yards. Germany was on her knees in April 1945, but still had formidable forces and all that was possible was being done to damage communication and supply lines. Lodder and his crew were among the small mixed force of bombers that roamed over the rest of Germany, bombing aerodromes and dropping target markers to spread confusion and thin out German defences. In this they were successful; only one Lancaster was lost between the two main raids.

On the other hand, the five men from Lodder's crew who were killed were statistically very common. They joined the list of over 70,000 RAF aircrew who had been killed in the last six years. Of these 57,000 were from Bomber Command alone, and more than two thirds of them had no known fate.[2] Around the world, 41,881 men and women had simply disappeared and were listed as missing, believed killed.

* * *

Result of investigation and findings:

Information received from Burgomeister's office in Eningen (T 2504), via the American Graves Registration Unit (GRU), stated that two or three Australian fliers were buried in the cemetery there. A letter from the Rural Police, forwarded also, stated that the dead men were found in a wood thicket near Ehingen on 28th October 1945 and were presumed to be from a crash at Ortelfingen (T 2503), the dead being one body and the remains of another one.

A covering letter from American GRU lists two unknown Australians saying that these had been disinterred and, on being identified as Australians, had been reburied in the same place.

* * *

From the deserts of North Africa, over the mountains of Italy and the Balkans to the forests of Germany; through Dutch marshes to the frozen wastes of Norway; tens of thousands of RAF personnel still lay in their aircraft, or buried in hurried and poorly marked graves. Each missing aircraft had been logged by the Air Ministry, and a file started. Identifying marks and serial numbers were recorded along with operational details of the circumstances of the loss, and to this was added information gleaned from survivors, intelligence sources and the German authorities themselves. Every possible effort had been made to account for these losses during hostilities, and keep the next of kin fully informed of their fate. Armed only with flimsy evidence, in December 1944 the RAF and Air Ministry formed the Missing Research and Enquiry Service (MRES) and sent them to Europe to find their missing people and lay them to rest.

* * *

Ortelfingen was visited and the actual crash location determined. The aircraft crashed in the woods at Ahlingen (T 2503).

Parts of the aircraft were found at Ahlingen, two engine numbers being found and sufficient other parts to identify the aircraft as a Halifax.

A signal was sent to you, by us, on 15th January 1947 requesting the engine numbers of this Casualty Enquiry. Your reply proved this crash to be coincidental with this Cas. Enq.

A visit to the head town of the Landkreis, Vertingen (Y 1790), revealed that [in] fact two more English fliers were buried at Westendorf (T 2801). Visiting this latter town it was established that these two had come from the same crash at Ahlingen. No details could be obtained regarding the description of these two, rank, trade, etc.

From your Cas. Enq. F/O Lodder, F/S Naylor and Sgt Casterton are safe. The two other Australians would appear to be buried at Ehingen. Of the other three, two would appear to be buried at Westendorf.

The eighth man is possibly buried at Ehingen as one report from that village states 'two or three'. On the other hand the Americans, who have exhumed these men, report only two. However, in the near future, [Graves Concentration Units] will be here to concentrate these bodies and when this is done a check will be made to see if the eighth man is at Ehingen. If he is not found to be there a further search will be made.

During this concentration a check will be made to establish the identities of those buried.

* * *

Evidence on the spot was usually inadequate. Aircraft crashes, particularly with heavy fuel or bomb loads, leave little in the way of coherent wreckage. The German authorities lacked the expertise and, increasingly as the war went on, the will to clear crash sites properly. Wreckage could be cleared for recycling or left in situ. Bodies, which would have suffered severe trauma, were sometimes buried with honours, sometimes buried in haste by the crash site, and sometimes simply left in the wreck. Little effort was made to identify or even separate the bodies found.

* * *

Investigation Report

From: No. 3 M.R.E.U., B.A.F.O.

To: Air Ministry, P.4 (Cas), 73/77 Oxford Street, London.

Copy to:

Date: 4 February 1947 **Investigation Officer:** F/Lt. J.L.N. Canham **Section:** 17

A.M. File Reference: P.431026/45   **A.M. Cas. Enquiry No:** G 126

Unit Reference: **Section Reference:** 17MRES/G126

Aircraft type & number: Halifax MZ467

Date & Time: 16/17 April 1945

Position of crash: In woods near Ahlingen **Map Reference:** T2402

Crew:	**Particulars of burial:**
AUS 426118 F/O Lodder	Safe UK
161430 F/S Naylor	Safe UK
1601854F/S Windus	Westendorf
AUS 434183 F/S Foster	Ehingen
1694825 Sgt Casterton	Safe UK
1572467 Sgt McGarvie	Westendorf
1595698 Sgt Gray	Westendorf
AUS 432388 F/S Tisdell	Ehingen

Cemetery & Map Reference: Ehingen T2504 Westendorf T2801

Articles found: Signet ring enclosed as 'appendix' to exhumation report.

Any further action: Identification of dead and registration of graves.

* * *

For five years teams of the Missing Research and Enquiry Service, led almost entirely by ex-aircrew officers, scoured Europe, the Middle East and the Far East. Crash sites and graves needed to be found, and then identified. With the minimum of training or guidelines, search officers would enlist the help of the army to exhume the bodies of their erstwhile comrades. Pathology was in its infancy, and DNA undreamed of, and sometimes several exhumations would be needed as slender clues were sought which may lead to the identification of bodies which had suffered severe trauma and remained buried for up to ten years.

* * *

Result of investigation and findings:

Further to our report on this Cas. Enq. dated 28 January 1947:

The graves of the five missing members of this crew have now been exhumed by No. 85 GRU. The results of the findings were:

At Westendorf were found two coffins. One of these contained one nearly complete body and the remains of a second one. There were definitely two bodies. The other coffin contained one complete body. On a hand on the nearly complete body in the first coffin was found a ring on which were engraved the initials 'RM.'

At Ehingen the remains found amounted to only a small pile of fragments of clothing and a few bones. These came up in the earth that was thrown up whilst digging. The disintegration being probably due to the previous examination carried out by the American Graves Unit.

The grave-digger at Ehingen stated that when he buried these remains he buried two sacks but he did not know what they contained. The Americans, on exhuming these bodies, found identification to prove the dead to be Australians.

The complete body found at Westendorf was a Sgt so with the findings of the exhumation the fate of the crew would be as follows:

F/O Lodder, F/Sgt Naylor and Sgt Casterton safe U.K. The two remaining Australians, F/Sgts Foster and Tisdell buried at Ehingen. At Westendorf are buried the other three. Sgt McGarvie who was identified by his ring. The Sgt, being the only one not accounted for must be Sgt Gray and the last remaining crew member being the remains in the same coffin as McGarvie must be F/Sgt Windus.

These findings would appear to be definite and it is suggested that when final concentration takes place F/Sgts Foster and Tisdell be buried under a joint cross, the others being buried under their names.

* * *

One member of the Missing Research and Enquiry Service would describe their task as 'the greatest detective job in the world'. Most search officers were volunteers. After six years of war, all had good reasons to go home. Every case solved carried a physical and a mental cost. Every case solved laid a ghost to rest for a family back home.

CHAPTER ONE

A Corner of a Foreign Field

With proud thanksgiving, a mother for her children,
England mourns for her dead across the sea.
Flesh of her flesh they were, spirit of her spirit,
Fallen in the cause of the free.

Lawrence Binyon 'For the fallen'

Homer tells us that after Achilles killed Hector of Troy, he added insult to injury by dragging his body around the city walls from his chariot. This was not the way dead heroes were supposed to be treated, and caused as much despair in Troy as his death had done. Hector's father, King Priam, felt so strongly that he even entered the enemy camp incognito twelve days later in a successful attempt to secure the return of his son's body so that suitable honour could be shown to it.

What Homer does not tell us is what happened to the other hundreds of dead warriors, who were probably either flung into a pit, or left for the birds and animals. For millennia that was the accepted conclusion of the soldier's 'hard bargain' – an unmarked mass grave. By the eighteenth century technology, warfare and society had advanced enough to see the burial and memorialisation of soldiers, almost invariably officers, by those families who could afford it. Generally this would be in the place they had fallen, but occasionally bodies, or parts of them, were returned to their own countries. In the early nineteenth century, Britain would bring the body of Horatio Nelson home in a vat of brandy for a hero's funeral, and France would bring Napoleon's heart back from St Helena. For the majority, the enlisted men and non-commissioned officers, fate still held only the nameless corner of a foreign field. Soldiers were regarded, as the Duke of Wellington so succinctly put it, as 'the scum of the earth', and in his army as well as most others, an announcement on the Parish notice board at home was the best eulogy they could expect.

By the 1850s, in Britain at least, this began to change. A religious resurgence in the country led to widespread reformation of the way the

1

dead were treated. Graveyards had until then been almost temporary resting places, with graves being reused again and again as space ran out. Now new cemeteries were being laid out on the edges of towns to accommodate permanent graves, but even these were still subject to grave robbers and body snatchers. Criminals would still often have their bodies used for instruction at medical schools, and have their bones displayed for future doctors to study. Plots and headstones were expensive, and as often as not the dead would receive little or nothing in the way of identifying marks on their graves. But, things were changing.

As early as the Sikh Wars (1845–46 and 1848–49) regimental monuments such as that in Christchurch Cathedral, Canterbury, for the 9th Lancers, began to list in stone the names of all the dead. By the Crimea, individual soldiers faced the possibility of a separate and named, albeit temporary, grave. In Britain the armed forces were slowly being afforded more respect and dignity within society, although this process would take another half a century to make much headway, and battlefield conditions also came into play. Unusually for a British campaign, in the Crimea the army remained essentially static for several years. Without the need to break camp and march on in pursuit or retreat, more care could be taken over burials. Still, though, there was no permanence. A cross may be placed over the grave, but no-one would be entrusted to care for the grave, or replace the marker when it rotted.

The South African War, 1899–1902, would be the first to see any systematic care for British Army dead. The government provided each casualty a metal grave marker, and with the colonial authorities on hand after the war more care of the graves was taken. The impetus for this can be seen clearly in changes in society. Across Europe and America the late Victorian period saw a growth in individualism. With greater literacy rates, wider suffrage and a growing middle class came a society where the individual wielded greater power and received greater recognition than ever before. The South African campaign saw the recruitment and deployment of a largely civilian army by Britain for the first time since the English Civil War, two and a half centuries before. Men joined the army on a wave of patriotism just to fight the Boers, and with the regular army hard stretched, thousands of men from what would become the Territorial Army – the Militia, Volunteers and Yeomanry – volunteered and were sent to fight. For the first time the British Army had both a large middle class contingent and roots in the wider society, with a huge number of enlisted men who were essentially civilians in uniform. They, and their families, still thought in civilian terms, and were reluctant to accept the traditional approaches of the regular army.

Similar movements had already happened abroad. During the American Civil War (1861–64) directives had been issued for the separate burial of all fallen soldiers, whether their identities were known or not. Most often this would occur on the field of battle, but there was also a booming business in travelling embalmers and coffin-makers with the field armies. For a fee, a soldier could arrange in advance for his body to receive proper treatment and a coffin, and be shipped back to his home-town and family. After the war permanent cemeteries were laid out and maintained for the dead from both sides. A similar arrangement occurred after the Franco-Prussian War (1870–71). The subsequent Treaty of Frankfurt included stipulations regarding the burial of the dead, and the proper care of those graves that were on enemy soil.

These were wars held in relatively settled and populated areas. Frontier wars were still understood to be subject to different standards and conditions. After the loss of 268 men of the 7th Cavalry at the Little Big Horn in 1876, it would take the United States Army almost exactly a year to send an expedition to clear up the battle site. This was despite the area having been cleared of 'hostile' tribes and forts established along the valley. Eventually it was pronounced pressure from the public and the families of the dead that stirred the authorities into sending a party to conduct a sweep of the field, collecting the remains of most of the officers for shipment home, and burying the remains of the other ranks. Even then, the job was hurriedly done and a year later most of the graves had washed away to leave the bones open to the elements again. A second expedition was mounted the next year to rebury the dead.

This pattern repeated itself almost every year until 1881 when the first mass grave was dug and properly lined against the elements. Even so, remains are still being discovered today. What perhaps makes this, and the treatment of the dead in so many other colonial campaigns, ironic is that the enemy was one who was often demonised and dehumanised based upon their behaviour towards their enemy's dead. The Zulus, for example, were vilified for their practice, meant as a sign of respect, of cutting open their enemy's stomachs. This let the warrior's spirit leave the body and proceed to paradise. The British found this horrifying when they came to clear up the field of their defeat by the Zulu's at Isandhlwana (1879). However, as they tipped their own dead into mass graves, unidentified and marked only by white-washed boulders, they paid little or no heed to the occasional officer who wandered through the unburied Zulu dead collecting skulls or other bones to send back to Britain for anthropological study.

This trend is an interesting one. Throughout the late Victorian period it was a widespread phenomenon. While the British were decrying the likes of the Maori or the Ashanti (another tribe for whom mutilation was a sign of respect) for their treatment of the dead, they simultaneously gave little regard to their own soldiers, and packed off large quantities of the enemy's dead to Britain for evaluation and study. What this all proves, if nothing else, is that treatment of the dead in military circles had always been as subjective and erratic as that in the civilian world.

This all changed with the First World War. Social, religious and educational improvements by the beginning of the twentieth-century had changed people's expectations, and a new realisation of political power helped to enforce them. In Britain's mass, civilian field armies it became expected that relatives would be informed of a soldier's death and the circumstances. The British Army, though, had not expected a campaign on this scale or of this complexity, and in the early days of the war, in the chaotic retreats and scrambles for tactical advantages of 1914, much of this work was done by the Red Cross Mobile Unit, under Fabian Ware. Although primarily concerned with the treatment and evacuation of wounded, the Mobile Unit also logged graves and, through their connections via Geneva with the German Red Cross, traced missing men and prisoners.

From 1915 careful records and lists began to be kept, cross-referenced and utilised to send telegrams on their way to homes to break the news of the death or wounding of a loved one. Frequently, a letter from the commanding officer or friend would follow with more details. Even as battles raged, every effort would be made by Graves Registration Units (GRU) to recover and identify bodies, bury them, and then mark and record their location. One officer, from 3 Graves Registration Unit, explained their task in a letter to his young son:

> We go away to a place to look after the graves of the poor English soldiers who have been killed. We keep them ever so neat and presently we are going to sow some fresh seed around them. We have put up a cross at the head of each with the poor soldiers name on, so that when the Mummies come to see the graves they know which is their own soldier boy. There are lots of German soldiers buried near here too.[3]

In time these records would be handed over to Fabian Ware. His Red Cross Mobile Unit had, in 1915, been reconstituted as the Graves Registration Commission. In 1917 they became the Imperial War Graves Commission (IWGC). Under all of these guises, they oversaw the concentration and permanent marking and care of the graves of the fallen. Records of each casualty and the known details of their burial were kept, graves were marked where possible, and photographs of those graves sent to the families. It was decided, partly on symbolic grounds but also with a heavy consideration for practicality and cost, that fallen servicemen would be buried in the countries where they fell. For the most part the host nations donated the land needed, and suitable preparations were made.

This task took many years. Work on laying out proper cemeteries could not begin until after the war, and even then not until the battle-fields had been at least superficially cleared up and made safe. The Treaty of Versailles helped clarify the process, with Articles 221, 225 and 226 all dealing with the international exchange of information on casualties, missing persons and graves, the repatriation of bodies, and future burial sites. Contrary to the popular belief, none of these clauses dictated that German graves should be black to denote guilt for starting the war. Germany had even less resources than Britain for marking their dead, and tarred wooden crosses, black in appearance, were all that could be afforded. Throughout the inter-war period the IWGC carried on replacing their temporary crosses with permanent headstones, landscaping their cemeteries with flowers and arcades, and compiling lists and memorials to the missing, all the while receiving more bodies recovered from the old battle lines. Ironically, the Commission finally declared their initial tasks, notwithstanding the steady stream of newly discovered remains, finished in 1939.

In Britain, the scale of the loss was unimaginable. Virtually every family had lost someone. Everyone knew someone who had been killed. Only around forty towns, the so-called 'Thankful Villages'[4] had not lost a single resident. In this environment of death and loss, a culture of mass mourning and symbolism grew up. The simple, even naïve, air of unity and patriotism that had held the country together as they faced an unparalleled struggle and unimaginable horror was still in force. There was little room for individual mourning, and with most of the 908,371 British and Imperial dead being buried overseas (at this time over one third of them with no known grave), there was little chance for relatives to indulge in personal grief. Instead, symbols such as the Cenotaph, the Unknown Warrior and local war memorials became the focus of mourning across the country.

The Second World War brought another round of killed and missing servicemen across the world. For the British, this meant much the same routine of Graves Registration Units and IWGC burials. The Americans too adopted this approach, although with the extra consideration of allowing the families to choose whether they wished their relatives to lie in the country they had fallen, or to be brought home for burial. In the Far East neither side paid much attention to the proper burial and marking of their enemies graves; much the same could be said of the war on the Eastern Front, with the added complication that each side actively sought to destroy enemy cemeteries during their advances. In most other areas, though, the dead were respected and recorded as far as was practical.

The Air Ministry decided that simply leaving the recovery of remains to chance was not enough. Casualties were dealt with by P.4 (Cas) Branch of the Ministry, and by 1941 they were coming under public pressure to do more about the hundreds, perhaps thousands of RAF aircrew who were officially listed as 'missing'. Something was needed to bring them out of this limbo of uncertainty, and so the Missing Research Section (MRS) was set up to investigate just these cases. Despite their incredible work, by the end of the war in Europe nearly 42,000 aircrew were still missing without a trace and tens of thousands more had fates identified only by shaky evidence provided by the Germans, and an extended version of the MRS, the Missing Research and Enquiry Service (MRES) was established. A worldwide organisation, the MRES took the search to the battlefields, and systematically scoured millions of squares miles to account individually for and bury their list of missing men and women. Unlike anything that had gone before, they began with a list of every known missing person, and as they were found, they were ticked off.

But, why did the Air Ministry feel that these added measures were necessary? Public opinion was certainly an issue. The aftermath of the Great War had brought a social and political awakening to much of the country. The nation was more willing to question the powers that be, rather than just accept what they were told. P.4 (Cas) had an open door policy, and visitors could write or call, either on the telephone or in person, at any time. Questions could and were asked in Parliament, as well as to the Ministry in person, and increasingly relatives demanded answers.

There was also perhaps an added factor. Everyone in the senior echelons of the Air Ministry, be they politicians, civil servants, or serving officers, had been through the First World War. Most had held combat commands, and most had been decorated for bravery. Some had sons in the services. Air Marshal Sir Philip Babington MC AFC, Air Member for Personnel 1940–42, had commanded 49 Wing in 1918 as a 23 year old, and his son was killed in a Mosquito crash in 1942. Sir Arthur Street MC, Permanent Under Secretary of State for Air 1939–45, had been an infantry officer until wounded, and his son had been in Bomber Command until shot down. In 1944, he became one of the fifty British officers executed by the Gestapo after the Great Escape. Viscount Stansgate DSO, Secretary of State for Air in 1945, had been a combat pilot and now had two fighter pilot sons. The eldest was killed in a night fighter crash in 1944. Air Marshal Sir John Slessor DSO MC, Air Member for Personnel in 1945, had also been combat pilot and had been appointed straight from commanding Coastal Command. Air Chief Marshal Sir Arthur Tedder, Chief of the Air Staff 1946–49, had commanded squadrons on the Western Front and in Egypt during the Great War, and in 1921 had commanded No. 207 Squadron during the Chanak Incident, when war with Turkey appeared possible. His eldest son had been a Blenheim pilot, and was reported missing in August 1940. His body was only found and identified, by the MRES, in December 1945.

These men had seen the original war to end all wars from the sharp end, and many had all too close a personal experience of the second one. They had seen how their comrades had been treated during and after the First World War, and knew that nearly a thousand of them from the flying services on the Western Front alone were still missing, with no known graves, twenty years on. There is not enough documentary evidence to say for sure, but their experiences as soldiers and as parents must have had some effect on their actions.

The same enthusiasm permeated every level of the organisation. All officers in the MRES were theoretically volunteers. Their task involved long hours, often seven days a week, in arduous conditions. To close a case would involve the exhumation of bodies that had been extracted from wrecks and may have been buried, often several to a grave, anything up to ten years previously.

By December 1950, the Air Ministry was reporting that of the 41,881 personnel listed as missing in August 1945, 23,881 had been accounted for in known burials. Another 9,281 had been formally recorded as being lost at sea. This left just 8,719 personnel known as otherwise unaccounted for, and this total included around 800 who had been located in Burma, but on whom no clear information had arrived as yet.[5]

The operations of the MRS and MRES would, at least in the long term, set the trend for future generations. While the tail end of the MRES was still active, the Royal Australian Air Force was listing more of their personnel as missing in the air war over Korea. In the final days of December 1950, Squadron Leader E. W. New and Sergeant T. S. Henderson were sent from Australia to Pusan to trace two missing men from 77 Squadron RAAF[6]. Squadron Leader Graham Strout had been lost in his Mustang on 7 July 1950 near Mukho, and Pilot Officer William Harrop had been shot down on 3 September 1950 while escorting B-29 bombers on a raid over Taegu. New and Henderson headed in-country even as the Communist North Korean and Chinese troops swept south and retook Seoul. Despite the evident dangers, they visited the areas where the pilots had been lost to see the crash sites and interview the local population. On the 18 January 1951, both Strout and Harrop were buried with full military honours on the outskirts of Pusan in the presence of their fellow pilots.

Interestingly, another point is raised by New and Henderson's report. While the armies of the United Nations, and particularly the United States, made little effort to account for missing men (although in fairness their governments' fought for the rights of their prisoners of war despite the issue holding up peace negotiations for a full year), the bodies of the dead retained all of the symbolic importance they had gained in the last thirty years. Even as the Allies were being rolled seemingly inexorably back to the sea and it appeared that all was lost, both the British and American high commands were considering the future of the graves of their killed. New and Henderson record that the Americans were preparing to exhume their dead and take them back with them, so as to prevent them falling into enemy hands. The British were publicly stating that they would do no such thing; they intended to stay and protect them. The location and treatment of the dead had not lost any of its symbolism.

This could be a double-edged sword. Few acts in the round of counter-insurgency operations that accompanied Britain's withdrawal from her Empire caused as much distress, anger and frustration as the murders of two sergeants in the Intelligence Corps in Palestine in 1947. Sergeants Paice and Martin had been captured by the Palestinian Irgun group in mid-July 1947. Three weeks later the bodies of the two sergeants were found hanging near Nathanya. The areas around the bodies were checked for booby traps and mines, but as the first body was cut down an explosive device strapped to it exploded, severely wounding an officer. Even the local mayor, O. Ben Ami, was shocked by this act, stating that 'Of all the crimes which have been committed in Palestine, this is the most dastardly, and most abominable, and will sully our struggle for the liberation of our people.'[7] No strangers to provocation and terrorism, the British Army found this desecration of the dead to be an outrage, and direct reprisals by British soldiers can be traced back to this act.

By the end of the Korean War, 8,000 American and 82 British service personnel were still officially missing in action. Thanks to New and Henderson, no Australian aircrew were unaccounted for. These figures were nothing compared to the Second World War (for example, 78,000 Americans were still missing from that conflict), but a factor now came into play that would blossom over the next 20 years. The Korean War did not enjoy the popular support that the wars against Germany and Japan had done. Even less popular would be the Vietnam War, and even though by the time Saigon fell in April 1975 only 2,583 men were officially unaccounted for, the public backlash was far in excess of anything that had gone before. Although initially a peripheral issue, it gradually captured the public interest, stoked up by lurid Hollywood treatment and sensational novels, to become a part of the national psyche.

The figures of missing aircrew were lower by the end of Vietnam for several reasons. Partly, aircraft were more technologically advanced. Ejector seats gave aircrew a better chance of escaping doomed aircraft. Improvements in designs and engines meant that smaller aircraft could carry heavier loads, with correspondingly smaller crews. A single-seat Douglas A-1 Skyraider, for example, carried a heavier ordinance load than that habitually carried by the ten-crew Boeing B-17 Flying Fortress only a few years before. Perhaps a more important factor was the advent of combat search and rescue (CSAR). It had not been unknown for pilots to land during both the First and Second World Wars to pick up downed comrades, but this needed a large open space to land their aircraft in and then room to turn and take off again, a requirement that most crash sites did not have. But the development of helicopters from the mid-Second World War had given air forces the capacity to get to even the most inaccessible sites. The Americans had experimented with CSAR in the late 1940s, and had used helicopters in a limited way in this role in Korea. By the 1960s helicopters had progressed enough in reliability, payload and performance to make them a much more serious proposition.

This new capability meant not only that downed aircrew could be lifted from danger within a matter of minutes, but that a procedure was in place to deal with these situations. It became common practice for rescue activities to be factored into operational planning. Take for example the last year of the British counter-insurgency campaign in Aden (1966–67). It became policy that RAF anti-guerrilla operations, usually conducted by ground attack Hawker Hunters, would only take place when a Westland Wessex CSAR helicopter was available to accompany them. This extended to other air operations too; when an Army Air Corps Sioux scout helicopter was shot down over Crater during the mutiny of the national guard, an RAF Wessex successfully landed under heavy fire and pulled out both crewmen. Meanwhile further east the American forces were making CSAR an art form in Vietnam, although also proving that this capacity could lead to pyrrhic victories.

Perhaps the best known, and most spectacular, CSAR operation began with the loss of a US Navy A-7 Corsair, call-sign Streetcar 304, over Laos on 31 May 1968. Over the next three days and two nights, 189 sorties were flown before the downed pilot, Lieutenant Kenny Fields, was rescued. In that time seven further aircraft were lost: one US Navy pilot had to be picked up from the sea, five US Air Force aircrew had to be rescued from the jungle, and a US Air Force pilot was captured by the Viet Cong and added to the list of missing men.[8] This was a drastic case, but almost every day aircrew needed extracting somewhere in the war zone, often by definition in extremely hostile areas. Rescue aircraft were lost as a result, and the audit sheet did not always come out in favour of the Americans. Perversely, CSAR sometimes led to more names being added onto the lists of missing men than struck off. Despite this the efforts still went ahead; it was now an implicit part of the serviceman's unwritten contract that no-one be left behind, alive or dead. In 1982, for the first time British service dead were brought home with the fleet returning from the campaign in the Falklands. The Argentineans on the other hand declined offers to have their dead returned home, and they remain in the Falklands as a visible symbol of that country's claim on the islands. Since 2003, it has become an all-too familiar sight to see flag-draped coffins being unloaded from transport aircraft from Iraq or Afghanistan.

Today, things have swung even further the other way. In 1993 a US operation in Mogadishu went badly wrong when a Black Hawk helicopter was shot down.[9] Although a Combat Search and Rescue team landed within moments and extracted the wounded, they could not extract the dead crewmen who had been trapped in the cockpit when the nose was crushed. Instead, the area had to be secured, and in the resulting operation a second Black Hawk was shot down. Most of the crew were killed, as were two Special Forces members. Soon the whole area degenerated into a fire fight that lasted the rest of that afternoon, through the night and into the next morning. American casualties mounted to a total of nineteen killed, while Somali casualties ran into the hundreds. As the Air Ministry discovered in the 1940s, it had simply become politically and socially unacceptable to leave your service personnel behind: it is part of the debt that they are owed.

CHAPTER TWO

The Missing Problem and Wreck Recovery

Less said the better;
The bill unpaid – the dead letter.
No roses at the end
Of Smith, my friend.

Last words don't matter
And there are none to flatter;
Words will not fill the post
Of Smith – a ghost.

For Smith, our brother,
Only son of loving mother,
The ocean lifted – stirred –
Leaving no word.

John Pudney, 'Missing'

The Army tended to pick up their dead and wounded as they went along. Front lines were more or less defined, and units tended to move and fight in fairly large groups. Even in small patrol or platoon size actions in confused landscapes like Norway, Italy or the Western Desert, larger units would be nearby and almost certainly there would be survivors to witness any casualties. The Royal Navy faced a more complex situation. On lonely, featureless seas, the disappearance of surface or submarine vessels was far from unusual, but the Navy, like most sea-faring organisations, has always followed the ethos and practice of burial at sea. If a ship is sunk, the dead go to the sea bed with it, and it would have been not just impractical but simply impossible with the technologies of the day to recover them. In naval terms, bodies that are not accounted for are not classified as missing unless the fate of the ship itself is unknown. For this reason sunken ships are deemed to be

11

war graves. The RAF, as we have seen, was different. The challenges they faced were more severe, but most of those men who were listed as missing would have crashed over land. In theory, their bodies would have been recoverable. Recovery of those bodies would not only be a necessity for identification, laying to rest the fears or hopes of relatives, but because as we have also seen it was culturally unacceptable in a Western, Christian society not to give them a decent burial.

This makes one of the more perverse aspects of the missing question even stranger; that some of the aircrew still reported as missing were in fact lost over the United Kingdom. This has been particularly high-lighted in the cases of Battle of Britain pilots, and bears some examination to emphasise the issues involved. Particularly since the late 1960s, after the classic film *Battle of Britain* was released and captured the imaginations of the post-war generations, there has been a growth in interest in excavating crash-sites, especially those from the Battle. Aviation archaeology groups sprung up and soon began work on sites across the South East. Before long, to the surprise and shock of all, human remains began to be found.

This has become the cause for some fairly major conflicts between the Ministry of Defence and the enthusiast groups. On the one hand the enthusiasts see it as a travesty that pilots, particularly but not exclusively those from the Battle of Britain, have lain under British soil all of this time without any efforts being made to give them a proper burial. The Ministry, on the other hand, has been reluctant to condone enthusiasts digging up RAF pilots without any form of permission or supervision. Wrecks often contain unexploded ammunition or occasionally bombs, and can prove dangerous if anyone except qualified specialists deal with them. Apart from this obvious safety aspect, there are the ethical issues surrounding the exhumation of bodies. The MoD felt strongly enough over this issue to pressure Parliament to pass the Protection of Military Remains Act, 1986, making, among other things, digs on aircraft suspected of containing human remains illegal without permission from the MoD, the land owner, and the next-of-kin of the aircrew thought to be down there.[10]

This was undoubtedly necessary. Whatever the motives of the many, there is a small minority of aviation archaeologists who are only interested in recovering valuable artefacts to the detriment of all other issues. There were cases of bodies being disrespectfully treated; in one case a dig on a German aircraft unearthed the remains of the pilot stuffed inside a carrier bag.[11] The law has gone a long way towards guarding against this kind of abuse, but has at the same time constrained more legitimate groups. To take the example of Battle of Britain groups further, even though they are operating in relatively small areas of this country, archaeologists and researchers face many of the same problems that the

Royal Air Force and Air Ministry faced in Europe after the Second World War. Records, particularly as regards locations, are sketchy at best. Locals confuse dates or places. After all, many airmen may have disappeared in roughly the same area at around the same time.

The legislation demands that the identity of the pilot should be known, and the agreement of the next of kin received, before a dig can begin. This requires either exemplary documentary evidence, usually impossible, or the type of evidence that can only be gleaned from the wreck itself. This Catch-22 infuriates enthusiasts, but is understandable from the MoD's point of view. Some families are bound to feel that, at this length of time, the bodies of their loved ones are better left in peace where they lie and a memorial mounted nearby, as in the case of Pilot Officer Arthur Clarke of 504 Squadron. After being posted missing in September 1940, his Hawker Hurricane was later located on the Romney Marsh. Today he still rests in his aeroplane, with a simple memorial by the side of the nearest road. Even if the relatives do not object, and the dig goes ahead, the multiple problems involved in identifying crashes from above the ground frequently lead to mistakes. On the one hand, this results in having to tell the family of a different airman, out of the blue, that their relative has been found and exhumed. On the other, it involves disappointment for those whose relative was not found. Either way, it can lead to grief and trauma to all concerned.

But perhaps a more important question than whether aircrew should be recovered now is why were they not recovered at the time? The simple answer is that in 1939 the mechanisms for dealing with crash sites were in their infancy. Between the wars most maintenance and salvage operations had been contracted out to civilian firms for budgetary reasons. In the mid-1930s world events, particularly those in Germany, sparked a series of expansion schemes in the RAF in an attempt to make them again capable of fighting a war on the scale and distance from home of that of 1914–18. These accelerated after 1935, when talks with Adolf Hitler in Berlin led to the belief that the German *Luftwaffe* was now of a sufficient strength to rival the RAF. Half a dozen schemes were enacted to bring the Air Force up to strength over the next four years, but all of them focused exclusively on front-line fighting squadrons. No attention was paid to either reserve forces or to the many administrative or technical branches that would be necessary to keep those front-line squadrons in the fight. The emphasis was on a show of strength, a deterrence, and the Air Ministry 'put almost everything into the shop-window, and very little into the store-cupboard.'[12]

As late as September 1938 Air Vice-Marshal W. L. Welsh CB DSC AFC, the Air Member for Supply and Organisation, was warning that since the only RAF repair depot, based at Henlow, had been converted to a training unit, the RAF needed to take immediate action in this area.[13] This finally galvanised reform, but it was limited and slow. Maintenance Command was embodied, covering all manner of repair, maintenance and supply matters. Repair, including salvage and wreck recovery, came under the remit of 43 (Repair) Group, who had control of six repair depots across the country. Three of these were to be run by the RAF: 13 Maintenance Unit (MU) at Henlow, 30 MU at Sealand, and 32 MU at St Athan. The other three would be run by civilian contractors: 34 MU at Abbotsinch, 47 MU at Burtonwood, and a final MU probably to be at Stoke.[14]

At the outbreak of war, very little of this had been implemented. 43 Group had taken a backseat within the Command in deference to 40 (Equipment) Group, 41 (Aircraft) Group and 42 (Ammunition and Fuel) Group. The Group HQ had not been officially established, just one of the service depots (13 MU) had become operational, and only two further depots were even under construction. To make matters worse, many of the civilian workers at the HQ and depots were reservists who were recalled and then posted to other duties.[15] The war left little choice but to press ahead, and within weeks the HQ had been firmly established at Andover and the Group officially came into being. It still, however, did not achieve much in the way of repair or salvage. The first priority handed to the Group was to participate in the RAF-wide programme to fit all aircraft with wireless telegraphy sets, and then the repairing and maintaining of all ground and air wireless equipment. This left the task of wreck recovery in the hands of already overstretched MUs from other Groups.

To return to using the Battle of Britain as an example, and as the bulk of the fighting had occurred over Kent, let us look at 49 Maintenance Unit, based at RAF Faygate, near Horsham. They were responsible, under the overall command of 49 (Maintenance) Group, for all crashes in Kent, at that time an area of around 1,400 square miles. Their field strength consisted of teams of 8–10 airmen with a non-commissioned officer, working under the direction of a crash inspector, usually a Pilot Officer. The inspector would consider each case, and then give a broad judgement on how it should be dealt with. Options varied from complete recovery of the airframe and engine, plus obviously any aircrew, to simply filling in a crater and moving on to the next site.

Usually the course of action was somewhere between the two. A single seat fighter would create quite a debris field, depending on the angle of dive. The wings and parts of the rear fuselage would most likely break off on impact and spin away across the ground. At any angle, the engine, being the heaviest part and probably pulling the cockpit section behind it, is likely to have dug itself 15–20 feet into the ground. This may not seem to be much, but with the technology available (nothing more complex than shovels and a mobile crane) then a full recovery operation was likely to be extremely difficult and perhaps even hazardous. In areas like the Romney Marsh, Thames Estuary or other coastal regions, soft ground would only add to the scale of the task, and probably make it altogether impossible.

Time and the sheer size of the task were also factors. The Air Ministry appears to have issued instructions that the priority was to be clearing up visible RAF wreckage without delay. Presumably, at this most precarious point of the war, the sight of downed RAF aeroplanes littering the countryside was simply unacceptable, while these wrecks could also contain much needed spares. By all means leave the German wreckage, which would have to remain in situ until studied and cleared for removal by the RAF Technical Intelligence office anyway, but any potentially morale damaging Spitfires or Hurricanes should be dealt with at once. Between 1 September and 29 November 1940, this amounted to 618 RAF aircraft within 49 MU's remit alone.

To make matters worse, wreck recovery was not even their main function. The primary role of Maintenance Units was to support front line squadrons by repairing and returning damaged aircraft with the minimum of delay. Added to this vital, and massive, work load was the need to render assistance to the Kentish RAF stations which were the subject of heavy German raids during the early phases of the Battle, which left very little time to deal thoroughly with each wreck recovery case. And the commitment to keep these vital stations operational cost 49 MU dear. On 14 August a raid on RAF Hawkinge cost them two vehicles, including a heavy low-loader, destroyed, while a raid on RAF Tangmere on the 16th cost not only three low loaders, a mobile crane and a 3-ton truck destroyed, but Leading Aircraftsman Albert Gainey and Leading Aircraftsman Ronald Hewlett killed as well.[16] This was the same week as teams were sent to recover aircraft from all over Kent, East Sussex, the Isle of Wright and even Wiltshire. In all, August saw 49 MU called to 371 aircraft crash sites. Soon the RAF was forced to make up the gaps in their own strength with civilian contractors. Usually working in teams of only two or three men, they were completely inexperienced at this work and had even less specialist equipment at their disposal.

The net result of these strains on the system was that most crashes were only dealt with in the most perfunctory way. If the pilot's body, or parts of it, were visible, they would be recovered, but very little would, or could, be done to extract and thoroughly search cockpits. It is not uncommon now for the wrecks of aircraft whose pilot has a known grave to be excavated only to find the remains of limbs or lower torsos still in them. In the Hurricane, for example, the fuel tank was right in front of the pilot behind the instrument panel. Apart from regularly causing severe burns to pilots who were shot down, this arrangement may have centred any explosion on impact just a few inches from the pilot, disarticulating any remains. This meant that sometimes only partial remains were recovered, although the airman was officially recorded as found. One extreme example of this would be Sergeant Dennis Noble, of 43 Squadron. Shot down in his Hurricane on 30 August 1940, Sergeant Noble had crashed in the middle of a street in Hove, Sussex. His body was recorded as having been recovered at the time, although the wreckage was left in situ. In November 1996 an amateur enthusiasts group applied for and received permission to excavate the crash site. In the process, they unearthed what the local coroner estimated to be 80% of Sergeant Noble's remains.[17]

It was also far from unusual for bodies not to be identified. Fires or the impact could easily destroy or obscure the serial numbers on an aircraft, particularly on the canvas-covered fuselage of the Hurricane. The aircrew themselves would also probably bear little in the way of identification. It was officially forbidden to carry personal papers or items on operations, and the fibre identification tags worn by every serviceman were known to be highly flammable. It would often become necessary to call out a member of the squadron to identify a pilot by whatever means possible. For a front-line unit this would often mean the intelligence officer, who, although probably swamped with interviewing returning aircrew and maintaining the proper paperwork and combat reports, at least would not be missed from the fighting strength of the unit. Flying Officer Tom Waterlow, Intelligence Officer with 610 Squadron, would record that:

> I don't enjoy my work ... when it entails rushing around the countryside looking at crashed aircraft and identifying my friends by the numbers on their machine guns.[18]

The gruesome task of clearing up human remains did not always fall to the RAF. In urban or inhabited areas, a guard from the local authorities, be they police, Air Raid Precautions, Army, Home Guard, or whoever, would be placed on the site, and the first priority would be to recover visible remains for the sake of decency and morale. When Flying Officer Robert McGregor Waterson of 603 Squadron was shot down over Woolwich in August 1940, Bombadier John Cross, Royal Artillery, was called out to help with the recovery:

> On the 31st, because of the aerial activity, we were confined to the ground floor of the barrack block when there was the sound of an explosion close to the west of the block. Shortly after, a sergeant announced that there had been a plane crash by the roadside and that a guard was required. I was told to take five gunners with rifles and to block the road at the south end of the incident, the intention being to protect the public from the dangers of live ammunition and to prevent looting. Similarly, another NCO took the north end.

On arrival at the site we were met with a tragic mess. The impact of the crashing Spitfire had resulted in the pilot being thrown through a corrugated parade shed at the side of the road. The impact was so great that his body had fragmented. His head was found on top of the shed.

My guard was kept busy holding back the gawping civilians who were arriving in numbers. Civilian undertakers arrived with a coffin, which was no more than a wooden box with a tarpaulin cover. Assisted by several gunners, we began the gruesome task of gathering the human remains. The job was carried out very thoroughly and it took us about an hour.[19]

Occasionally the apparent lack of concern from the RAF sparked off recovery efforts by the local population. When Sergeant Dennis Hayter, a pupil of 5 Operational Training Unit at RAF Aston Down, crashed his Hurricane near the village of Aust in Gloucestershire in October 1940, 50 MU deemed his recovery impossible. The aircraft had come down in a pond in the middle of a water-logged area, and with the limited time and resources available from their point of view they were correct. However, the local Superintendent of the ARP, Mr L. Hawkins, felt that: 'It was a matter of some concern to the people of Aust that the RAF had made so little attempt to recover the pilot's body.' Leading a team of ten ARP Rescue Service workers, Mr. Hawkins drained and excavated the area, finally recovering the body of Sergeant Hayter from a depth of 25 feet, after five weeks of effort.[20]

Despite the somewhat sporadic official approach at the time, and the occasional effort such as that at Aust, there was little outcry or public concern about the Air Ministry's tardiness in recovering the bodies of fallen air crew. One reason was that the families of these men simply would not have known. The authorities did not make it public for obvious reasons, and any official documentation that was sent to the families, including letters from commanding officers, would not mention the location of the crash site. Most people on receiving notification that their son or husband was 'Missing, believed killed', would most likely assume that they had gone down over the Channel or an equally inaccessible place. It would not be until after the immediate national emergency had passed that questions would be raised. Increasingly through 1941 the Air Ministry began to receive requests for more information about losses from the Battles of France, Norway and Britain, as we shall see.

Another point that should be raised at this juncture is that some of those who were missing had no families to ask these questions for them. In the summer and autumn of 1940 the RAF increasingly accepted Polish, Czech, French, Belgian, Norwegian and other foreign asylum seekers who had fled to Britain after the fall of their own countries. For the majority of these men the closest they had to next of kin was their comrades, and with their families still living in Nazi-occupied territories it would be months if not years before they were informed of a loved one's loss. In other cases there were the simpler problems of distance. Increasingly the Commonwealth sent their own established forces too; air crew from the Royal Australian Air Force, Indian Air Force, South African Air Force, and Royal Canadian and Royal New Zealand Air Forces found themselves posted to Britain to protect the motherland. More were recruited from those areas without their own forces: the Caribbean, territories in East and West Africa, or dozens of other far-flung colonies. Other men and women from all across the Commonwealth flocked to Britain to join the indigenous forces and help in the fight, as had others from North and South America, Ireland or other neutral countries. Some came through a sense of adventure, more through a determination to stand up to Nazism. Even in the early days of the war the wickedness of the Nazi regime was clear, and thousands came to the British Isles to take up the last ditch defence against what Winston Churchill had rightly predicted to be the threat of a new Dark Age.

Although a fascinating social and political phenomenon by itself, it also has one other relevant point to make. For all that the Royal Air Force was predominantly British, it was a multi-national force. Europe, as the main focus of the RAF's war, is the predominant focus of this work, and while in Europe all of these nationalities and contingents came under the umbrella of RAF control. Therefore, for the purposes of this work, unless otherwise stated the term Royal Air Force will be taken to mean all of those forces who served under the direction and command of the British RAF, wherever they originated from, and whatever shoulder flashes they wore.

Once the chaos of the Battle of Britain and the opening phases of the Blitz had passed, the Air Ministry found the time to reorganize the wreck recovery system. In July 1940 Sir Arthur Street, Permanent Under Secretary of State for Air, had issued orders for the splitting of the Air Ministry into two separate Departments.[21] This followed the Cabinet decision on 17 May to establish a new Ministry for Aircraft Production. Although the Air Ministry would remain as an entity, there would now be a separate department responsible for all matters pertaining to the development and production of aircraft parts. Included in this new organisation was 43 (Repair) Group, although strangely, Repair and Salvage Units (RSUs) overseas were retained under the authority of the Air Ministry.

The reorganisation reinvigorated 43 Group. Street struggled successfully for the personnel and resources for them only to not raise depots, but also designated Repair and Salvage Units to handle the recovery and processing of crashed aircraft. Like the MUs, their primary remit would be in bolstering the front line strength of the Air Force, in their case by salvaging any pieces of equipment that could be recycled or repaired and then entered back into the system as spares. These new units were established along very similar lines as those of 49 Group, with individual units assigned to geographic areas according to need. Kent and Scotland, for example, were both assigned a single Unit each. Scotland was fairly remote and had relatively few RAF stations, whereas Kent, although less than one-tenth the square mileage in size, was a front line area.

Even with Street's help, the desperate situation of late 1940 still slowed progress down. By October, though, the Group was taking shape, and for the first time began to take on their intended role. Even then they were often under-manned and crammed into whatever accommodation or facilities were available. We have already seen the scale of operations faced by 49 MU covering only one corner of England over a three month period. Once operations began, the task faced by 43 Group was gargantuan.

Throughout the rest of the war, the procedure for dealing with crash sites for the most part improved steadily. Sufficient manpower became available, as did specialist equipment. The organisation found its feet and established a firm method of working. Crashed aircraft would immediately be placed under guard by the local military or civil defence authorities, and the local RAF station informed. They would pass the message to HQ 43 Group, who would send the details down to the relevant unit. A recovery team would be despatched and, after exam-ination of the wreck by Bomb Disposal officers to check for unexploded bombs or ammunition, the wreck would be searched and if applicable the crew extracted. Those parts of the wreckage deemed salvageable would then be recovered and loaded onto low-loaders (they would need six for the average four-engined bomber, or two for a single-seat fighter). Some aircraft would be worth sending back to the manufacturer or another specialised workshop for repair or reconditioning, but for the most part they would be broken up and transported to a depot for processing. Any collateral damage would be shored up and the crater filled in. In October 1940, 348 crashes were reported to 43 Group, and 336 inspections carried out. Of these, thirty-nine aircraft were classed as fit for repair on site, 183 sent for repair in factories, and just 114 declared as write-offs.[22] As the Battle of Britain faded and the RAF drew breath, more personnel and resources were poured into the Group. From fifteen RSUs and 13,700 personnel in October 1940, it grew to twenty-nine units and 26,000 personnel 18 months later.[23]

By 1944 the organisation had spread considerably, although still only within the UK. With 750 low-loaders and 170 cranes at their disposal, it was a far cry from contracting out to removals firms in 1940.[24] Some 31,668 aircraft were referred to and dealt with by 43 Group in some way during 1944[25] and 12,089 aircraft passed through the hands of the RSUs for inspection or recovery, including almost 2,500 heavy bombers. The Group even took on the bulk of the responsibility for American crashes. The USAAF that began to arrive in Britain in 1942 was as woefully unprepared as the RAF had been three years earlier. By 1944 their own repair and salvage organisation was still in its infancy, and 1,400 American aircraft were dealt with by 43 Group in that year.[26]

In a similar vein, the RAF also dealt with enemy crashes. Any survivors would be rounded up and delivered to the local police station, and then passed on for interrogation at Trent Park, Cockfosters. The wrecks themselves had to be reported to and inspected by RAF Technical Intelligence Branch before anything could be removed. Once they had been assessed, they could face several fates depending on their condition. If the airframe was considered repairable, or any of the equipment salvageable, they would be removed to the Royal Aircraft Establishment at Farnborough for evaluation, or from November 1941 possibly to 1426 (Enemy Aircraft) Flight at Duxford. If the wreck was of no technical or intelligence interest, but still in a recognizable form, or all appropriate tests had been completed, it would probably be handed over to various local or national authorities for use as centre pieces in drives to raise War Bonds, Spitfire Funds, or similar uses. Those that were beyond recognition or use would be scrapped and recycled.

Just as prisoners were treated with respect in the western theatres, so were the enemy's dead. Crashes were to be reported to HQ Fighter Command in the UK, or the nearest Air Head Quarters if overseas. The relevant salvage control units would then be informed, and the bodies recovered. In the United Kingdom the bodies would be sent to the local civil mortuary. The superintendent of that facility would then forward a statement of the effects found on the casualty to the Prisoner of War Information Bureau. As soon as possible an RAF intelligence officer would take charge of the effects, and the local RAF station or unit the body. The authority processing the casualty would then send a signal to P.4 (Cas) at the Air Ministry, the same department that dealt with RAF deaths, listing the aircraft type, the exact location of the crash, the date and time, and the current location of the crew.[27] Curiously, there was no section on the forms for the identity of the crews. Presumably these would be sent in at a later date by RAF Intelligence, and cross-referenced by the other details provided.

Naturally, the problem of broken and unidentified bodies still existed, but every attempt was made to do the decent thing. When a Messerschmitt Me 410 was shot down over Essex on 22 April 1944, the local Home Guard was called to collect what human remains could be found:

Walter Cain, on duty with another Home Guardsman, had the grisly chore of collecting human remains mingled amidst pieces of aircraft. It was a task not for the squeamish. The two men wandered the field using their bayonets like park-keepers, transferring what they found into sacks.[28]

The bodies would then, for the most part, be buried in the local, military approved graveyard. Of the 3,800 German service personnel buried in Britain, 2,728 were concentrated after the war at Cannock Chase, Staffordshire.[29] Funeral costs were dealt with as for members of the RAF, although a limit of £5 was imposed for the cost of the plot. Funerals would be conducted with due ceremony, complete with a national flag (in the case of Germany, the Swastika does seem to have been used) drawn from either the local general equipment depot, or 3 MU. Photographs of the funerals and grave would be taken and passed, along with full details of the dead, through the International Red Cross to the Germans.

This, then, was the system in place for the recovery and identification of fallen aircrew. Although somewhat slap-dash to begin with in the UK, as the war progressed the home and overseas systems improved and streamlined. But nothing could be done for those who fell behind enemy lines, and these would begin to be a weight heavy on the Air Ministry's mind.

CHAPTER THREE

The Air Ministry Regrets: Casualty Procedure 1939–45

Deeply regret to inform you that your husband Flying Officer John Smith is missing and believed to have lost his life on 6 June 1944 as a result of air operations. Letter follows. Please accept my profound sympathy.

Wording of official telegram notifying next of kin.

For three generations of service families, the most dreaded sight was a telegram. The small buff envelopes would, with the Air Ministry's (or War Office's or Admiralty's) condolences, inform them that their relative had been killed, wounded, was ill, or was missing.

Considering the circumstances, the Air Ministry system was surprisingly swift and efficient. Ground battles have clearly defined front lines where bodies are easily accounted for while the fighting is still in progress. Usually only in cases such as the Western Front during the First World War, where the lines remain static and prevent the recovery of bodies for long periods, do large numbers of soldiers become officially 'missing'. Prolonged fighting often further damages and buries the bodies or destroys grave markers, particularly when heavy artillery is in use. In addition papers or identification disks disintegrate over time.

With the Royal Air Force, the question of missing airmen was both more widespread and more acute. Unlike land warfare, in aerial conflicts there are no front lines. Even during the Battle of Britain, with clear geographical barriers between the opposing sides, aerial battles could wage across hundreds of square miles of land and sea. An air raid on Britain could see German bombers flying over almost any part of the English Channel and North Sea, and over south-east England, the south coast, East Anglia, the north east, or the areas to the north and west of London. At least one distressed German bomber landed in south Wales, while further attacks incorporated Ireland and the industrial West Midlands and north west of England. Following British victory in the Battle, for Fighter Command alone the area of operations expanded even wider. Fighter units now conducted their own raids, sweeping across northern France, Belgium and the Low Countries. Over the winter of 1940–41 and on into the spring and summer these operations saw the RAF losing heavily, albeit against a background of propaganda victories. Sweeps could quickly degenerate into chaotic chases over miles of open countryside. With few landmarks and the pilot too preoccupied with flying and fighting to be able to pay much attention to navigation, aircraft could easily become separated from its unit and stray miles from their recorded area of operations.

Further complications ensued as both sides expanded their night bombing arms. After dark navigation was even harder. In the early days of the war it was rudimentary, still largely based upon dead reckoning and celestial readings. Even years later, as both the British and the Germans developed lattice works of radar beams and beacons across Europe, navigation could be extremely hit or miss. A fault with the rudimentary equipment, a cloudy night, or the slightest variation in wind direction or strength from that forecast could see single aircraft or entire formations scattered across a vast area. The worse night of the war for the RAF, the Nuremburg raid of 30 March 1944, was made significantly worse by poor weather forecasts, which then saw the attacking force scattered and disorientated.

Then of course there were the human factors. The merest mathematical miscalculation, or slip in pilot concentration, could have drastic results. A mistake of half a degree – a pencil's width drawn on the navigators map – could see an aircraft drifting miles off course and never arriving anywhere near it's objective. Even if the objective and the flight plan of a missing aircraft were known, these possibilities made the knowledge potentially useless. Simply searching along the route would most likely be a waste of time; the missing aircraft could be dozens of miles to either side.

Outside the confines of Western Europe, the question of tracing losses became even harder. Over the Atlantic or Pacific oceans on long range reconnaissance or anti-submarine operations, or over the equally remote and featureless deserts of North Africa, the chances of an aircraft's loss being witnessed were even less. The same can be said for the air lanes used for ferry and communication flights across the South Atlantic, India, Africa, or those including Greenland. In Burma the chances might be higher. But in an environment where aerial and long distance views were severely limited for those on the ground, and rolling hills and jungle provided few concrete points of reference for locations, there would be little hope of gaining firm intelligence on where the loss had occurred.

The Air Ministry, in 1939, was hopelessly unprepared for a war, even more so than the Royal Air Force, and for losses on such a scale. The Casualty Branch, S.7 (Cas), was a small and relatively new department and nothing could have prepared them for what was to come. The Air Ministry War Book, the inches thick, multi-volume plan that laid out how the organisation would expand in time of war, and what new posts would be needed to cope with the increased workload, did not even mention S.7 (Cas).[30] On 5 September the RAF suffered its first casualties, Blenheim crews from 2 Group, Bomber Command, on a raid on Wilhelmshaven. Far from being able to carry out its intended role of collating and disseminating information to the RAF and to the lost men's relatives, S.7 (Cas) was stymied. What information they had was gleaned from the BBC and other media sources.[31] Gradually firm details began to filter through from survivors of the raid in German prisoner of war camps, via letters to their families. Clearly, this situation was unacceptable, but the Air Ministry moved fast to reform the system. S.7 contacted the International Red Cross Committee to ask for their advice, and with their help a proper system was established whereby lists of casualties could be exchanged as promptly as possible through Geneva. The Germans quite bluntly called these *Totenlisten*: 'Death lists'. The first one arrived on the 14 October 1939.

The reforms did not end there. On 16 October Sir Arthur Street MC, the Permanent Under Secretary of State for Air, announced the formation of a new Branch, P.4 (Cas). Under the command of Commander R. Burges RN (Retired), with the honorary rank of Wing Commander, P.4 (Cas) would take on sole responsibility for dealing with officer casualties and the main responsibility for dealing with other ranks. Some areas such as the updating of records, processing of accounts and allowances to families, and the handling of personal effects were retained by S.7 working out of their Records Office in Gloucester. Until 1943, all initial casualty paperwork was dealt with by P.4 (Cas) at the Air Ministry offices in London, with subsequent reports and communications being split: London dealt with officer casualties, but other ranks were dealt with through the offices in Gloucester. This obviously led to problems. Communications were not perfect and cross-referencing files a major headache. In April 1943, both offices were brought together in London, setting up over Drages the furniture shop at 73/77 Oxford Street.

The challenges facing the new branch were manifold, given the scale of operations that would develop over the next 6 years and the very nature of air fighting itself. Operations frequently occurred at night, and almost always a long way from friendly territory and witnesses. Gathering information on even the location of a loss, let alone the fate of the crew, was difficult and, as often or not, unsatisfactory. For full details of how this system worked, see Appendix C. Suffice to say here that every effort was made to ensure that information was promptly and accurately gathered and then, with their personal effects, passed to the other departments of the Air Ministry, the Royal Air Force, and of course to the next of kin. Whatever else this issue is, it is fundamentally about people, not paperwork.

The simple telegram, adopted as a fast and reliable way to inform relatives of what had happened, would shatter the world of whoever received one. In late April 1944 Peggy Ryle received a telegram telling her that her husband, a Squadron Leader with the Pathfinders, was missing on operations. Even though, as a senior officer's wife, she had the advantages of close friendships with and the support of other senior officers on the station, the information was devastating:

> But none of them can possibly know what an agony it is. I have heard people talk of heart-ache and never know what it meant or thought anything about it. But I have a pain round my heart night and day and I feel raw inside. I have lost a stone and a half in ten days.[32]

For Mrs. Ryle, it would be five long months until the fate of her husband was confirmed, each day recorded in her diary as a running monologue to the missing man:

> My own beloved man, I heard today that Guy and Johnstone's bodies have been found and that there were five unidentifiable bodies there, which means you my darling.
>
> God help me.[33]

Most other families would not have the benefit of close contact with their relative's unit. For most there would be simply the agony of waiting. The telegram would be followed by a confirming letter from the Air Ministry, officially to arrive two or three days later. However, a longer delay was usual. Burges had decided that it was better to send out a late letter than one devoid of news, and so often the letter was delayed until news was received from the German authorities. At busy times, for example after a particularly bad air raid, the Branch was known to fall anything up to two or three weeks into arrears.[34]

Likely to arrive at the same time would be a letter from the commanding officer of the casualty. Air Ministry regulations stated that these should be sent as soon as possible, and should be as personal as possible. Stock phrases or the use of standard templates were to be avoided. Again, at times these could fall behind the ideal schedule. During the

Battle of Britain, for example, when squadron commanders could be leading their men on several sorties a day, administration naturally began to take a back seat. The circumstances of a casualty would also affect the time scale. On the morning of the 31 January 1943 Sergeant Henry Jones of 9 Squadron was killed when his bomber crashed in Yorkshire on its way back from an operation. Because of the close proximity to his home station, news was quick to come through, and his parents received their telegram that same afternoon. The next day the squadron commander was able to follow the telegram with a letter:

1st February 1943

Dear Mrs Jones,

It is with the greatest sorrow that I write concerning the telegram I had to send you yesterday, notifying you that your son, Sergeant Henry Summers Jones, had been killed as the result of operational flying.

He was the Wireless Operator of an aircraft which had carried out an operational mission on the night of the 30/31st January, 1943, and crashed on return to this country. It may be some consolation to you, however, to know that you son's death must have been instantaneous.

Your son had only recently joined this Squadron, but in the short time he was with us gave every promise of becoming a most efficient Wireless Operator. He always showed the utmost keenness in the performance of his duties, and his death has been a heavy blow to us all.

All the officers and airmen join me in sending you deep sympathy in your great loss. If there is anything I can do for you, please do not hesitate to write to me.

Yours sincerely,

J. M. Southwell

Wing Commander, Commanding

No. 9 Squadron, Waddington[35]

The next day the local Methodist chaplain joined the Wing Commander in passing on his sympathies. Although not required officially in regulations, this was to be a common and much appreciated gesture, perhaps as these letters usually focused on the personality of the individual, rather than their professional abilities:

Dear Mrs Jones,

This morning I have received official information of the dreadful accident in which your son, Sergeant H. S. Jones, lost his life. I wish that I could adequately express to you and to all to whom he is dear, the deep sympathy felt for you by all of us at the camp a Waddington.

Your loss is grievous. We knew him as a young man of character, highly capable and courageous, trusted and well-liked by both officers and men. He was one of those who went out to give himself without stay or stint for others. You have cause for pride in the memory of one who had placed all lovers of righteousness in his debt; one of those who make our ultimate victory certain.

We hoped his gifts would have had years of usefulness in happier times. I pray that you and yours may have the divine consolation and believe that he goes:

> *'Where every gift finds sweet employ,*
> *In that eternal world of joy.'*

God bless you.

Yours sincerely,

E. C. Raynes[36]

Over the next few weeks and months more letters and forms would follow. The Air Ministry accounts offices at Worcester would be in contact over any allowances that the family may be due, or the settling of the deceased's accounts (including the payment of death duties). Personal effects would be forwarded by the unit to the RAF Depository at Colnbrook, near Slough, until death was confirmed, when non-service items would be returned to the family. The Royal Air Force Benevolent Fund would be in contact to offer their services, be it either financial assistance or advice on the casualty procedure as a whole. If the casualty was deceased and their body in the UK, further paperwork would concern the fate of their mortal remains. Families could claim the body for burial at their local cemetery, or leave it to the unit to organise a funeral at the closest cemetery to their station. Either way, the Imperial War Graves Commission would write to the family. Initially they would arrange for the temporary marking of the grave with a wooden cross, and lay out their responsibility for the care of the grave. Later, further forms would concern the permanent marking of the grave with a headstone, and the family's choice of personal inscription. In the case of Sergeant Jones, the squadron also provided his family with the names and addresses of the next of kin of each other member of the crew.

This case was a fairly straight forward one. Death was instantly confirmed and the body recovered and identified immediately. When men were simply missing the process would be much more drawn out, with the presumption of death following anything from six months to a year later. Only then could outstanding accounts be settled and personal effects be sorted. In the meantime, all the family could do was wait.

Likewise, the further the casualty was from the UK, the longer the process could take. Warrant Officer Charles Walter 'Wallie' Gentry, 155 Squadron, went missing in his Spitfire over the India-Burmese border on 5 November 1944. His wife did not receive a telegram to this effect until the 8 November[37], or the confirming letter until the 15th.[38] The commanding officer did not write his letter until the 18th.[39] Communications were slowed by the distances involved, and these also meant that personal effects could not be claimed so readily. These would have been packed and sent to the nearest Air Headquarters, in this case AHQ Burma, until death was confirmed and shipping space found. Presumption of death was much harder in the Far East. If, as we shall see in the next chapter, the German *Totenlisten* were often inaccurate, they were at least regular. The Japanese had no such system, nor cared about setting one up.

Over the winter of 1941 and into the spring of 1942 Japanese forces swept through Singapore, Java and Malaya. By the end of March 1942, nearly 7,000 RAF personnel had disappeared and were unaccounted for. In London, the Air Ministry decided to wait for the Japanese to provide an equivalent of the *Totenlisten*, confirming who was a prisoner at least, before contacting the families of the missing.[40] As time dragged on and still nothing was heard from the Japanese, the Air Ministry decided to follow the War Office's lead and declare their men as 'unaccounted for', and therefore outside of the established system. By September there had still been no official news but questions were being asked in Parliament[41], and pressure was being applied by the Australian government regarding those members of the RAAF whose fate was unknown in the Far East. Despite this, it would not be until February 1943 that these men would even be reclassified as 'missing', thus allowing the families to receive certain benefits and allowances. By the end of the war, most of these men still had not had their fates confirmed. In the case of Warrant Officer Gentry, even as late as January 1946 his wife was writing to the RAF asking for news. The reply, from the Base Personnel Office of South East Asia Command on 6 February 1946, could merely report that enquiries were still being made, and no firm information had been found.[42] It would not be until August 1946 that Warrant Officer Gentry's accounts would be closed and settled, and his back-pay could be released and the income tax paid after his date of death refunded.[43]

Long before this, though, Warrant Officer Gentry's last letter had been forwarded from his squadron. A common phenomenon, last letters were written and then held by the unit only to be sent in case of death, and are perhaps the most beautiful, emotive and tragic of all papers written in war-time:

To my Darling Wife Phillis,

Should you read this before hostilities cease, it will be because I had no chance to say goodbye to you in person. Although those many goodbyes we said were the most painful minutes of my life, I would have preferred to have seen you in person once more, because it is so hard to say in a letter, all the things I want to say.

Foremost, is my desire to express my gratitude for your love and faithfulness, which honour is as great as any for which man could wish. You brought into my life something worth living for, and, if necessary dying for – love for a woman, the sweetest of all.

You no doubt wonder at the seeming unfairness of life. Whilst so many couples enjoy a full life of happiness, we, like others have never had the chance to share each others' joys and sorrows for a very long period as husband and wife.

However, we must remember that if the cost of freedom is high for many of us, (have no fear of the final issues of this war, while England breeds such men as those with whom I have flown, no power on earth will be greater) that price must be paid for the benefit of the children of this bloody world, that they might not know the anguish and suffering of war for years to come.

Think not, my sweet-heart, that if you have not given us a son and heir (or daughter) that I think you have not been the perfect wife. You have for years past meant everything to me.

You have, my dear, for long known my philosophy, the chief principle of which was to accept life as a teacher, and experiences not as a fallen tree on life's road, or down-grades which are liable to put you off the track, but as foundations for a better and straighter, if not narrower highway.

So let not this separation be to you as a fallen tree, my darling. If ever you fall in love with some other lucky man, I pray that he has fewer faults than I had.

I put my trust in your practical character to spend no time on reminiscences of our happier days, unless they bring back to you some of too infrequent but precious happy days of love and understanding.

To all our families and friends I have but one message. Sincere apologies for any hurt I have caused them. Thanks for their friendship and much good advice, and finally, the wish for a pleasant future.

And so, I leave you, my darling beloved wife, pal and sweetheart, until we meet again.

All that was mine is yours, to do with as you will. Though, in life I gave all to the RAF with willingness, you have my spirit forever with you.

Your devoted and adoring and loving husband,

Wallie.[44]

Last letters were unfortunately not always comforting to the recipients. Pilot Officer Glyn Machin, 252 Squadron, was shot down on 1 August 1942 in a Bristol Beaufighter off the coast of North Africa. He was later reported as killed in action, although potentially his last letter could have had the effect of actually prolonging his family's grief and uncertainty:

17 June 1942

Dear Dad,

I wanted to save someone the trouble and embarrassment of writing to you in the event of my going into the wrong end of the casualty lists. You see I have done some of that sort of writing myself and I do not like it.

First of all rest assured that so long as I am merely posted 'missing' or 'missing believed killed', there is a chance – quite a strong chance in fact – of my turning up again. Only a few days ago a chap got back after wandering up and down occupied territory for more than seven months. If I became a prisoner of war I shall make every effort to escape and, especially with so much anti-Nazi feeling in Europe, I should stand an excellent chance of returning.

If I am posted as 'Killed' then there is still a slim chance that I will be all right; mistakes have been and are being made in compiling casualty lists. Anyway I have outlasted a lot of my pals and will be able to meet them again.

The fact that I have lost several of them lately is the main reason for my writing this letter, that, and the explanation I gave in my first paragraph. Please do not think I have not enjoyed this life of suspense. I think it is great never to know from one day to the next where you will be – anywhere on earth ... or elsewhere. It gives one an appreciation of the value of a peaceful existence which normally one takes for granted.

I have actually liked it all – being bombed in Malta and Africa, being five hundred miles from the nearest friendly soil, your life hanging on two British built engines and two British built wings, fighting a Heinkel fifty miles from any land, hunting for trouble three hundred miles over hostile land, believe it or not I have enjoyed it all. And when that last action comes, I shall like that too. It is a great game this, one's life is in one's own hands. One can sell one's own life dearly or one can throw it away. When I go I will have cost Jerry a few hundred thousand pounds. If I haven't I will come back and haunt him.

Well don't worry about me Dad. If there is one iota of a chance I will be back, and if not ... Well 'I'll see you later'.

Look after yourself.

Love

Glyn[45]

Human nature is to cling to false hopes and any glimmer of relief. Hopes of administrative errors or oversights could keep families in unrealistic conditions of optimism for years after their loved one had been listed as killed or missing, or even after the end of hostilities. Soon after the war the Air Ministry received a letter from a man convinced that he had recognised his son in a photograph in a newspaper from one of the concentration camps in Germany. Enquiries were made, but no evidence found to support his hopes.[46] In 1948 the father of Flight Sergeant William Sutherland came from Canada to Britain to better pursue his own efforts to trace his son. In an event widely reported in the newspapers of the time, one day at King's Cross railway station Mr Sutherland came face to face with a man whom he was convinced was his son. By the time he recovered his composure the man was gone, but the father spent days at the station fruitlessly hoping to see the man again.[47] Flight Sergeant Sutherland had been a bomb aimer on a Short Stirling lost in December 1943 on a 'Gardening' operation, dropping mines off the Frisian Islands. Today he is still missing.

These sorts of feelings were far from uncommon across the country, and the Air Ministry learnt fairly early that public appeals for information on particular cases were likely to receive a lot of attention, very little of it useful. In September 1945 a Frenchman handed in some personal effects that he had found near a crashed aircraft to the headquarters of the Second Tactical Air Force. The crash had apparently been a fighter, and the pilot was known to be buried nearby as an 'unknown airman'. As the effects included two photographs of a young lady, signed 'To Bob from Barb', the unusual step was decided upon to publish one of the photographs to see if anyone recognised her. A later report on the case recorded:

The response was extraordinary; telephone calls, telegrams and letters poured in. Barbara was recognised from Land's End to John O'Groats, and many points between. She was a WAAF, a WREN, a dentist, a nurse ... Barbara was also a very bad girl, at present in a Remand Home, and the wife of a baronet – this last suggestion was anonymous. Two letters, apparently from lunatics, had a certain entertainment value, but did not add to the sum of our knowledge. One contained complimentary references to Lord Dawson of Penn[48], and stated the writer had hurt his head, but was better now.

One writer enclosed the photograph of a girl he did not know, but which he stated 'had fallen out of a library book at Hammersmith', thus presenting us with a second unknown. Another writer enclosed the picture of a lady described as 'the pin-up girl of the 14th Army'. The lady, who was in native attire, was attractive but not Barbara.[49]

Eventually a practical lead was offered, and 'Bob' was identified as a crew member from a Vickers Wellington.

A heavy weight also fell on those who were involved in casualty procedure from the other side of the correspondence. The Air Ministry, and P.4 (Cas), were not simply offices or organisations. They were groups of men and women undertaking a difficult and sensitive job. The Casualty Branch was principally made up from civilian clerks, but there was also a significant number of WAAF staff. These people were very aware of what they were doing, and the effects it could have at its final destination. Particularly later on and after the war, the WAAF clerks were women who had served on active stations and seen the war first hand before being re-mustered. Leading Aircraftswoman Iris Walter would recall of her time at P.4 (Cas) after the war:

> We had to be very sensitive about what we were doing because this was going out to the next of kin who even some years later would still be upset about it all. And then we'd put that phrase in 'We have now discovered the last resting place of your son/husband/brother' and then we would tell them a little bit about anything the MRES team had discovered about the crash, if there'd been a funeral or military funeral of some kind ... So that would be the next few paragraphs and then we'd have to say 'You're son/husband had been reclassified from "missing in action" to killed in action'[50]

These efforts were usually appreciated, another WAAF recalling that 'we often had some very nice letters back from parents.'[51] Regardless of this, it was not a pleasant job:

> Later on we got some [reports] from the Far East, and these were quite distressing because [if the crew] got out and managed to land, the Japanese simply beheaded them, which of course ... I found it very upsetting.[52]

The staff had few illusions about the subject they were dealing with. Part of their job was to receive the bare, stark facts of the case and then soften them into something more sensitive and acceptable for public consumption. Some of their dealings bought them into very close contact with the tragedies that they were cataloguing. Personal effects from crash sites would be sent to P.4 (Cas) for processing as sorting these could help identify the crew, and for selecting which could or should be passed on to the families:

> I used to go downstairs sometimes with rubber gloves on and smoking cigarettes because [of the smell]. We had lots of effects come back from the 'planes, so we used to sort them through and see if we could identify any of the objects ... Day after day, different 'planes, sorting them out.[53]

Of particular importance as the war entered its final phase, and the Allies liberated increasing tracts of Europe, would be the Missing Research Section of P.4 (Cas). Increasingly enquiries and visitors arrived seeking information on missing men.

CHAPTER FOUR

Missing Research Section, P.4 (Cas)

Empty your pockets, Tom, Dick and Harry,
Strip your identity – leave it behind.
Lawyer, garage-hand, grocer, don't tarry.
With your own country, with your own kind.

Leave all your letters, suburb and township,
Green fen and grocery, slipway and bay,
Hot spring and prairie, smoke-stack and coal-tip,
Leave in our keeping while you are away.

Tom, Dick and Harry; plain names and numbers,
Pilot, Observer and Gunner depart.
Their personal litter only encumbers
Somebody's head; somebody's heart.

John Pudney 'Security'

A t the end of October, 1941, Wing Commander Burges of P.4 (Cas) Branch, Air Ministry, wrote a memo to Air Vice-Marshal Douglas Coyler DFC, Director of Personal Services, Air Ministry, on the subject of missing airmen. 'From time to time', he wrote;

the question arises in the Casualty Branch as to what steps can be taken, and how far we should go, in the conduct of enquiries into the fate of personnel who have been reported missing.[54]

He went on to explain that the public view was often that 'an omniscient Air Ministry must have in its possession full details of what has become of aircraft and crews' but has withheld the information due to reasons of security. Burges gave three examples of officers who had been posted missing during the Battle of France, May 1940, and listed the special efforts

34

made to locate information on their fates. Two, Pilot Officer Saunders and Flight Lieutenant Cogman, had finally been traced, the former after eight months of enquiries and the later after 'a considerable time'. Both searches had involved numerous letters and 'almost endless telephoning'. The third case, Pilot Officer Henry Peter Dixon, had not been solved and after eight months of searching had been abandoned.

Burges's point was that P.4 (Cas) had no remit or guidelines on dealing with unsolved cases. Theoretically their job was to process new casualties, inform the next of kin, and then deal with the paperwork regarding funerals and estates. No forethought had been given to the problem of investigating cases where the status of the casualty was unclear, and with RAF casualty rates increasing as Bomber Command stepped up their offensive and the war in the Middle East picked up pace, there was less time to devote to these cases. Normal work was getting in the way of investigations, and investigations were hindering normal work. In conclusion, Burges asked that the policy on missing aircrew, and the task of investigating their current status, should be clarified, and that if it was decided that it fell within P.4 (Cas)'s remit (as, he points out 'there is no doubt whatever that the public would appreciate it if it were'), that a special section be set up to deal specifically with retrospectively assessing and examining these cases.

Coyler passed Burges's memo on to Air Marshal Sir Phillip Babington MC AFC, the Air Member for Personnel. His covering note recorded that although 'we want to make every effort to meet the wishes of the relatives',[55] he also felt that P.4 (Cas) did not have enough staff to meet both duties. Babington in turn passed the matter on to the Permanent Under Secretary of State for Air, Sir Arthur Street MC, and the Parliamentary Under Secretary of State for Air, Lord Sherwood, for comment and advice. His own position was vague on the matter, but he felt that perhaps the best policy would be to collect and collate evidence for the families, while leaving the 'onus' of actually investigating the matter on them.[56]

A fortnight later, Street's and Sherwood's replies came through. Sir Arthur, an infantry veteran of the First World War with a son in Bomber Command, was ultimately responsible for public relations within the Air Ministry. His view was that 'it would be bad for morale if the idea were to get abroad that the Air Ministry was disinterested in the fate of people who were no further use to the Service'.[57] He suggested the establishment of a small sub-section within P.4 (Cas), one serving officer and two clerical staff, to begin work immediately. Lord Sherwood, answering a day later, was in complete concurrence. Interestingly, he voiced the opinion that the view quoted by Burges about the 'omniscient Air Ministry' was due to the excellent work of P.4 (Cas) to date, implying that nothing should be done to inhibit this work now.[58]

With these agreements came the establishment of the Missing Research Section, P.4 (Cas), on paper at least. The physical establishment took a little longer due to wrangling with the Secretarial Branch of the Air Ministry over the provision of staff. Their view was that if the new investigative team was to lighten the load on P.4 (Cas), then P.4 (Cas) could afford to lose two clerks to form the new Section. It took a terse memo from Burges shortly before Christmas to convince them of the need to assign new staff.[59] Even then, the beginnings were slow. After barely a few weeks in post, the first commanding officer, Pilot Officer Kinnaird, was posted to other duties in February 1942. Flight Lieutenant Alfred Peveril Le Mesurier Sinkinson, an officer already serving with P.4 (Cas), was seconded in his place, but only on top of his other duties. No new personnel would be appointed until July, when Flying Officer Fortreath arrived. His inexperience meant that through July and August 1942, only twenty-five cases could be investigated, of which ten were closed successfully and two unsuccessfully.[60] By the end of the year Fortreath was transferred on, and Flight Lieutenant Sinkinson had officially taken over the MRS, although with the proviso that he could be called back to supplement the main casualty office when needed. Eventually, two further officers would be appointed to assist him, but all would be subject to secondment to other parts of P.4 (Cas) as a matter of last resort. The Air Ministry had an open door policy for this Branch, and personal visits or telephone calls from the relatives of missing airmen were common. Even in the last weeks of the war this problem was still being flagged as a drain on MRS time, although requests for more staff were consistently turned down.[61] Some of these visits would be to the MRS, or even at their request to identify artefacts or provide other information. These rose from an average of ninety-five visitors a week in January 1945 to 145 in April. The MRS had handled an average of two of these visits per week in January, but by April they were dealing with twenty-three, constituting a serious drain on their time and inhibiting their work.[62]

For all the obstacles and shortages faced, the MRS met with a remarkable level of success. Even through July 1942, when staff problems were perhaps at their worst, valuable work was done and the basis of a system of operation laid down. The first MRS progress report, July 1942, recorded the solution of several long running cases. The Pilot Officer Henry Peter Dixon whom Burges had cited nine months earlier as an impossible case was not only traced, but a witness to his death found and his grave located in Dunkirk.[63] Further information on two other men missing from the Battle of France was also obtained, and passed to the families. Although neither case, Pilot Officers Leonard Thomas Dixon and Thomas Borg-Banks, were actually solved to the extent that graves were located, dates of death were confirmed. In all three cases it had simply been a matter of time and consistency to trace those who held the relevant information.

Two further cases were covered in the report. The first was acting on information obtained from the German authorities about a body washed up in Norway in mid-June 1940. The man had no identifying papers, discs or features beyond an RAF uniform with an Air Gunner's brevet. He was estimated to have been dead for approximately 24 hours. Apart from this scant information, descriptions of two personal items and two photographs of the man were passed on. One of the personal items, a signet ring, bore the monogram 'AJH', and in the end it proved a relatively simple operation to compare these initials to a list of air gunners reported missing in the first half of June 1940, and it is proof of the heavy workload of P.4 (Cas) that this had not been done before. One match was found: Corporal Alfred John Hull of 224 Squadron. His wife was approached and she identified his personal effects, and his squadron identified him from the photographs. The photographs were not shown to his wife.[64]

The second was similar, but both more recent and more complex. In this case the body of a Sergeant had been washed up near Whitby in mid-May 1942. Medical examination had produced a time of death of 6–12 weeks ago. Again there were no positively identifying artefacts, although his shirt did bear a service number. Again there were personal items: another monogrammed signet ring, this one with 'AJP', and a Ronson lighter with the same initials. There was also a watch and a bunch of keys. The service number was the obvious place to start, but this number had belonged to a Sergeant Kenneth Elkins in 88 Squadron who had been killed over Le Havre in March. It came down to the initials, again, although this time there was a much broader time period to deal with than before. Eventually, two possibilities were thrown up, and the families of each were shown the artefacts. The wife of one, Sergeant Arthur James Pratley, positively identified them.[65] The MRS was already proving its worth in both clearing the backlog of missing cases, and actively helping in the more complicated of the new cases.

Sinkinson's August 1942 report displayed an even more remarkable range of problems solved and techniques used. Six cases were reported, and in their way are representative of the work of the missing research organisations over at least the next three years, if not the next seven. The first two followed the relatively straight forward pattern already developed in the previous report: the body of a Canadian Sergeant washed up near Worthing in mid-July was identified by his standard issue wrist watch, and the badly decomposed body of an officer found on the Essex shoreline in March was identified by a laundry label. Both of these methods became part of the staple of the MRS. Although often time consuming, following service reference numbers and other numerical clues often yielded the best results. In the case of the Canadian, the RAF and Air Ministry's strict bookkeeping and generation of mountains of paperwork paid off. The reference number stamped on his watch was traced to a batch delivered to 25 Maintenance Unit, from there on to RAF Station Bircham Newton, and from the stores there to Sergeant Alexander Norland Urquhart of 407 Squadron, who had been reported missing, believed killed a month earlier.[66] Serial numbers on almost any piece of kit could be traced. A year later, Flight Lieutenant Sinkinson was to report on the case of a Wellington, which according to intelligence sources had crashed on the night of 12/13 July 1942 near Thildonck. The intelligence report listed a series of numbers found on parts of the wreckage, and these were passed on to the aircraft's manufacturer, Vickers Armstrong Ltd, for identification. They were traced to the fuel tanks of Wellington X3798, which, after cross-referencing with RAF records, was found to have been lost on the 12/13 August 1942. Despite the discrepancy in dates, the known facts fitted. Two bodies had been found and buried, and even without being able to identify the remains at least a start had been made in preparation for any future visits to the site and exhumations.[67]

Harder to follow, at least initially, were laundry labels. Most RAF personnel had their laundry done at either Station laundries or, more likely, contracted local firms. A few made private arrangements. In order for the laundries to keep track of the different items, labels with reference numbers for both the customer (sometime, but by no means always, the person's serial number) and the laundry were sown in. Sometimes these would include the customers name. By definition, these labels were indelible and usually proved to be remarkably durable. Even if faded or decayed, infra-red photography was found to be able to bring out at least partial details. As early as September 1942, Flight Lieutenant Sinkinson had correspondence with the General Secretary of The Institution of British Launderers,[68] as well as the editors of Power Laundry,[69] The Laundry Journal and Laundry Records[70] magazines, asking for advice and issuing appeals for information. On that occasion, full descriptions of three labels were listed, hoping to find the issuing business. The editor of the latter two magazines sent back a detailed description of the standard methods and materials used in marking laundry, which became the foundation of the MRS database of label designs and reference numbers.[71] Close links were maintained with the laundry industry by the MRS and many thousands of men were identified by these means, the first being Pilot Officer Kenneth Le Roy Holder of 121 Squadron, listed as missing since December 1941 and the subject of the second case in Sinkinson's August 1942 report.[72]

The laundries were just one of many organisations that the Missing Research Section began to foster links with. The bulk of their information from overseas still came from the Germans through the *Totenlisten* passed via the International Red Cross. These were not the most reliable of sources, though. In the spring of 1944, the Germans informed the Air Ministry, somewhat belatedly, of the burial of 'Haidee Silver, 40851', supposedly the pilot of a Short Stirling which had crashed near Mons, Belgium, on 15 May 1940. Apart from the obvious discrepancy that Stirlings had not been in service in 1940, the name did not match any known RAF personnel. The number, however, was the service number of a Pilot Officer Michael Henry Grayson Rawlinson, who had been lost at around that date. This officer's father was contacted, and it transpired that his son had been given a silver bracelet from a female relation engraved 'From Haidee'. The body was undoubtedly that of Pilot Officer Rawlinson, but the German report had been garbled at some stage in its process.[73]

These types of confusions were no rarity, and obviously wore a little thin with the officers of the MRS. In October 1944, Sinkinson was informing Wing Commander Burges that 'The Germans have surpassed themselves with an entry in the *Totenliste* which states than an airman called "Lhude Sing Cuccu" was shot down in a Typhoon on 10th January, 1944'. Records showed that a Pilot Officer James Bassett had been lost on that date in a Typhoon over France. Sources confirmed that Bassett had had a verse from the Elizabethan song Llude Sing Cuccu, recently parodied in the flight safety publication Tee Emm, emblazoned across his Mae West. This allowed Bassett's body to be identified and his status confirmed in a remarkably unlikely way.[74]

Although the International Red Cross acted as the official conduit to the Continent, national Red Cross organisations also conveyed information to Britain, even if it was often less detailed than the German records. In March 1944 Sinkinson was reporting that information had been received from the Netherlands Red Cross on a Whitley that had come down near Culemborg on 18 June 1940. The crash and survival of most of the crew had long been known, but the Netherlands report confirmed that the two outstanding members of the crew had been buried in the nearest town. After more than three and a half years the families of the missing men could at last find out what had happened.[75] Even though the individuals had not been identified, again enough information had been gathered to allow positive identification as soon as the Allies reoccupied that area.

Other national organisations had their uses too. For example, incredibly, the German Aero Club maintained links with the British Royal Aero Club, and particularly early in the war was known to pass information on casualties, presumably gathered by its members, on to London.[76] Immediate information would be gained from the intelligence debriefs of other crews on a particular raid or operation. Although, particularly at night, positive identification or knowledge of survivors was slight, perhaps the rough location of the loss could be established, or an idea of how many of the crew escaped gauged by whether an aircraft blew-up in mid air, flew into an object, or fell more slowly to earth. Any and all possibly relevant information would be gathered and noted. At a later date, members of missing crews or other aircraft lost in the same period but who had managed to escape back to Britain would also be quizzed to find out if they had heard or seen anything or anyone of significance.

Less immediate information also flowed across the Channel from many other sources. Allied intelligence provided the RAF with a wealth of material, either from British agents on the Continent, or indirectly through any of the various national resistance movements. As in the case of Wellington X3798 these reports were not always completely accurate, but even the smallest detail could help. Sometimes there was a genuine bonanza, such as in the summer of 1944 when the Mother Superior of Grand Hospital, Caen, handed over a list of all Allied servicemen who had passed through her hands since 1940. The list provided information on forty-eight servicemen, most of them RAF, and some of whom were still officially missing.[77]

Any snippets, no matter how vague or small, would be carefully noted against future use. Dossiers on each missing aircraft, with details on the aircraft, the engine serial numbers if possible, information on the operation on which they were lost, plus any additional intelligence information, were carefully kept, monitored and where possible updated. Inside each dossier separate files were raised on each crew member. Each file was given a reference number, and a simple reference system was used to categorize the cases by location. Cases where the aircraft was presumed lost over France were given the prefix F, Germany were given G, Norway an N, and so on. This system, and these reference numbers, stayed with the dossiers and were subsequently used by the MRES.

When the third case in the August 1942 report came in, of seven aircrew found in a crashed Halifax in Belgium in August 1941, it was a straightforward matter to cross-reference this loss and whittling the possibilities down to being L9572, and the graves of the crew, although not identified individually, were at least logged and their families notified of their deaths.[78]

Slightly harder was the next case, although again it largely came down to a process of elimination. An airman with no identifying clues was found at Ostend following a crash nearby at around 2300hrs on the 24 October 1941.[79] Investigations found that the only unaccounted for aircraft in the area at that time on that night had been Wellington X9828, on its way to raid Frankfurt. The only member of that crew still untraced was Flight Sergeant Arthur John Page. Although there was no direct evidence to confirm that this was Page's body, there was simply no-one else it could be. This type of reasoning did not always bring concrete results, though. For example, another early MRS case was based on information received from the French underground that they had buried an airman called Chapman at Landercies (Nord) in May 1942. No other information had been received on the date or circumstances of his death, or on his rank or initials. There were many missing airmen with the surname Chapman, but a trawl through the records narrowed the options to two men who may have been in that area: either Flight Lieutenant Paul Geoffrey Chapman, lost in a Blenheim on 18 May 1940, or Sergeant G. B. Chapman, a Spitfire pilot lost on 9 August 1941. Only in August 1944 was the identity of the airman confirmed as Flight Lieutenant Chapman, after the discovery of the grave of Sergeant Chapman by the Army at St Omer.[80]

The fifth case from August 1942 was far more complicated. The same source in Belgium had passed on a few fragments of leather and other materials from a crash site.[81] Two of the leather fragments had markings – 'R61780', 'Oida' and what could possibly be 'RCAF'. One of the miscellaneous items was the beginning of a spool of film marked 'Start 7 A/C 7520 S'. In these cases, even the scantiest of details could be used. The prefix R applied, among other things, to RCAF service numbers. With the added evidence of the possible RCAF marking, this avenue was pursued and a name found to match the numbers – Sergeant William Henry Bracken, who had been lost on the 19/20 May 1942. The serials on the film was also traced, and came back confirming that it had been issued from 7 Squadron to Stirling N7520. The crew of this aircraft included Sergeant Bracken and a Pilot Officer Irvine Frank Hoidas. All clues led to the same place, but this crash and the burial of the crew had already been logged a few weeks before.

This sort of fragmentary evidence was the bread and butter of the MRS. As we have seen, it often involved some kind of reference or serial numbers, or a partial name or other standard issue equipment clue. Another common clue was letters, although officially these should not have been taken on operations. By definition these were all the more individual, but this meant that there was less in the way of standard guidelines to follow. Having said that, a good starting point would be to trace, if possible, the sender. In August 1943 the *Totenliste* reported an unidentified body found near Dunkirk. The only identifying item was a letter from 'K Cox 953851, SHQ, RAF, Manston'.[82] Cox was traced and found to be now stationed in Malta. The internal evidence of the letter indicated that it had been written in May or June 1940, so the MRS wrote to him asking who he had written to in that period.[83] His reply indicated that the only possible candidates could have been his two cousins in the 4th Battalion, Royal Berkshire Regiment, both of whom had been listed as missing after the Dunkirk evacuation. It was not unusual for the unidentified cases in the *Totenlisten* to be investigated by the MRS, only for it to transpire that the person had in fact been in the Army, the Fleet Air Arm, or the Royal Navy. The odds were in favour of any new bodies being discovered on the Continent being aircrew, but whenever evidence to the contrary was found the case would be turned over to the Admiralty or, as in this case, the War Office.

Sometimes the sender of a letter could not be traced. A case from the late summer of 1944 involved an airman who had been washed up on the shore near Messina in November 1943.[84] The only clue on the body was a letter from 'Reg' at an address in Wiltshire to 'Jock'. Again, internal evidence provided a date: Wednesday, 30 June 1943. The local constabulary for that address was contacted, and they confirmed that the address belonged to the father of Sergeant Reginald Brown, who unfortunately had been listed as missing at the end of August 1944. Apart from highlighting the long backlogs that the MRS still endured, this case also demonstrates a technique often employed by the Air Ministry. The local police would almost always be consulted when following a lead concerning an address, rather than cold calling the house. At every turn, efforts were made to cause those involved in investigations as little trouble or trauma as possible. In this case Mr Brown, even while waiting for news on his own son, was able to help the investigators, and informed them that his son had had a friend called Jock from Glasgow. He could not clearly remember the surname, but provided a list of possible names and derivates. One of these led to Sergeant John 'Jock' Hagan, from Glasgow, who had gone missing on 24 October 1943 after a raid on an airfield in Italy.

The final case on Sinkinson's first report back in August 1942 was somewhat less than orthodox. It concerned Walrus L2312, which had last been seen leaving RAF Mountbatten in the early hours of 18 June 1940 on a secret mission to the coast of Brittany.[85] Onboard had been the three crew members, Flight Lieutenant John Napier Bell and Sergeant Charles William Harris of the Royal Australian Air Force, and Corporal Bernard Felix Nowell RAF, plus one passenger, a British Army officer employed by the Admiralty, Captain Norman Hope. The aircraft was neither seen nor heard of again, or at least not until two French boys escaped across the Channel in October 1941. They reported that an aircraft had crashed at Ploundaniel, near Finisterre, and the crew had all been killed. Their bodies had all been recovered and buried. Three had been positively identified as Flight Lieutenant Bell, Corporal Nowell and Sergeant Bennet. The fourth appeared from their description to be Sergeant Harris. The problem here, of course, was that there had not been a Sergeant Bennet on the aircraft, nor was there any sign of Captain Hope. Enquiries were made with the units and parent units involved, as well as individual officers to double check the known details and seek any possible explanations. Letters were received from as far afield as Plymouth, Northern Ireland, Thorney Island and Iceland, but no-one could shed any light on the situation. The best guess of any of the correspondents, and at the end of the day of the MRS, was that Hope had taken on the fictitious identity of Bennet due to the secrecy of his mission. This view was, and still is, officially supported.

This was not the only case where all was not always as it seemed. *Totenliste* 177 reported that 440176 Eden M, had been washed up in Schleswig-Holstein on the 14 August 1943. There was no information on how this identity had been established, which was unfortunate as Leading Aircraftswoman 440176 M. Eden was very much alive and well and stationed with 17 Operational Training Unit at RAF Silverstone. At this point, Sinkinson reported, the MRS made 'tactful enquiries by telephone and letter to the WAAF officer i/c WAAF Section, Silverstone'. She replied that Eden's fiancée had been missing, but was now a confirmed prisoner of war. Further digging revealed that Eden had corresponded with one other airman previous to her engagement: Flight Sergeant Dwain Nowell Hunter RCAF, an air gunner on a Lancaster reported missing on the night of 29/30 July 1943. This evidence was considered enough to identify formally Flight Sergeant Hunter's body.

No definitive statistics exist for the work of the MRS. Only a fraction of their work was ever reported on in their bi-annual reports, a representative sample to help Wing Commander Burges in his never ending struggle for manpower and resources. Only the tip of those cases have been reproduced here. By the middle of the war the families of all missing personnel were receiving an Air Ministry leaflet – 'Advice to the relative of a man who is missing' – which assured them that they 'make every endeavour to discover the fate of missing men, and draw upon all likely sources of information about them.'[86] The leaflet outlined the various options of where information could arrive from, and asked them for patience and not to listen to enemy broadcasts, which were often (intentionally or otherwise) misleading. It ended with the promise that 'this official service is also a very humane service, which well understands the anxiety of relatives and will spare no effort to relieve it', hence the P.4 (Cas) open door policy.

Hundreds of missing airmen were identified and their cases closed through the work of Sinkinson and his assistants, and information gathered on thousands more. A complete database was compiled of missing aircrew, with all the known details and evidence filed and referenced. By the end of 1944, most of the open cases could not be resolved from London: it may be that the Germans lacked the expert knowledge to identify fully a wreck or body, or that the burial site of some or all of a crew was known, but not the individual identities. These types of cases could only be solved by physically visiting the sites and examining the remains, be they human or machine. Thanks to the MRS, the information needed to locate and analyse these sites was in place. All that was needed was the manpower and command decision to pursue the matter onto the Continent.

In December 1944, Supreme Headquarters Allied Expeditionary Force authorised a field unit of the MRS to enter France. Squadron Leader William Mace Mair RCAF was appointed as commander of the new unit, termed the Missing Research and Enquiry Section. Six Flight Lieutenants were selected from volunteers as search officers, each with a driver, and a general duties clerk appointed to assist Mair. The search officers were carefully selected with several criteria in mind. All had lived and worked in France before the war: a lawyer, a farmer, a travel agent, a wool merchant, a tailor, and the owner of an English bar in Paris.[87] Of the six, three were RAF, one RAAF, one RCAF and one RNZAF roughly to reflect the proportions of men still missing in Europe (see Appendix A). Apart from that, there were few selection criteria, simply because no-one quite knew what to expect in France, or what skills would be needed.

Squadron Leader Mair had spent the war in various staff posts, including a short period in the summer of 1944 with the casualty staff of HQ 6 (RCAF) Group of Bomber Command. Now, he faced a completely blank slate. There were no procedures or guidelines for the task he faced, and almost everything had to be developed from scratch. Ironically nature and transport delays acted in his favour. He had arrived in France in the first week of January 1945[88] to take up residence in the British Army Staff Building in Paris, but severe weather prevented the rest of his team from crossing the Channel for another month.[89] By this time, the motor transport that had been earmarked for their use had been diverted to another theatre.[90] Replacements would not become available until April, thus beginning what would become a recurring theme in MRES operations. At least this enforced immobility gave the team time to find their feet and begin establishing operating procedures and filing systems. This was ground breaking work, summed up in January 1948 in the citation for Squadron Leader Mair's Order of the British Empire, by which time he was Senior Officer in Charge of Exhumations and Identification:

He joined the Missing Research and Enquiry Service in December 1944 and has taken a large and responsible part in the initial organization of this Branch of the Service. He is entirely responsible for the exhumation procedure now in use, which he evolved from his own experience of research work in the field, and the application of his methods has enabled a large number of missing aircrew to be traced. Apart from being a most efficient officer, Squadron Leader Mair subordinates everything to his official duties and does not spare himself. He has continuously worked for long hours in an endeavour to perfect the organization and much of the success of the

Missing Research and Inquiry (sic) Service is due to his foresight, planning and energy. The Missing Research Enquiry Units have a thankless and at times horrible task to perform but their importance cannot be too strongly emphasized. Squadron Leader Mair's work is particularly noteworthy.[91]

Despite the problems, the search officers began work in the cemeteries in and around Paris, although a major administrative proving ground soon came their way. In November 1944 Wing Commander Burges had visited Paris and met with Madame L'Herbier of the Amicale des Infirmieres Pilotes et des Secouristes de l'Air (Union of Pilot Nurses and Air Rescuers), a section of the French Red Cross.[92] Madame L'Herbier, who later also received the OBE, had spent the war travelling around French hospitals gathering information on initially French Air Force, and then all Allied, air crew casualties. This had extended into gleaning information on crash and burial sites, too. All of these records were now in MRES hands, and they provided the first significant inroad into the incredible task of tracing those Allied air crew still missing in Europe.

In March 1945 the Air Ministry Weekly Orders included 'A.247 – RAF and Dominion Air Forces' Missing Research and Enquiry Service', announcing the establishment of No. 1 Missing Research and Enquiry Section. The order clarified their role, and appealed to all units, whether those undertaking their own research or those who came across or were given evidence, to pass their records on to P.4 (Cas). The last paragraph noted that an 'Announcement will be made of the establishment of additional sections when their formation is found necessary and approved.'

CHAPTER FIVE

Missing Research and Enquiry Service

This is a preliminary warning letter, the object of which is to enlist your support and assistance in what I regard as a most important activity, namely Missing Research and Enquiry .... We have got to undertake this work on a very much larger scale than at present if we are to have a hope of tracing anything more than a very small percentage of our missing aircrew before all clues are obliterated and local inhabitants forget or lose interest in evidence which we know is often still available ... Relatives naturally wish to get information on the fate of missing aircrew, and unless we can show that everything reasonably possible is being done to trace them, we shall be failing in our duty.[93]

Letter from Air Marshal Sir John Slessor, Air Member for Personnel, to Air Chief Marshal Sir Sholto Douglas, commander British Air Forces of Occupation, 10 August 1945

I n the summer of 1945 the Royal Air Force faced reverting to a peacetime footing. In the years since 1939 they had expanded and developed almost beyond recognition. The small, professional inter-war force had become a sprawling beast full of new technologies and purposes. Metal aircraft and jet engines had replaced the string and fabric biplanes of 1937 and 1938. Entire air forces had sprung up across the world, with vast training and logistical organisations developed to support them.

In the Far East Japan was still to be knocked out of the war, a process RAF planners confidently expected to take another 18 months. To this end, quite apart from the fighter and tactical bomber forces supporting the army in Burma and the maritime reconnaissance and strike aircraft patrolling the Indian and Pacific Oceans, a large segment of Bomber Command had been allocated to contribute to the campaign against the Japanese home islands, known as Tiger Force. This would entail a dock being built on the island of Okinawa, with infrastructure being constructed to connect it to the site of an entirely new airfield. The men, machinery and materials for this would have to be transported half way around the world, and then supply lines maintained. Everything this new air force would need to operate, from rations to bombs, toothbrushes to fuel, would need to be shipped 20,000 km (12,000 miles). Meantime, the bomber force of ten or more squadrons would need to be flown the same distance, with fuel and maintenance available along the way. Two of these squadrons, 9 and 617, had reached India by the time Japan unexpectedly surrendered in August 1945.

Even then, the RAF's duties did not slacken. Allied prisoners of war had to be located, food and medical supplies dropped to them, and eventually the prisoners evacuated to a safe place. As the Allied powers, particularly Britain, France and the Netherlands, reclaimed their colonial possessions air power was needed for transport and communications as well as suppressing local nationalist forces. From Java to Indo-China the RAF provided the bulk of these forces. So short were resources that in Indo-China Japanese pilots and aeroplanes were conscripted for use. As Task Force Gremlin, this arrangement would carry on for over a year.

In the Middle East many of the same problems applied. Egypt and Palestine were vital to Britain's communications with the rest of Africa and with Asia. Airfields and radio relay stations maintained the flow of material and information each way, while also guarding the strategically vital Suez Canal. Libya also needed occupation until a new government could be arranged, and for several years after the war German prisoners had to be guarded until shipping or aeroplanes could be found to take them home.

Across Europe the British Air Forces of Occupation maintained a strong presence to deter resistance, and be ready to rebuff any threats from the east. Air power had been vital to winning the war, and the threat of continued bombing was perceived as vital to keeping both the Axis powers and the Soviets in check. Meanwhile fleets of transport aircraft and bombers dropped supplies to the starving population of Holland, and began flying liberated Allied prisoners home.

In South Africa, Canada, Rhodesia and America training units kept up the flow of new pilots and aircrew. In these and dozens of other countries maritime patrol units kept the sea lanes open and safe. Over laying all of these commitments were the RAF's transport roles; a global, pioneering network of air routes supported military and political movement, communications and control. Scheduled flights could move men or despatches from one side of the globe to the other in a matter of days, and were vital to the post war strategies of the British government. Even where these routes were flown by civilian companies, the radar and radio latticework that maintained safety and control over them was run and manned by the RAF.

All of these commitments and drains on resources were against a background of public and political demands to cut budgets and to initiate and then accelerate the process of demobilizing its wartime members. Even as all of these calls on the RAF flooded in, radical new technologies and types of aeroplanes were entering service, each needing ground and air personnel to be trained, and appropriate maintenance facilities and techniques established. Everything possible had to be done to keep up at least the pretence of being able to revert immediately to a war footing should the Soviets strike west.

In short, over the summer of 1945 the Royal Air Force was providing the sinews that held the new world together, and was gradually being stretched apart by an incredible range of conflicting demands on resources and manpower. Even as arguably the most dynamic and adaptive of the three armed services (neither of the other two had faced such rapid development of technology or tactics over the previous six years) it was hard pressed to meet all of these calls, as such radical policies as Task Force Gremlin demonstrated. This just makes it all the more extraordinary that in July and August 1945 a most remarkable set of meetings occurred at the Air Ministry.

The first was held on the 26 July. The minutes[94] record that the Air Member for Personnel, Sir John Slessor, and senior staff from his and other relevant departments, both RAF and Civil Service, gathered to discuss one thing: the men who were still listed as missing from the war so far. The estimates available were sketchy, fluctuating between 20 and 30,000 aircrew; the real figure of just shy of 42,000 would not be calculated until the following year. In fact, the number needing Air Ministry attention was much higher. On top of these, there were tens of thousands more men whose fate was only known through German communiqués. Experience had shown much of the evidence produced by the Germans to be shaky, and as much as anything these men needed to be properly accounted for. The focus of the meeting was the work of the Missing Research and Enquiry Service (MRES) in Europe, and whether the expenditure in men and resources in these austere times could be justified.

Already the original Missing Research and Enquiry Unit team had expanded.[95] Plans had obviously been afoot since at least March 1945, when the Air Ministry Order was issued on the MRES. After explaining the function of the unit, and the chain of command, the Order laid out how officers in the field could pass on any information relating to missing airmen that they came across. The Order concluded with the implication that further search sections would soon be formed. This had become the case in May 1945 when No. 2 Section was raised in Belgium, and based in

Brussels. In June No. 3 and No. 4 Sections were created to act as mobile units in France, trawling through the countryside. In July No. 5 Section was formed in The Hague to cover Holland, and No. 6 Section in Oslo to cover Norway. Even as this meeting took place, moves were afoot to create No. 7 Section in Denmark, based in Esbjerg, and No. 8 Section in Germany, with its headquarters at Bunde, both of which came into being in August. In July the decision had been made to place these units, for administrative reasons, in 28 Group, Technical Training Command.

The Air Ministry committee firstly considered the policies then in effect with the Army on the continent, based around the Graves Registration Units. These swept across Europe following the old front lines, cataloguing and identifying bodies as they went. This was the standard practice in most countries and forces, but the committee agreed that the RAF 'missing problem ... requires special and different treatment'. Due to the unique nature of aerial operations, the traditional system was no longer sufficient, and if the missing aircrew were to be accounted for, a new system was needed. The crucial question was, was every missing man to be accounted for? Was the MRES to be proactive or reactive?

In this they were adamant. 'The Air Ministry', they stated, had 'an obligation to elucidate the fate of "missing" personnel'. Partly this was due to the public interest in the issue, but there were other possible motivations too. But whatever the cause, it was decided that 'the public interest in the missing problem [demands] that the highest priority be accorded to the requirements of the Missing Research and Enquiry Service'. It was proposed that the MRES would be radically expanded, with three main field units one each based in France, Germany and the Low Countries, all under the operational control of P.4 (Cas) in London. Each would consist of fifty search officers, with individual transport and drivers, plus clerical staff. Significant in this was the specific mention of motor transport, something from which the ground forces suffered a perennial shortage.

To minimise the impact on operational capacity, the search officers for the field units were to be drawn from the RAF's pool of redundant air-crew[96] or from officers due for demobilisation. Another, more enigmatic, source of recruits would be repatriated prisoners of war. The reasoning behind this is obscure – it would have been thought that after years of enforced captivity far from home they would not have been willing candidates for further duties abroad. Perhaps the reasoning was that, as men out of touch with modern types and techniques, they would be no loss to the RAF's front line strength. It is also possible that these men were expected to have language skills and first-hand knowledge of processes that shot down air crew went through that could help them in their investigations. For equally enigmatic reasons, the policy of systematically recruiting ex-prisoners of war was abruptly ended soon after.

The July meeting closed by setting up a sub-committee to examine the practicalities of expanding the MRES more closely. It was emphasised that 'the matter is to be pursued as one of great urgency', and that future plans had to produce a Service capable of accounting for all missing air crew within the rather hopeful target of one year. A week later, 2 August 1945, this new committee met in the office of, and was chaired by, Air Commodore C. Grierson, Slessor's Deputy Parliamentary Secretary.[97] It included many of the same staff, including Group Captain Burges (head of P.4 (Cas), and Director of Missing Research), and Mr. F. H. Denny from the Air Ministry's Secretarial Branch, S.1. Strangely, two faces from the previous week were missing: Squadron Leader Sinkinson, who had perhaps the widest experience in the work of tracing and identifying missing airmen, and Wing Commander (soon to become Group Captain) Eustace Hawkins DSO, who would eventually lead the MRES in the field.

Wing Commander Lancashire had been tasked after the last meeting to develop a draft table of strength for the expanded MRES. He presented his findings in two parts. Firstly, there was the Headquarters for each of the three projected units, comprising: a Wing Commander in charge, a Squadron Leader as second in command, a Flying Officer as adjutant, and three further Flying Officers respectively in charge of equipment, motor transport, and accounts. At this time, each would have come under the direct operational control of P.4 (Cas) in London, albeit with a designated Group Captain as liaison officer. This meant that their movements and actions would be controlled centrally from London. However, administrative control would come from the nearest appro-priate major RAF unit; from their existing stores and systems the MRES would draw pay, rations and supplies. Secondly, there were the field units. Each of the units would have six sections on paper, but the arrangement would be fluid. Any of the eighteen sections could be trans-ferred between units if additional men were needed. For example, one of the three projected units could lend a section to become the nucleus of the fourth unit it was now being proposed should be set up in Scandinavia to help get that running. Each section would have a Squadron Leader (in command), three Flight Lieutenants and one Flying Officer as search officers, each with an airman as driver.

The composition of these sections, nationality-wise, would continue to follow that of the original No. 1 Section. Indeed, the whole of the MRES would be roughly proportioned with the broad breakdown of RAF casualties during the war, for the time being at least. As time went on and the search passed through the one year limit, the Dominion governments increasingly clamoured to have their officers returned for demobilisation. This problem was in the future and beyond the year originally planned. All that mattered for the time being was that the expansion had both been approved and, now, a clear plan set out.

Within a week arrangements were being made for the expansion of P.4 (Cas) to cope with the increased administration expected to accompany search efforts. Slessor personally wrote to Air Marshal G. Johnson at the RCAF Head Quarters in Lincoln's Inn Field in an attempt to procure space there to act as an overflow for P.4 (Cas)s main Oxford Street offices.[98] A day later, 10 August, Slessor was also writing to Air Chief Marshal Sir Sholto Douglas, commander of the British Air Forces of Occupation in Europe, asking him to place 'a very high priority' on the MRES's requirements regarding rations, accommodation, and the supply and maintenance of motor transport.[99] After outlining the role of the MRES ('a most important activity'), he added that a Group Captain would soon be appointed to join HQ BAFO to oversee the MRES and co-ordinate meeting their requirements.

In August 1945 the Missing Research and Enquiry Service underwent the sought after expansion, but would take a larger shape than even the sub-committee had envisaged. Once the Air Ministry began, they found that five units were required, with a few odd sections extra. The existing sections in France were grouped together as No. 1 Missing Research and Enquiry Unit (MREU), with the added remit of searching Luxembourg.[100] In Brussels No. 2 MREU was formed to cover Belgium and Holland, although it later moved on to search Czechoslovakia and the French Zone of Germany.[101] No. 3 MREU was formed around No. 7 Section in Esbjerg, and tasked with clearing Norway and Denmark, and later the American Zone in Germany.[102] The old No. 8 Section became the nucleus for No. 4 MREU, who were faced with the unenviable job of searching the British and Russian Zones of Germany, and later Poland. Their HQ was to be in Hamburg; not a pleasant posting considering the potential hostility of the local population, who would vividly remember the fire storm raid of 1943. This one would also later be the parent unit of the Berlin detachment.[103] These four units came under the umbrella of HQ MRES North-West Europe (NWE), commanded by Wing Commander Eustace Fellowes Hawkins DSO. Hawkins had been a Colonel in the Royal Artillery during the First World War, and during the inter-war period had lived in France, first as the Paris manager for Rolls-Royce Motor Cars Division, and from 1936 as Continental Sales representative for the Hawker Siddeley Aircraft Company, Ltd. He had attempted to rejoin the Army in 1939 but was turned down on grounds of age, and so he had applied instead to the RAF, this time taking a slightly more liberal approach to the enlistment forms. After spending most of the war on Air Ministry duties, he had joined the MRES in December 1944 and became Deputy Director of Missing Research.

The last fully fledged unit, independent of Hawkins' HQ MRES NWE, was the Mediterranean and Middle East Unit, renumbered as No. 5 MREU in July 1946.[104] Their task was to search the Mediterranean area and North Africa, moving on later into Italy, Austria and the Balkans.

Now that areas of responsibility had been assigned, some form of structure was needed to maximise coverage with the limited resources available. Each of these five main units followed a similar pattern. A central headquarters, under a Wing Commander or Squadron Leader, exercised more or less control over the unit's area of operations. The commanding officer would be supported by an Operations Officer, usually a Squadron Leader, and an Adjutant, usually a Flying Officer, and between them they controlled, co-ordinated and monitored all field operations and maintained contact with London. Fresh information or requests for help moving either way passed through their office, where several airmen would be employed as clerks, and orders issued to sections or teams as appropriate. They also handled the more standard duties of command – ensuring adequate logistic support and rations, keeping an eye on morale and work loads, and dealing with personnel matters. There would be a cadre of civilian interpreters and secretaries also on hand to provide local knowledge and clerical support. In the larger areas of operation – France or the Mediterranean, for example – these HQs would move around the country as various areas were cleared. In the smaller areas, such as the zones of Germany, they would more often be static.

Each unit HQ usually controlled eight sections. These radiated out from the HQ, spread around the surrounding countryside. Usually a section would be allocated to a local government district. Sections would on average consist of five search teams, with each team being an officer (of Flying Officer rank or above) and an airman driver. The commander of the section, a Squadron Leader, would himself be one of the search officers. He would also have had a clerk and some local staff to help him administer his teams.

This chain of command was flexible to say the least. Work loads for each section and team were left to the, usually impeccable, conscience of the officers involved. As we will see, the highly motivated unit personnel were left largely to decide their own schedules and methods of working.

Finally, there were the stray sections established in the Far East. These were never grouped together as a numbered unit, but acted semi-independently, probably due to the distances between them. Initially four search teams were established in Burma, and one in Siam and Indo-China.[105] Unlike Europe, the terrain was simply too dense and difficult to sweep, and so their searches would be intelligence based. Perhaps operations in the Far East could be handled on this reduced scale because of the efforts being made by the Australian Contact and Enquiry Service which was sweeping through New Guinea and the Philippines, contacting local tribes for information on crashes, and the Dutch Death Investigation Service, working on a similar project.

This all amounted to a significant outlay of men and resources. A memo from July 1946 stated there were 172 officers and 300 airmen in the four northern European units alone, with corresponding locally employed interpreters and clerks, plus the secretarial staff in London.[106]

However, just because their offspring were growing up, this did not mean that the work of the MRS had ended. In London they still sorted out the paper trail of the MRES's work. A major part of the work of the Casualty Branch, which had become absorbed back into their pre-war home, S.7, in 1946, was in trawling back through their archives to see which of the tens of thousands of still-open cases had any chance of success now that teams were operating on the continent. These cases would be sorted and sent, with all appropriate information, to the nearest field unit, to be passed from them down to a section and finally to a team for investigation. However, cases often turned up clues that could only be made into meaningful information by cross-referencing with official files that were too extensive to be carried into the field, or by checking details with the families of the suspected airman, and here again the London offices came into play. For example, there was the case of the Canadian Halifax that had been shot down near Bracht during a raid on Duisburg in 1944. Four of the eight man crew had been captured. Two bodies had been found and identified by the Germans. Two more were unaccounted for. In 1949 a team from 4 MREU investigated the case and uncovered part of the wreckage, and the two missing bodies were found inside the fuselage. They were no longer at their original stations, and there were no clues left as to their identities except a well-worn and patched pipe on one of them. The solution to the case involved extensive leg work on the part of both the Air Ministry and the RCAF in Ottawa. Eventually the next of kin of both of the missing men were contacted and those of one confirmed that their relative had been a pipe-smoker. Furthermore, they produced evidence that he had damaged his pipe shortly before being posted as missing and had in fact written home to request a new one. This tied in to the evidence of damage and basic repair work on the pipe that had been found. This was enough to formally identify one of the missing men, and of course the other by default. Shortly afterwards all four of the Canadians were re-interred in the Reichswald Cemetery.[107]

Some that they came across simply needed more time and effort spent on them. Such had been the backlog that had built up over the war years that some relatively straight-forward cases had been put to one side. For example, a few months after the case of the Canadian pipe, the MRS re-examined a case that had come to them through the *Totenlisten* in

January 1944. An unidentified airman had been found at a crash site near Berlin. The only distinguishing feature had been a pocket Bible, inscribed on the fly leaf with the name 'E. G. Ashby' and an address in South Woodford. No-one by that name had appeared on the casualty lists of the time so the case had been set to one side. Five years later it was re-examined and it was decided to check the address given. Investigation showed that Mr E. G. Ashby was alive and well and living at the said address. He had no relatives or direct links to any missing airman, but it transpired that during the war he had, among other things, belonged to a religious organisation and had distributed copies of the Bible on his various travels. Thankfully for the MRS, he had kept a list of all those servicemen he had given a Bible to, and a copy of this was checked and cross-referenced with the casualty lists. One man stood out: Sergeant William Currie. Mr Ashby had given him a Bible in 1943, and Currie, by this time a Pilot Officer, had later been reported as missing from a raid on Berlin in early 1944. Armed with this new information, the Berlin Detachment of the MRES were asked to exhume the unidentified body from the grave in the Russian Zone of Berlin. They did so, but absolutely no positive information was found to help identify the body as Pilot Officer Currie. Now stymied, the Air Ministry contacted the officer's father and laid the facts before him. He announced that he was satisfied with the evidence of the Bible, and so the Air Ministry formally identified Pilot Officer Currie and marked his grave accordingly.[108]

The evidence received by the Missing Research Section was not always case specific. Large numbers of files had been taken from the German authorities at the end of the war. These included the master files for the *Totenlisten*, and the files from the *Dulag Luft*. This was the prisoner of war camp located a few miles north-west of Frankfurt used as a clearing station for all downed aircrew. Run by the *Luftwaffe* Air Operations Staff and the *Abwehr* (German intelligence), the site included a designated crash-file building. During their stay, aircrew would be interrogated in what could be fairly rough methods. Any form of abuse and discomfort short of physical violence could be brought to bear to extract information, one result being a comprehensive list of crashes, the names and fates of the men involved, and the rough locations.[109] Although imperfect and work intensive to use, they did add another layer of information to the Air Ministry's files. Further snippets would also arrive from the most unlikely of sources. At the end of the war a photograph album was received from a member of the Dorsetshire Regiment. The album had been picked up as a souvenir from a *Luftwaffe* airfield near Bremen. It had belonged to a member of a long-range Junkers Ju.88 squadron, which had operated over the Bay of Biscay and the Atlantic from 1943. From the photographs and ephemera contained in the album the MRS were able to pin point the location of nine RAF casualties, and confirm the fate of ten other aircraft.[110]

Not all cases involved men lost on operations in the air. On 7 November 1944 a landing craft, LST 420, moving personnel up the coast of Belgium sank. Various unidentified airmen were subsequently washed up along the Channel. One was distinguishable only by an Indian rubber found in his pocket, with the name 'Evans' and a partial service number on it. The landing craft's passenger list was checked, and a Leading Aircraftsman Evans with a matching service number had indeed been on board. However, he had survived the sinking. Contact was made, and he reported that he thought he may have lent his rubber to Leading Aircraftsman William Williams, who had been killed. In all conscience, the Air Ministry decided that this was not enough to formally identify the body, though, and the remains were interred as an unknown airman.[111]

Before turning to the field work of the Missing Research and Enquiry Service, perhaps one more example should be raised. It should be remembered that the role of the London 'tail' of the organisation was not merely checking facts, or carrying the investigations further than could be done in the field, but also to act in direct liaison with the families of the missing men. All three aspects can be seen in this last case. A search team from No. 1 MREU in France sent back a propelling pencil, the only clue found in the wreckage of a bomber. The pencil was marked 'Ardhallow, Dumbarton'. Initially it was assumed that Ardhallow was a surname, but an extensive search of the files found no missing airmen of that name. Next they searched for manufacturers, but again could find no-one. Finally the MRS wrote to the Chief Constable of Dumbarton asking for his advice. The Chief Constable replied that Ardhallow was the name of a house in the town, occupied by a married couple. These people were approached and it transpired that the lady's brother had been a sergeant in the RAF and aircrew, reported missing in 1941. She recognised the pencil as one that she had given to him. Although this case had been successfully resolved, with not only the sergeant but by extension the rest of the crew being positively identified, the involvement of the MRS did not end there. The sergeant's sister requested the pencil be returned to her as a keep sake, but he also had a widow who, as next of kin, was entitled to all of his effects. Before closing the case and moving on, the pencil was sent to the widow with a letter laying out the sister's desire to have the pencil returned to her and tactfully requesting that serious consideration to her case be made.[112]

CHAPTER SIX

Around the World I Search For Thee

There was [no training] as far as I was concerned, nor was any necessary. My experience as former aircrew was sufficient for the purpose: to find a designated place, question local German authorities and independent citizens about aircraft crashes or associated burials in the area, dig holes, record evidence from recovered uniform and aircraft remains and, therefrom, to complete an exhumation report for onward transmission to the Air Ministry. Recovered aircrew remains were wrapped in Service blankets and handed over to the Army Graves Service for transportation and re-interment in the nearest Allied Military Cemetery.[113]

Sqdn Ldr Bill Lott
OC 20 Section No. 4 MREU

T he task facing the MRES was unpleasant to say the least. The men filling the ranks would know the trauma, and had likely witnessed first hand, that an aircraft crash could inflict on a body, and that is not even considering the likelihood of a fire as well. Include anything up to ten years of decomposition, and few would have any illusions about the graphic nature of the task before them. Identifying these bodies would not be an easy job, let alone finding them in the first place.

With the framework for operations in place, the personnel were now needed to form the units. Recruitment was a varied process. Some officers appear to have been 'head hunted'. Wing Commander Angus Mclean RCAF was appointed from the Test and Development Establishment to command No. 2 Unit in Belgium. Squadron Leader Philip Laughton-Bramley was also selected, and with ample qualifications by the lights of the MRES. A member of the Royal Naval Air Service during the First World War, he had settled in France after the war. He had retained a commission in the RAF Reserve, and had been reactivated in 1939 and attached to 60 Wing, British Expeditionary Force, in France. He had become separated from them during the hectic retreat of May 1940, and had arrived at Dunkirk too late to be picked up. Gathering a group of stray RAF personnel, successfully evading capture, he eventually found a Belgian fisherman willing to ferry them to Britain, from where he was posted to Singapore, and from there to Australia. Here he fulfilled several staff roles, including on the staff of Admiral 'Bull' Halsey, the US Naval commander in the South Pacific. Here was a resourceful officer of strong character and wide experience, quite apart from the language skills acquired from twenty years living in France.[114]

Officers lower down the line were also liable to being picked out of the crowd of officers and aircrew that the cessation of hostilities had left suddenly unemployed. Squadron Leader Bernard Moorcroft DSO DFC had entered a generic application for a posting to the Air Ministry in the hope of being stationed in or near London, where his new wife was living.[115] The interview for an appointment to the MRES was completely unexpected, as it was also for Flight Lieutenant Colin Mitchell. He was simply called to the Oxford Street offices of P.4 (Cas) and, as with most of the other officers, found himself facing Group Captian Hawkins and one or two other officers in a formal interview.[116]

Most members were recruited through more orthodox channels. The announcement about the unit in the Air Ministry Monthly Orders and other official publications had encouraged some to volunteer their services. Flight Lieutenant Roger St Vincent was stationed at No. 1 Air Command, Canada, when he had heard of the new unit. He had been sent with a draft of volunteers from Halifax by ship via Southampton and the aircrew transit centre at Bournemouth to the MRES cadre at RAF Gatwick. Here, after some initial problems, he joined Maclean's 2 MREU.[117] Hearsay could also be a factor. While kicking his heels at a holding unit at RAF Harrogate, a friend of Flight Lieutenant Ron Myhill mentioned to him that the MRES was being formed. Apart from appearing to be a worthwhile and interesting job, it was a way out of a state of limbo.[118] Flight Lieutenant Harry Wilson DFM had a similar experience, except that he was watching the formation of the units directly:

> *In February 1946 I was stationed at RAF Gatwick when I became aware of a unit that was forming there before proceeding to Germany. The formation of the unit, RAF, RAAF, RCAF and RNZAF, seemed like being back on [a] Bomber Squadron and the job they were about to undertake seemed to me as a job well worth doing.*[119]

The selection process for the new units was scant to say the least. Some officers recalled interviews with Hawkins, estimated at having lasted anything from fifteen minutes to two hours. Recollections of the content vary but some kind of language test was involved. Flight Lieutenant

St Vincent sat on the panels testing officers for their French skills before talking his way into the field, but recalls little else of what was involved. It appears that career prospects were discussed (it would be pointless employing anyone coming up for demob in the next year) as was the nature of the job. No-one had any illusions over what the task facing them involved.

Even less clear are what qualities the interview panels were looking for. Official paperwork on these issues remains frustratingly illusive, although it is clear that initially efforts were made to particularly recruit ex-prisoners of war. Why this policy was halted is not known. What is certain is that throughout the life of the unit it was aircrew who were most coveted and courted to act as search officers.

In some ways aircrew were the obvious choice. Apart from their availability now that the war was over, these men had to have had certain qualities to do their jobs, not the least of which was high intelligence. Add to that attention to detail, methodical minds, and tenacity, and they had the makings of first class detectives. Flight Lieutenant Mitchell saw it this way:

> Every search officer had to have been aircrew, because by their training they would have to be obstinate, and pedantic, with an eye for detail. The 'quick flick' was not good enough for this type of work.[120]

Another reason was familiarity with the subject matter. Aircraft recognition was part of their job, making the identification of wreckage easier. They would also have had certain expert knowledge that would have made identifying bodies easier. Flight Lieutenant St Vincent recalled:

> Most officers who had served on mixed squadrons composed of British, Australians, Canadians, Newzies, Rhodesians and others knew of their country flash and even material of the uniform.[121]

They had worked with the subjects of their searches. You will not find any Pilot Officers, the lowest commissioned rank held for one year after qualifying as an officer, on the lists of search officers, and relatively few Flying Officers. Most officers in the MRES would be Flight Lieutenants or above; men with experience of command and the RAF. With their expertise they would be able to identify and date equipment and clothing, while arguably the experience of the war and the heavy losses suffered by the RAF would have hardened them to their task. It must have brought a certain amount of commitment into play, too.

The only solid condition that the Air Ministry set on the make up of the MRES was that the nationalities involved should roughly reflect the proportions of those who were missing. About 69 per cent of these were

RAF, 17 per cent RCAF, 7 per cent RAAF, 3 per cent RNZAF and 4 per cent from the Allied Air Forces, be they Polish, Czech, French, Norwegian, Greek or any other nationality. By July 1946 the 172 officers on strength under HQ North-West Europe consisted of about 62 per cent RAF (106), 17 per cent RCAF (30), 13 per cent RAAF (22) and 8 per cent RNZAF (14), with 40 of the 300 airmen also being Canadians.[122]

Once selected, training was minimal. The days at RAF Gatwick as the teams waited for arrangements to be made to send them to the Continent were long and empty. Short courses by Air Ministry staff provided basic information on the task ahead, but little in the way of practical advice. Case studies were drawn from the experiences of the Missing Research Section, but the nature of their work had been suitably different to make the illustrations of limited use.[123] Pathology, for example, would naturally be a significant part of the search officer's skill base, but was something that the MRS had barely needed to touch on. Beyond lectures on basic physiology no instruction was given on these areas. Most of the training received was of the 'on the job' variety. Through the last few months of 1945 resources and transport became available to begin sending staff to the Continent. Here they joined the cadres formed by the original eight search sections, and it became a case of the older hands instructing the more recent ones in the finer points of their new trades. Officers and men joining No. 3 MREU at RAF Uetersen in October 1946 found themselves attending seven solid days of lectures by Squadron Leader Rideal and Flight Sergeant Ledger, before being detailed into search teams on the eighth.[124]

Other ranks had a somewhat less elaborate introduction to the MRES. They were simply selected and posted through the usual Royal Air Force channels. Corporal Douglas Hague was working with an Air Disarmament Unit in Germany when his orders came through:

Our postings came through and mine was to this Number 4 MREU, and I said to the Sergeant 'What's that?', and he said 'I dunno, search me. You'll find out when you get there.'[125]

Around the world each unit or section would face its own local difficulties or issues. There would be some standard challenges, mainly coming from the higher echelons of the RAF and Dominion Air Forces. For the most part this centred around the desire to close the MRES down for reasons of economy and manpower. At any one time, at full strength, over 600 RAF plus scores of civilian staff were being tied up with tracing missing airmen, a number which the Air Ministry was keen to lose from their pay roll. The British Air Forces of Occupation were also complaining of a drain on their resources.[126] Fortunately, there was enough opposition to the accountants not only to keep the MRES alive, but to extend its existence. In the meetings of July and August 1945 the Air Ministry had somewhat optimistically predicted that the MRES would need just one year. By August 1946 the impracticality of this became obvious. Due to the problems and delays in establishing each unit, most teams had not begun operations until early 1946. The Air Member for Personnel, Air Marshal Sir John Slessor DSO MC reported to the Under Secretary of State for Air in this month that of the estimated 31,000 missing airmen in north-west Europe alone, only around 7,000 had been accounted for. Furthermore there had been hundreds of enquiries from the public, including over 300 from Members of Parliament (there had also been over the same period five questions asked in the House of Commons about missing airmen, two of them about specific men or crews[127], and at least one letter direct to the Prime Minister). He concluded that 'relatives of *all* of the [remaining] 24,000 expect the maximum to be done' to find their sons. He therefore proposed that a new end date for the MRES be set at April 1947, with the option to extend for a further three months.[128] His plan was accepted.

The July 1947 target would also be missed, although in that month No. 1 MREU was closed down in France, leaving behind detachments of liaison officers to clear any outstanding or new cases.[129] By the end of September No. 2 MREU was also disbanded in Germany[130], but this was still not enough for the bureaucrats. Now pressure was even coming from the Chancellor of the Exchequer to close down units, release personnel and cut costs.[131] Still, Slessor stood by his convictions and would not countenance any suggestion that the MRES should be prematurely shut down, stating:

> *I feel that the work which the Missing Research Units are doing is of such importance that if we abandon the task before it is given a reasonable chance of completion, there might be serious repercussions.*[132]

Some serious problems were already looming, but from the opposite angle. The Canadian government was applying pressure to speed up the work and expedite the closure of the MRES. This was caused by a desire to bring home their living airmen as well as metaphorically bring back the dead ones. In February 1947 the headquarters of the Royal Canadian Air Force wrote to Slessor to remind him that the majority of the fifty-five RCAF personnel engaged in MRES work in Europe were men who had enlisted only for the duration of the war. The RCAF were working to a deadline. These men had to be released from their duties and repatriated back to Canada by August in order to be demobilised in September.[133]

Demobilisation became a steady drain of MRES personnel. Even with units shutting down there was still a need for more officers and men to make up numbers. Such were the shortages that some men were simply drafted in. Squadron Leader 'Tommy' Thompson, who had seen operations as both a bomber and a fighter pilot during the war, found himself posted to the MRES in Denmark in early 1946 from the Air Disarmament Unit, whose job it had been to ensure the complete and irretrievable dismantling of the *Luftwaffe*. His training consisted of a basic briefing from an Army officer in charge of the German prisoners who were to help with the exhumations.[134] Volunteers were still sought wherever possible. In mid-1946 Squadron Leader Bill Lott, ex-Bomber Command and ex-prisoner of war, was working for the Control Commission for Germany (known as the CCG, or Charlie Chaplain's Grenadiers) as an interpreter, living in Detmold and walking to work every day. Often in the morning he would see RAF blue Humber staff cars passing, with RAF and MREU markings.

> The occupants of these cars were RAF personnel in uniform and persons in civilian clothes. I was intrigued: here was I, obliged to walk to work, while these characters were swanning around in top-class transport. I was determined to discover what kind of 'racket' they were on.
>
> I managed to get one of them to stop; the persons therein were two RAF officers, an RAF airman driver and a German civilian. It transpired that they were members of another 'Special Duties' outfit charged with establishing, where possible, the fate of RAF aircrews missing from operations over Europe, of whom there were a very great many. The German civilian acted as interpreter/translator during their investigations.
>
> After a short conversation I was convinced that their function was far more interesting and worthwhile than what I was currently doing; I managed to contact one of the senior Commanders of the organisation ... and persuaded him to organise my transfer to MRES.[135]

These new officers would find that the units had now settled down into a solid working pattern, partly based on the Standing Orders issued by Burges in December 1945, and partly on the Missing Research Memoranda which had begun to be regularly issued and which contained orders and guidelines. Searches were approached geographically. Just as, in Europe at least, each MREU was allocated to a country, so each section of the MREU was allocated a sub-section based along the local political boundaries. A section would typically take the local equivalent of an English County: a Kreise in Germany, a Fylke in Norway, or a Department in France. There were exceptions to this rule, with areas being combined if there were not thought to be many cases to be traced, as, say, in the south of France, or more than one section sent in if there was a particularly heavy work load expected, such as with the Ruhr. Once in their allocated area, a section would establish a roughly central headquarters, and the individual teams would spread out to begin work.

Sections received their tasked assignments from several sources. The Air Ministry would send through Casualty Enquiries, essentially copies of the master files on a particular loss, for any missing aircraft that they thought may be in the section's area. A team would then be allocated to examine the most likely area, and question the local population and authorities. Potential witnesses and the local authorities were sought out, including mayors, clergymen, grave diggers, police, medical staff, scrap dealers, and anyone else who may have been involved in dealing with the crash or it's crew. Apparently, often the younger the witness was the better:

> The children, you'd be surprised, made much better witnesses than many of their elders ... When I heard that there were children who saw something I'd always try to find them. On one occasion I had completed the investigation and was walking away when I saw three boys standing on a street corner, and I called them over and through my interpreter I began to question them. They were on their way to school. They knew it was a Lancaster. I asked them why they thought it was a Lancaster and not a Stirling, as both had four engines, and they said yes but, the four engines on a Stirling are radial, but the four engines on the Lancaster are in line.[136]

It was discovered very early on that this type of questioning, while turning up information on the aircraft that was being sought, would also turn up information on other crashes, too. Information on these would also be taken down, and where appropriate the details sent back to the Air Ministry to see if they fit any known losses. Whereas Casualty Enquiries received a prefix of the first letter of the country where they were thought to have been lost (F files for France, G for Germany, etc), all of these locally established enquiries received the prefix X. In early 1947 a change of procedure was introduced. Heavily influenced by the proliferation of X-files, it became policy to instigate general sweeps as the first action of the section whenever a new area was begun. In No. 4 MREU in Germany, this became known as Field Operation X.[137] Questionnaires would be sent to all local authorities or related parties, and public appeals for information made. The resulting information could then be collated and compared to Casualty Enquiries, saving a lot of time before physical searching began.

Naturally the help of the local population was invaluable to the search teams, in gathering information and finding wrecks or graves. The help of individuals was to be recorded and rewarded by the MRES. Ornate diplomas were produced by the Air Ministry, and embossed with the person's name. Just as lengths were to be gone to ensure that those who had provided significant assistance were rewarded, so:

great care should be taken [to] ensure that recommendations do not include names of persons who have indulged in pro-axis activities and have since tried to curry favour with the Allies.[138]

These diplomas were only to cover helpers to the MRES. Anyone who had assisted downed aircrew during the war were to be reported to MI9 (Escape and Evasion). They issued their own diplomas, also known as 'Tedder certificates' after Air Chief Marshal Sir Arthur Tedder, Chief of the Air Staff 1946–9. MRES officers were at liberty to collect information on any likely candidates, to be passed via the Air Ministry to the War Office. Likewise, the War Office could ask MRES officers to look closer at a particular case to see if a certificate was warranted.[139]

Evidence on the ground varied greatly from case to case. Generally the biggest influence was the date of the crash. During the Battle of France most wrecks seem to have been perfunctorily dealt with, with the armies of neither side having the time to do much except bury dead crews near their aircraft. Frequently these bodies would be subsequently exhumed by the local population for a decent burial. A wonderful gesture, these efforts were perhaps not always as meaningful as they may have been. An officer from No. 1 MREU conducting a sweep in France came across a large marker stone recording the burial site of a Flying Officer Round. The marker was on the boundary between a village and what had been one of the advanced landing grounds used by the RAF in 1940. When the RAF had moved out in May 1940 the villagers had found a cross marking the grave of 'F O Round'. In an act of considerable bravery, the village had paid for a large marker stone and had maintained the grave throughout the war. Unfortunately the Air Ministry had no record of any outstanding casualties by that name from that time. An exhumation was ordered but extensive excavations could find no body. What they did find was a cross marked, in English, with the words Fouled Ground. This had been the station latrine, and the warning marker left behind had been misinterpreted.

In the early years following the Battle of France remains were much more respectfully dealt with. Bodies were recovered and buried properly, often with military honours. It was not unusual for survivors of a crash to be allowed to attend the funerals of their crewmates. Wreckage would be cleared up methodically, for intelligence purposes or salvage and recycling. From mid-1943, most search officers agree,[140] the treatment got steadily worse. The crews became the 'terror flieger' as Bomber Command's campaign was stepped up and became both more efficient and more destructive. German troops were now less likely to treat bodies with respect, and increasingly crews would be buried in joint graves at the local cemetery or even next to their aircraft. Wreckage was also more likely to be left lying around as the transport to move the remains of large bombers was not available. The incidents of aircrew found with suspicious bullet wounds also steadily increased. As the Allies swept through France and the Low Countries in 1944 and 1945, it became far more normal to find the crews of aircraft recently shot down over or close behind the battle lines to be found still at their stations. This also became the case in Germany in the spring of 1945 with the heavy bombers. Now the Germans had more immediate matters to deal with.

Wrecks and graves left search officers with two potential starting points for an investigation. Identification of wreckage, be it through the aircraft serial number, or engine or other component plates, would considerably simplify and narrow down the task of identifying any related graves. They could also act as an indication to look for graves that had not been marked at the time and would otherwise have been passed over unnoticed. Graves could be altogether harder. Although an established relationship to a known crash, or an entry in the cemetery records, could give an indication of whom they contained, it was seldom that simple. As time went by markers and official records became less and less reliable. Common estimates show as many as 50 per cent of records in German cemeteries to be inaccurate to some degree. Often bodies would be buried several to a grave. If they had been buried long enough this made not only identifying individuals hard, but even merely establishing how many persons were in a grave.

In September 1946 a team from No. 1 MREU looked into a case near Harcourt on the Somme. A Bristol Blenheim had been shot down, according to the locals, on 24 May 1940, and had crashed in a field near the village. The Germans had buried three men and a dog, a Cocker Spaniel, at the crash site, although two of these were later transferred by the French to the village cemetery. The area had been cultivated and whatever wreckage the Germans had left behind was long gone, along with any indication of where the third body may be. There were no means for identifying the aircraft and no Blenheims were outstanding from the 24 May, so for the time being the case was put to one side. In April 1947 another team from No. 1 MREU exhumed the bodies of the crew, and found evidence of an officer, with a clothing tag from Plumb & Son Military Outfitters of London, and a sergeant. With no further evidence, the case again went into hiatus. At the end of July No. 1 MREU was closed down, although a few stray liaison officers remained to take care of the outstanding cases.[141]

One of these officers was Flight Lieutenant R. Noel Archer, who had already built up a reputation as a skilled and tenacious investigator, especially in the field of exhumations. He continued with the case, and in September 1948 managed to find evidence that the crash had actually been on the 22 May 1940. As five of the six Blenheims found on this day had been accounted for it was logical that this was L9184 of 57 Squadron, crewed by Pilot Officer Roi Leonard Saunders, Sergeant Samuel Frank Simmons, and Aircraftman 1st Class George Rosse Pirie. Plumb & Son confirmed that Saunders had been a customer, and his father that he had been an avid dog lover, and was known to fly with his pet on board. The graves in the village were duly marked as the last resting places of Saunders and Simmons, but Pirie remained missing.

In April 1949 George Pirie's widow, Mrs. Doris Pirie, wrote to the Air Ministry informing them that she was travelling to France in order to visit the crash site and make her own enquiries. This was far from uncommon, and the Air Ministry wrote to Flight Lieutenant Archer that:

Apparently Mrs Pirie is doing some Missing Research on her own. It seems most unlikely that she will succeed. But we must do what we can to comfort her.

Archer lent every assistance, right down to procuring the Mrs Pirie an hotel room. Part of his efforts included tidying up the graves and markers of his crew mates. On a hunch, he arranged to re-exhume the two graves, and it was as well that he did. What he found were quite clearly three skulls and separate torsos, obviously completely missed for whatever reason by the original exhumation team. On her arrival in May 1949, Mrs Pirie was presented with the apologies of the Air Ministry, and her husband's grave after nine years on the missing list. She had every right to be angry at the mistake that lengthened her wait by two years, but instead Archer reported that:

She seemed very pleased and now thinks the R.A.F. Missing Research and Enquiry Service is a wonderful organization, having the interests of the next of kin of the missing airmen at heart.[142]

As time went by, investigations became increasingly focused on exhumations. Cases that could be cleared above ground soon were, leaving only the tricky ones that required closer examination of the bodies. This need had been anticipated and an agreement signed by the French Government on 16 October 1944 allowing British forces carte blanche permission to conduct exhumations as they saw fit.[143] However, British regulations were strict. Only the Army Graves Concentration or Registration Units were allowed to exhume bodies, often using either German prisoners or local labour. The MRES could watch, and then conduct the examination, but were not allowed physically to open the graves themselves.[144] Once a grave was opened, if the bodies were in coffins they would be raised to the surface. If, as was often the case, the bodies were not in coffins then the search officer would usually lower himself into the grave to study the remains in situ. Only once a careful examination had taken place would the process of raising the remains, which could damage or destroy evidence, begin.

Once exposed the MRES had a standard form to fill in, with a chart to show which body parts were retrieved. Standard identity tags issued to every serviceman were made of a composite material that was both flammable and biodegradable, and so the official means for identifying the airmen often no longer existed. Therefore every little clue needed to be examined carefully and recorded. The type of soil would be noted. This could be cross-referenced with the level of decay to establish a rough date of death.[145] A basic physical description of the body was taken, and a dental chart filled in, although this was often pointless. Only the Dominion forces kept regular or accurate records of dental work. Details of the uniform and equipment were carefully noted, as these would at least point to the nationality, rank and trade of the airman, based on the type and quality of the material, and the insignia. A rough date might also be established from the varieties of equipment and the dates it had been introduced. It was also always possible that personal equipment bore the name of the wearer, or at the very least a serial number that could be traced to the man issued with it. Laundry labels or other potentially important clues were taken for later analysis and cross-reference, as were personal effects. They would all be forwarded to the Air Ministry. Once they had been checked for any information that could help identify the owner, personal effects would be handed over to the next of kin. Once all useful information had been gathered, the bodies would be reburied, and the reports written up and sent to the Air Ministry. No changes could be made to the marking of graves based on the exhumation, for example if a name was found for an unidentified airman, or the identity was different from the one on the marker, or two bodies were found in a graves marked for one, until the Air Ministry had checked and agreed with the report.[146] One final act followed every exhumation. Standing Orders were quite clear that the first and last thing that a search officer should do on approaching or leaving a grave was to salute it.[147]

Flight Lieutenant Colin Mitchell, No. 4 MREU, described the process in more detail:

> They were all carried out under my control, because I didn't want anyone from the pick and shovel brigade ... [doing] any damage. We had what I'd call the ideal situation and the less ideal situation. The ideal situation was where you knew they'd been buried in coffins, and that made life much more easier. But it was when you get those who weren't buried in coffins, and I regret to say that in one instance they were in tea chests.
>
> I would arrange to have them exhumed, and the lids taken off. I'd then give my interpreter my clipboard and a pencil, then I'd put on rubber gloves,

and then I would start my investigation. I would look at the body. The first thing I would look at: what was the colour of the uniform? If it was a dark blue, it was an Australian. Was it a pilot, air gunner, bomb-aimer, navigator? Then I would look on the epaulettes: was he an officer, or a sergeant, or a flight sergeant? Then I would work down the body (I wouldn't touch it), just with my eyes I would be working down, and this I would call to my interpreter who would be recording exactly what I was telling him. Then I would unzip the flying boots to see if there were a number, rank and name inside. Having got so far, that was all I could see from the outside without disturbing anything. I would then try to get my fingers down the neck of the roll-neck pullover to see if I could hook up the identity discs. I think I only came across one with identity discs. If I was unsuccessful I would then go through the pockets, the two up here first, then inside the battledress, and then the trouser pockets. And then I would come to where I have got to turn the body, to see if anything had been thrown into the coffin. I would then look to see if they were wearing any rings, but I'm sorry to say that of all the exhumations I did I never once came across a personal item: a watch, a ring, a scarf, nothing. All these were removed by the Wehrmacht or the Russian prisoners of war [who had buried them].[148]

Despite the nature of their task, morale among the MRES teams appears to have remained high. The level of commitment felt by all the members to their jobs comes through their testimony loud and clear. Even if it was not felt to begin with, exposure to the task engendered it. Wing Commander Ray Sheppard RNZAF joined No. 1 MREU in early 1946 as a young Flight Lieutenant. His reason to begin with was, after training abroad and flying Spitfires in Italy and then Austria, a reluctance to return to civilian life in New Zealand. He wanted to use the opportunity of being in Europe to explore the continent a little more, and the MRES seemed to offer the perfect vehicle. In the end, the job grew on him. He stayed for four years and became RNZAF liaison officer to all the European MREU's. Flight Lieutenant Roger St Vincent RCAF also chose to stay in Europe rather than going home. He recalls the morale on No. 2 MREU being high, despite atrocious weather conditions, poor equipment and transport shortages:

I do not recall that anyone ever complained about work or assignments – it was done in a professional manner, improving as we learned from experience. Yes, the work was done with diligence and respect for those who gave their lives in service.[149]

Poor equipment was a perennial problem. Very little specialised kit was issued to conduct exhumations, and what there was tended to be basic.

Before going to a town reporting graves Unbekant Flieger *[Unknown Flyer], we were to ask the mayors to open the grave/s for a certain day and time. We would keep a supply of rubber boots, gloves and disinfectant in the basement where the coffins were kept. On each trip we were to take along knives, scissors and dental charts [to be filled in]. It was winter and inclement weather would at times prevent the opening of the graves. It was not the lack of willingness on the mayor's part, but the lack of transportation which would cause officers to wait in turn to proceed on a trip.*[150]

Motor transport was always in short supply across the forces of occupation in Europe, and some units or sections never received their full complement of vehicles. Sometimes something could be done about this, but not often. Flight Lieutenant St Vincent managed to obtain some extra vehicles for his unit, The Hague Section, No. 2 MREU, through contacts with the Canadian Army in Germany.[151] Usually, the situation had to be endured. Poor maintenance only added to the problems. Many of the units had their work delayed by this, with returns usually showing a 60 per cent serviceability rate. Generally speaking MT support was only available through the local RAF or Army framework. 'G' Section of No. 4 MREU were based at RAF Uetersen, and borrowed staff whenever possible. Len Hamer worked in Uetersen's MT section:

[We] looked after their vehicles: they had Humber cars and Bedford 15 cwts. They also ran a Glider Club and I looked after these vehicles, a Fordson winch and some motor cycles. They were a great team up to the rank of Squadron Leader, but in a way you are all the same to them, not quite Tom, Dick and Harry, but near enough.[152]

The MRES system was quite different to how the American forces approached the problem.[153] Perhaps as is to be expected due to the scale of resources available to them, they threw far more manpower and where-withal into the search. Although they too carried out Field Operation X-style questioning (and co-incidentally, designated their unknown cases X-files), followed by physical sweeps, followed by exhumation and examination, the three phases were each conducted by a different, specialist team. Once exhumed, bodies were taken to central clearing houses, or Central Identification Points (CIP), at either Strasbourg, France, or Neuville-en-Condroz, Belgium, if in Europe, or Pearl Harbour if in the Far East. Here professional pathologists would examine the body, and where possible identify it. The families of American casualties could claim bodies for repatriation to the United States, and in fact 171,000 of the 281,000 American service personnel killed during the war were sent home. To facilitate this, the American Graves Registration

Command (AGRC) claimed by the end of operations in 1951 a 98.7 per cent success rate in identifying European casualties. Even considering that this covers not only aircrew but also soldiers, who were much easier to identify, this is markedly better than the marginally over 50 per cent achieved by the MRES.

However, a closer examination of the MRES files throws up some interesting discrepancies in the American system. In March 1947 Flying Officer S. K. M. Powell of 17 Section No. 3 MREU had to chase up the AGRC about a Mosquito crew he had been investigating in Bubesheim. The bodies of Lieutenant Emile Van Heerden, SAAF, and Flight Lieutenant James Robson, RAF, disappeared and it transpired that they had been lifted from the crash site by an AGRC sweep. Although it was common for the Americans to relocate all unidentified bodies to central cemeteries for processing and identification, the strong implication was that they had known at least the nationality of the bodies at the time.[154] Nor was this an isolated case. A few months earlier Flight Lieutenant J. Endean, an officer on the same section as Powell, had been systematically clearing a cemetery at Benediktbeuren. The seven crewmembers of a Liberator of 178 Squadron, operating out of Italy, were known to be buried there from the local records. Once the rest was cleared, there was no sign of Sergeant Gill and his crew, though. Powell was to report:

> As all the British casualties in this cemetery have been dealt with, with the exception of the above mentioned men, who could not be found, it seems that the Americans have stolen these bodies. (Once again another incident of this happening).
>
> It is therefore requested that American Graves Registration be contacted immediately so that the bodies may be retrieved, if they are still in this country.[155]

The bodies were retrieved, and are now buried 250 miles from where they crashed, at Cholley in France. If the bodies are this far west, it would imply that they had already passed through one of the CIP's, had been identified as American and were heading for the Channel coast for repatriation. Others seem to have been less fortunate. One No. 4 MREU search officer recalls:

> On a number of occasions we had trouble with our American counterparts. I once visited a village cemetery where five Polish airmen were buried in 1941 after their Wellington had crashed. When I returned a short time later I discovered their bodies had been removed by the Americans. This despite the fact that the cross stated RAF and happened before America joined the war ... I complained to our liaison officer with the 'Yanks' in Frankfurt, but it brought no result.[156]

Just as there were common problems and issues facing the teams across Europe, and standard ways of meeting these problems, the job faced by the search teams was not always so straight forward. One of the reasons for employing ex-aircrew had been that they were of a certain level of intelligence, and able to use initiative. Every case, although frequently similar, was unique. Some were far from usual.

In July 1948 a search team from No. 20 Section, No. 4 MREU, investigated the crash of de Havilland Mosquito PZ316. This aircraft, from 21 Squadron, had taken off from RAF Thorney Island late on the night of 22 January 1945 to conduct an intruder patrol over Germany. The *Totenliste* would later record that this aircraft had been shot down at Allrath, Westphalia, about 13 miles south-west of Dusseldorf. The list recorded that the crew, Captain W. R. Roberts SAAF and Flying Officer E. Webb, were buried at Grevenbroich just north-west of Allrath. On arriving at Grevenbroich the search officer sought out the grave-digger, an elderly gentleman called Herr Oehmen. He could only give an approximate location for the bodies of the two aircrew, and extensive exhumations on this area did not find anything. Checks were made with the British Army and the Americans to see if any bodies had been removed, but none had from that area of the cemetery. Further checks were made with Herr Oehmen. The search officer explained how one of the men could be expected to have been wearing a blue uniform, and the other the khaki uniform of the South African Air Force. Herr Oehmen now directed the team to another plot, where there were several empty graves. These bodies had been relocated to the new Imperial War Graves Commission cemetery at Rheinberg. Cross-reference with the IWGC showed that neither Roberts nor Webb had been received there. An excavation of the areas around this plot was carried out, but the only bodies found were Russian prisoners. Despite the set backs, the search team kept at it. Over time more visits were paid to Grevenbroich and Herr Oehmen. The grave-digger confided that he sometimes woke up at night thinking about the case. This suggested to the case officer that there may be some information deep in his sub-conscious relating to the case. Therefore, with Herr Oehmen's agreement, he took the grave-digger to the University of Bonn, where they met a Dr Wicke, a psychiatrist. Dr Wicke hypnotised Herr Oehmen, and under his direction the grave-digger indicated a section of the cemetery that contained French and Russian prisoners. This row was exhumed, and the last grave was found to contain Captain Roberts and Flying Officer Webb, both of whom were subsequently moved to Rheinberg.[157]

One situation that was not uncommon was the wrong identity tags being found. These were a rare enough find to begin with, but occasionally the names on them did not tally to any known missing aircrew. This would cause various delays and confusion, and more often than not the stray name would be traced to a WAAF, the sweetheart of the missing man who had swapped tags as a romantic gesture.[158] At least once, though, the conclusion to the case was altogether more tragic. An exhumation in 'S-Hertogenbosch, Holland, recovered a body that not only carried the proper identification, but was undoubtedly that of a WAAF.[159] It was not uncommon for WAAF's from bomber stations to be smuggled on board aircraft by their crews for unauthorised joy rides, and even on to raids. To this day, eleven members of the Women's Auxiliary Air Force are listed on the Runnymede Memorial, five of them members of the Special Operations Executive.

Another occasional complication was the arrival of relatives to conduct their own search efforts, as we have already seen. In some cases, like that of Pirie, it was a positive influence. More frequently they were not, taking time and effort from the search teams that could have been better spent elsewhere. Sometimes it simply made a difficult job even harder. When a fighter was found in a canal near Eindhoven, a team from No. 2 MREU was sent to investigate. A local farmer was employed to drag the airframe far enough out of the canal for the serial number to be read from the rear fuselage. This information was sent back to the Air Ministry, who confirmed that the pilot of this aircraft had never been recovered. A team was sent back to complete the excavation of the aircraft, and with it the pilot. Unfortunately the news appears to have leaked out from the Air Ministry to the pilot's family, who arrived in Holland and demanded to be present as the aircraft was extracted. This just made the job harder, as MRES staff had to keep the family back away from their son's fighter while the search team extricated the remains and moved them as quickly as possible to a waiting coffin. Nothing would have been gained by the family seeing the condition of the body.[160]

CHAPTER SEVEN

France, Belgium, Holland, Norway and Luxembourg

I was driving up Carl Johangate when I met a Mosquito coming down the street.

From an interview with a Oslo taxi-driver regarding the raid on the Gestapo headquarters there in September 1942[161]

In the summer of 1945 the Missing Research and Enquiry Service blossomed across Europe. The small scattered sections formed the nuclei for the larger field units, able to cover much more ground and much more quickly. Individual sections and search teams spread like spider's webs across countries that were, at least as far as the population was concerned, friendly and receptive. The physical geography was a different matter. The rolling countryside of France gave way to dense forest in Belgium, marshland in Holland and finally the mountains and sub-zero temperatures of Norway.

By August the old Nos 1, 3 and 4 Sections had been gathered into No. 1 Unit and had grown to cover the departments along the whole northern and western coast of France from Dunkirk around to Brest. By mid-December most of the initial area had been completed, although in some areas delays were caused while minefields were cleared, and were not fully finished until the next August. One of the cases cleared in this area was Flying Officer Arthur Tedder of 139 Squadron, who had been shot down in a Bristol Blenheim on 3 August 1940 while conducting intruder operations against German airfields. With his crew, Sergeants Douglas Spencer and Owen Evans, he had been buried in a communal grave in Nacqueville Community Cemetery. He was the son of Air Chief Marshal Sir Arthur Tedder, who by 1946 was Chief of the Air Staff, and who would lend his weight in support for the continuation of the MRES throughout his tenure in that post until 1949. Later, in May 1948, the three would be re-interred in Bayeaux British Military Cemetery.

72

A lot of the work for No. 1 MREU originated in the first year of the war; Hawker Hurricanes, Westland Lysanders, Fairey Battles and Bristol Blenheims lost during the Battle of France or subsequent raids on the invasion barges in the northern ports. This could lead to considerable confusions due to the hectic nature of the fighting. Records could be sparse and inaccurate, and sometimes aircrew could turn up a considerable distance from where they were supposed to have been. On 11 June 1940 Armstrong Whitworth Whitley bomber N1362 piloted by Sergeant Norman Songest took off from a field on Jersey for a raid on Turin, northern Italy. The aircraft never returned, but shortly afterwards No. 9 General Hospital, with the British forces in France, reported that three RAF sergeants, including a Sergeant Songest, had been brought in dead and had been buried by them near Le Mans. The details were sketchy, and by the time the MRS came to examine the case the squadron records had been lost with the fall of Jersey and the hospital records lost in the evacuation from France. Enquiries were made through the International Red Cross, but no definite confirmation of burial of the three sergeants or any sign of the other two crew members could be found.

In June 1946 a unit from No. 1 MREU moved into the area, and uncovered the graves of two unknown airmen at the village of Le Grand Luce, about 24km (15 miles) south of Le Mans. An exhumation revealed only one identifying mark; a ring engraved NMS, Sergeant Songest's initials. The other body was almost certainly one of his crew, but this still left one man unaccounted for at this site, and two more out there somewhere. However, about the same time a grave was found by another section investigating the report of a crash 80km (50 miles) to the north-east at Orgeres-la-Roche. It had been marked as containing four airmen, but an exhumation could not confirm the exact number. The nature of the crash and the length of time since burial meant that the remains were inseparable, but one clue was found: a Ronson lighter engraved 'PB Dec 2nd 1939'. This was reported back to London, where a standard procedure for such artefacts had been established by the MRS. First, a list of all men with those initials lost in that very general area was compiled. Then, birthdays were checked. Experience had shown that date-engraved items were most commonly 21st birthday presents, but when no matches were found the search moved onto the second most likely occasion, weddings. Sergeant Philip Budden, the second pilot of N1362, had been married on 2 December 1939. This was deemed enough to connect these two distant graves. The discrepancy was finally explained by the Germans burying the three airmen near the wreck site, while the other two had been carried south by the retreating No. 9 General Hospital before being laid to rest.[162] Eventually, all five were interred in a collective grave in Lignieres-La-Doucelle Communal Cemetery.

France proved in some ways an easy country to clear and in others very hard. The country was mainly open and easy to traverse, while the population was mostly friendly and willing to help. Canadian officers were used where possible to help with the language problems, although this did not always work. When Flight Lieutenant Ralph Laronde of No. 5 Section, No. 1 MREU, approached the mayor of one town to explain that he was here from the British unit tracing missing airmen, that he understood some were in the local cemetery and that he wanted to arrange a collection, he was slightly nonplussed when the mayor became agitated and called the town council together. It transpired that a slight mispronunciation had led the mayor to understand that Laronde was seeking a collection of the monetary kind rather than to relocate bodies.[163]

French civilian help certainly eased the task facing the MRES. The files collected by Madame L'Herbier had shed light on dozens if not hundreds of cases, while the contribution from the French Resistance was even greater. Not only information had been kept, but also physical evidence and personal effects. Much of this had found its way back to London and the Missing Research Section during the war, but there was still plenty left for the field teams to examine. Difficulties did arise from the actions of the Resistance, though. Apparently, it was not unknown to find an extra body in supposedly RAF graves, where a collaborator had been conveniently disposed of. Having said that, Flight Lieutenant Archer was also approached twice in the back streets of Calais by shady characters asking him how much he would charge to put an extra body back after his next exhumation.[164]

In one case severe complications arose through Resistance involvement. In October 1946 the graves of four unknown airmen were found in Avesnes Communal Cemetery. Flight Lieutenant E. J. Dawes of No. 2 Section was sent to investigate, and he linked them back to probably being from a Vickers Wellington of 460 Squadron that had crashed in May 1942. Three of the crew had become prisoners of war, but four were presumed killed. The name of a local family, the Coolbrandts, cropped up as having helped one of the crewmen who was subsequently captured and now may or may not be one of the buried men. The family was traced and questioned, if for no other reason than that if they had helped an airman they would be eligible for a so-called Tedder Certificate. It transpired that their son had met the airman in question wandering in nearby woods and had brought him home. The family fed him and relieved him of his bulky and conspicuous Irving jacket and flying boots. The next morning he was passed on to a nearby farmhouse where he was kitted out with civilian clothes and given false papers. He remained hidden for a couple of days while preparations were made to smuggle him across the border to Belgium. Unfortunately, before this could happen the French police arrived and the airman, Sergeant R. Ferry RAAF, was arrested. The Coolbrandts were already suspected of being collaborators, and rumours spread about their collusion in the arrest. In July 1944, with the Allied land forces approaching, the Resistance began settling old debts. A detachment arrived at the Coolbrandt's house and, after opening fire, threw two grenades through the windows. The son, who had initially helped Ferry, was killed outright and his father severely wounded and crippled for life. The only family member to escape injury was Madame Coolbrandt.

Flight Lieutenant Dawes carried out extensive research to see whether the Coolbrandts deserved a Tedder Certificate and full exoneration and pieced the story together. The tale was tragic to say the least. One of the local Resistance workers had approached Mde Coolbrandt to secure Ferry's Irving jacket, to cover the trail effectively, but Mde Coolbrandt had refused to give it over. She insisted that she should keep it as evidence in case, after the war, rewards were given to those who had helped escaping airmen, which was fairly far sighted for 1942. The discussion had become heated, and eventually Mde Coolbrandt had stormed off to see a neighbour, Mde Bon, and they had gone together to see the mayor. The mayor was a known collaborator, who at the time of the investigation was serving seven years in prison for his crimes. It could not be proven what had transpired with the mayor, but it was known that Mde Bon's husband was a prisoner of war and that she believed that by turning in an airman some kind of swap could be made. It was also clear that Ferry's arrest was a direct result of whatever conversation they had. The longer term results were that Mde Coolbrandt served four months in gaol for collaboration, lost her son who had genuinely helped Ferry in good faith, and had her equally innocent husband crippled.[165] After Dawes finalised his report, it was discovered that in fact five other members of Ferry's crew had become prisoners and only one of the men in Avesnes Cemetery was from his crew; his pilot, Flying Officer William Kennedy RAAF from New South Wales. The other three bodies were later identified as being members of another crew, probably a 7 Squadron Short Stirling shot down about five weeks after Kennedy.

One of the remarkable points of the Coolbrandt case was that even in late 1946, eighteen months after the end of the war, it was not until well down the line of investigation that Flight Lieutenant Dawes even knew how many of Kennedy's crew had been killed or how many had been captured. This was quite unusual for an RAF crew, but less so for one of the Allied or Dominion services. In June 1945 No. 1 MREU took over responsibility for the investigation into the location of two Supermarine Spitfire pilots, Adjutant Rene Porchon and Sergeant Chef Marchal of 345 (Free French) Squadron. They had been lost on 19 November 1944 while conducting ground attack operations on the German garrison of Dunkirk, which had been bypassed by the advancing Allies. One of the pilots had been hit by flak and lost control, and the second then collided with him. Reports from nearby ground forces, in particular the Czech Independent Armoured Brigade, stated that one parachute was seen and patrols sent out to try and rescue the pilot, but he was seen to be captured. Given the low altitude at which the accident occurred, this seemed unlikely.

Marchal was Belgian, and the Belgian Inspectorate General had begun search operations before the case was passed on to the MREU, and they had found the crash site of one of the Spitfires. Cross-referencing of the makers plates identified it as PT855, Marchal's machine. The area had been evacuated by the Germans during the fighting, but one witness was found, who stated that the Germans had recovered the body and buried it nearby. By January 1947 neither the other crash site nor any bodies had been found, and the case was closed. However, when passing through the area sometime later Flight Lieutenant Archer heard of the case and reopened it. An extensive ground search uncovered the severely fragmented remains of a second Spitfire outside Dunkirk and the original search area, which was identified as Porchon's PL427. Enquiries at the nearest churchyard uncovered a grave of an unknown Allied pilot ('Aviateur Allie Inconnu') with a date of death marked as 19 November 1944. An exhumation uncovered a pilot with RAF equipment, a khaki battledress and dark blue shirt of the type favoured by the Free French. There were no definite marks of identification, as indeed would be expected with a European pilot who would not want to reveal his genuine identity and so put his family at risk, but there was enough to identify the body as Porchon. Marchal was never found. Very noticeable in the file on the investigation is that at no point was it revealed that Marchal had been operating under an assumed name (also for security reasons) and was in fact called Toussaint, nor was it ever definitely stated whether he ever became a prisoner of war as some reports suggested. Due to communications problems with the Belgian authorities, the entire investigation was completed without knowing for certain whether one of the subjects was actually missing, or was still alive somewhere.[166]

Work problems aside, life in France was fairly pleasant. The food shortages that would later cripple efforts in Germany and the horrendous winter that bogged down movement in Holland were both much less serious in France. There was not the widespread destruction to deal with either, and surroundings were generally pleasant. Liaisons naturally formed with local women and not a few officers, including the redoubtable Flight Lieutenant Noel Archer, married French ladies. One of the officers had bought a house in the south of France with the back-pay accumulated from years of being a prisoner of war and this was made available for honeymoons and other holidays.[167] Work progressed quickly and on 31 July 1947 No. 1 MREU was formally disbanded at Chantilly.[168] The story, though, did not end there. Detachments remained in the field with Army Graves Concentration Units and in Paris with the Imperial War Graves Commission to help co-ordinate their combined efforts to concentrate the graves of airmen into properly cared for cemeteries. Part of this task would be tidying up loose ends on outstanding cases, or closed cases where new evidence was discovered. With the best will in the world, the inexperience of the search teams meant that there were quite a few of these sorts of cases, enough to keep Flight Lieutenant Archer and others busy for a further two years.

We have already seen how the team working on the case of Aircraftman George Pirie had overlooked the extra body in a grave. Other cases had also suffered by fairly simple mistakes or confusions. In August 1948 Archer was asked to reopen the case of the crew of Handley Page Halifax LW173, lost on the night of 12/13 June 1944. Six of the crew members had been killed and one survived. In mid-1946 No. 2 Canadian Concentration Unit had discovered three graves at Givenchy-en-Gomelle that they had exhumed and identified as airmen and then reburied at Leubringhen, where several other airmen were already interred. The exhumations had led them to believe that there were five bodies and so they were reburied in five graves. The Canadians had produced a report identifying the five bodies as Kyle, Alexander, Kelso, Ruber and Ball. The first three were missing members of LW173's crew, but the latter were not. In fact, it did not look unlikely that they were not names at all. Two of the other members of the crew were already in Leubringhen and had been identified. The only outstanding member of the crew now was its pilot, 26 year old Canadian Wing Commander Christopher Bartlett DFC and Bar. Archer's task was to exhume Ruber and Ball and see if either of them was actually Bartlett. In the end, it was found that both were Bartlett. The Canadians had been mistaken and buried two halves of the same body in separate graves.[169]

In this case it appears to have been a series of mistakes by the Canadians that had led to the problems. Sometimes it was problems inherent to the case. The identification of the crew of Westland Lysander V9673, for example, was never going to be satisfactorily settled. The pilot, Flying Officer James Bathgate DFC RNZAF, had been engaged on special operations with 161 Squadron when he was shot down on 11 December 1943. His body was easily identified, but there was no way to differentiate between his two passengers, Claudius Four and Abel Moreau, who as SOE agents were carrying no identifying matter.[170] On other cases the long arm of coincidence stretched out to baffle investigators. In June 1949 Flight Lieutenant Archer was called to St Maclou de Folleville where two Allied aircrew had been shot down on 8 July 1944. The problem here was not identification, but differentiation. One had been Sergeant Jeremiah Healy of 57 Squadron, the other John Healey of the USAAF.[171]

Some cases were reopened in order to make absolutely certain of the original conclusions. The case of Sergeant Percival Johnson was kept open despite considerable evidence to show that it had been closed nine years earlier. He had been shot down in a Bristol Blenheim in the Channel near Dungeness on 9 July 1940. The bodies of Johnson and his pilot, Squadron Leader Robert Batt, were found by HMS Brilliant, who then buried the pair at sea. In 1949 the case was ordered reopened because a grave had been found, apparently containing a body washed ashore, in La Plaine-sur-Mer Communal Cemetery and marked 'P. Johnson'. Local witnesses linked the body to an aeroplane that they had seen crash in daylight just off shore in January 1943, and reported that the body was dressed in khaki. An exhumation confirmed what had been heavily suspected, that this was the body of an American pilot. He was positively identified as 2nd Lt Paul Bouton. The odds of it having been Johnson were slim to say the least, but the job was too important to take chances.

On other occasions the pressure to re-examine cases came from outside. The father of Sergeant Reginald Priestley did not believe the official report that his son had been killed when Short Stirling EJ124 had been shot down near Amiens on 15 March 1944. His son's New Testament had been passed to him through the MRS and, adamant that his son had survived, he had taken it to a medium in what had been a common practise after the First World War. The medium had assured Mr Priestley that his son was still alive and probably living in Russia. Mr Priestley began lobbying the government to reopen the case and in October 1948 Squadron Leader Sinkinson wrote to Flight Lieutenant Archer asking him to re-examine the evidence. On the surface, there were certainly discrepancies. The principal witness, Abbé Henri Garbe, had told the original investigation in October 1946 that the bodies recovered from the wreckage of the Stirling were buried in two coffins. Only one could be found by the search party at that time, and they found and positively identified two complete bodies inside (the pilot, Pilot Officer Duncan Munro RAAF, and the navigator, Sergeant Arthur Skelton), along with parts of several more. Other witnesses stated that some of the bodies had been buried at the crash site (where a cross had been erected) or even at a different village. Again, no trace of these other men could be found, but given the evidence that the aircraft had exploded in flight at a low altitude, it seemed certain the rest of the crew had all been killed.

Flight Lieutenant Archer began his own investigation by re-interviewing Abbé Garbe. This time he stated that there was no second coffin, changing his story. He did confirm, though, that it was he who had recovered Sergeant Priestley's bible. He had taken it from the top pocket of a headless torso found inside the wreck. Archer then visited St Pierre Cemetery to exhume the grave for himself. He found two coffins, side by side; one had been disturbed, presumably the one originally examined in 1946, and Archer could confirm that it contained Skelton, Munro and parts of at least two other airmen. The undisturbed coffin also contained fragmented remains, and part of a flying boot that was stencilled with a name which could only be that of Priestley. Although the case had not ended the way Mr Priestley had hoped, it at least ended the uncertainty and gave him a grave to mourn at.[172]

Even by the standards of the MRES, Flight Lieutenant Noel Archer comes across as a tenacious and skilled operator. Perhaps the most famous case he would handle, and one that became more than usually obsessive for him, was that of Commandant (Squadron Leader) René Mouchotte, the highly decorated officer commanding 341 Squadron.[173] Mouchotte, who had escaped from Oran when France fell, was one of the top pilots of the Free French air force in exile. He had been shot down on 27 August 1943 while escorting American Boeing B-17s over Saint-Omer. His death was witnessed by his friend Pierre Closterman, who later dedicated his autobiography *The Big Show* to Mouchotte, but his body was never found. This was not unusual. As we have seen, most pilots of the Allied air forces flew under assumed names if they carried any identification at all, and Mouchotte usually called himself Ignatief.

As early as January 1945, the French Red Cross were scouring the country around Saint-Omer for Mouchotte/Ignatief's body. On formation No. 2 Section, and later No. 1 MREU, took up the case, scouring the area and exhuming various remains. Detailed work through into 1947 identified most of the remains in the area, and in March a process of elimination had left just one body unidentified. Apparently an Australian fighter pilot who had died soon after crashing, the body matched Mouchotte's general description. The dark blue of the Free French uniform could easily have been mistaken for the Australian one. Unfortunately, only a couple of months later more detailed work turned this certainty over and the body was re-identified as an American.

About this time Archer, whose friend Flight Lieutenant Laronde had been involved from the start, became interested in the case. As No. 1 MREU was wound down and closed it looked as if the Mouchotte case would be left unsolved. However, Archer took on the task and whenever his liaison duties took him into the area he chipped away at it a little more. He launched appeals in as many newspapers as possible, interviewed or corresponded with hundreds of witnesses and met with various ex-Free French airmen who were keen to help with the case in any way they could. He even began dreaming about Mouchotte.

In the end, though, Archer himself admitted that 'as time went on, other work came along and Mouchotte slipped into the background.' Archer was a busy man as a liaison officer, being kept moving around most of France, Belgium and Holland. Eventually it was this travelling that was to provide the break through. In March 1949 he was called on to look into a case discovered in Middelkerke, a Belgian coastal town. A Canadian pilot had been found in June 1946, and identified as Rene Martin. However, the serial number was that of a man repatriated to Canada in 1942, and no-one could be found by that name on any of the lists of the missing. When he re-examined the case, Archer found that the apparently Canadian service number (with the prefix 'C') had been misread or mis-transcribed during the first investigation. In fact, the supposition itself was also wrong, as Canadian numbers were given the prefix 'R'. Furthermore, the name Rene Martin did not appear anywhere. Archer visited the local mayor, and accessed the original coroners report put together by the Belgians during the war. Again, for whatever reason, this had been overlooked in 1946. This recorded that the body had been found washed up on a beach on 3 September 1943. It was also quite clearly recorded that the battle dress tunic (which had since disappeared) was marked 'Adjt. Rene Mouchotte'. Clearly, it was not only the service number that had been mis-transcribed.

On 24 March 1949, almost six years since he had been seen to crash, in fact into the sea, Archer was able to write to the Air Ministry asking them to confirm his findings and formally identify Mouchotte. The Air Ministry informed the French Government and personal thanks flooded into Archer from senior British and French figures. In October 1949 his body was exhumed for a final time and, on 3 November 1949, he was laid to rest in his family vault at Pere-Lachaise Cemetery, Paris.

A significant factor in solving this case had been Archer's movements across wide areas of Europe. In October 1948 his remit had been extended to include, in fact technically substituted with, Belgium. By the late summer of 1946 Belgium had been declared cleared, but as in France new cases or fresh evidence kept cropping up. Archer had already been picking up some of this work, and now the Air Ministry ordered him to move to Brussels permanently to take on these tasks. Almost immediately problems arose. For one thing, by now Archer was married, and he would need both permission to bring his wife to Belgium and accommodation for her. His clerk and driver would also need accommodation, and a living allowance. By this time the only RAF unit left in the country was a delegation attached to the Belgian Air Force, so lodgings and rations would need to be found through the local authorities. Likewise, office space was short. Neither the delegation nor the Imperial War Graves Commission, the two organisations that Archer was meant to liaise with, had space, and so an office was finally found some distance from them both. Garage space could only be found further away still, and servicing and spares would be unavailable in the country. The administration needed to run the section; passes, warrants, etc would need to be arranged through the delegation. They would also need to arrange for the transfer of the office furniture needed, which included eleven filing cabinets. All of this applied to one search team of three men. Consider what an organisational feat was needed to move entire sections around Europe.[174] Remarkably, Archer, his family and his team were able to move to Brussels and begin operations in mid-November.

Belgium, along with Holland, had been allotted to No. 2 MREU in August 1945. Command was given to Wing Commander Angus Maclean, a Canadian officer who had served with Bomber Command. He had been badly shot up over Germany, and had come down with his crew in Holland, but had managed to contact one of the escape networks and eventually evaded back to Britain via Spain. After two years with the MRES he would return to Canada and embark on a successful political career that saw him retire as Premier of Prince Edward Island in 1981. He died in 2000.

Unit headquarters had been set up at 23 Rue de la Toison d'Or in Brussels, with a local headquarters for Holland under Squadron Leader Philbin RCAF, based at a villa at Badhuisweg 85/7 in The Hague. Belgium was in many ways as straight forward as France, although problems were faced in the Ardennes region, where the fighting in late 1944 and early 1945 had caused widespread devastation.

> *What we had to do was go out to various places, wherever we got a report, and sometimes when you didn't get a report you'd go to a small town or village and see the mayor and ask for any reports of airmen buried or aircraft down, and they'd probably take you off to the cemetery and you'd see a grave. Some of them they knew who it was because they'd have taken the tags off them, but sometimes they didn't know but would give you the date that the aircraft was shot down.*
>
> *We had to collect our rations from Brussels each week, and we paid the hotel for accommodation and preparation of food, but we always did a bit of a fiddle to add a little bit because Belgium was very well off in those days for food. We got marvellous food in Belgium, so we usually augmented our food a little bit.[175]*

Again, the local population was friendly, and had helped in collecting information and evidence during the war. In 1942 a British bomber had crashed near Louvain, east of Brussels. A local resident had evaded the German guards on the wreck to recover an identity disc and the collar from one of the crew. In late 1944 the British had liberated this area and the Belgian had handed his relics over to the authorities. In time, these had reached the Air Ministry, where the MRS had uncovered the names of Sergeants Alan Wilson and John Simmons, and connected them to Short Stirling R9259 that had been reported missing on the night of

5/6 December 1942. A sweep of the area by a team from No. 2 MREU located a mass grave at Le Culot Military Cemetery. It was judged to contain an entire crew, and several items recovered: an identity disc of Pilot Officer Roland Boyes, one of Wilson and Simmond's crew; a parachute fragment with a label 'R9259'; a red scarf with a depiction of huntsmen and hounds, and; a Canadian sergeant's tunic. The scarf was recognised by the father of the pilot, Flight Lieutenant Hugh Arnott. Between the two sets of evidence, it was established that the whole crew had been killed in the crash, and had been buried together by the Germans.[176] They now lie together in Heverlee Cemetery.

Help from the locals was not always a positive influence on the teams, though. Naturally, the populace wanted to celebrate their liberation, and widespread rejoicing carried on into 1946. Just as naturally, many called on the local British units to send representatives, but in Belgium this almost always meant the MRES:

> There was a group who claimed to have been the Resistance during the war and they had a lunch to which we were invited as guests of honour. Well this lunch went on with drinking from twelve o'clock until about 6 o'clock.[177]

Belgium was declared complete in September 1946, although as we have seen there were still unsolved cases, and the local teams moved. There was more of a British presence in the next area, Luxembourg:

> We went down and we were in Luxembourg city and lived in a hotel there but there was a British Army unit already in Luxembourg training the Luxembourg Army, so the officers ate with the officer's mess there ... and the airmen ate with the troops in the barracks.[178]

The headquarters of No. 2 MREU now moved to Schloss Schaumberg, near Diez, in the French Zone of Germany. However, the section in Holland remained. Here the MRES had met problems from the start, not least in the severe weather encountered. Being a low lying country, Holland was liable to flooding, while the harsh weather froze the ground solid. Movement was impeded by mud and exhumations difficult until the spring. Limited trips could be made when one of the unit's two cars was available:

> Shortly before Christmas it was my turn to have a car assigned, and with my interpreter Cornelius we drove to a grave site to the north, along the west coast. It was an area where the locals often found bodies washed ashore and buried them in the soft, spongy clay. When the grave was dug up and the coffin opened, I was amazed to see how well preserved the body was. It was a simple matter to take down a good description, i.e.; the rank, crew

...til the 20th Century, care of military dead generally only extended to senior officers (Colonel Lake, ...ed at Roilca, Portugal, 1808). (Author's collection)

At best, a general monument would mark the death of soldiers (Fuentes D'Onoro, Spain, 1811). (Author's collection)

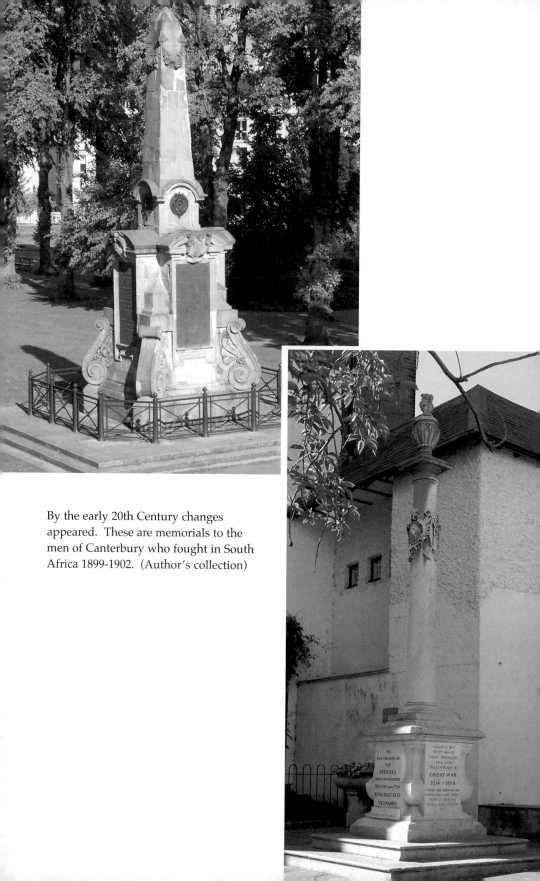

By the early 20th Century changes appeared. These are memorials to the men of Canterbury who fought in South Africa 1899-1902. (Author's collection)

megalithic monument to the First World War dead at Thiepval, France. (Author's collection)

ing the individual to rest: a First World War burial party, 1916. (Author's collection)

An unknown German airman from the Battle of Britain in Hawkinge cemetery. (Author's collection)

British and German dead side by side, Hawkinge cemetery. (Author's collection)

ypical case for a Maintenance Unit: an Heinkel He 111, April 1940, RAF Wick. (By kind permission wis Shelley)

e CWGC plot for German dead, Hawkinge cemetery. (Author's collection)

Memorial for Pilot Officer Clarke, who still rests in his aeroplane nearby. (Author's collection)

Vickers Wellington. Such aeroplanes were likely to fragment severely when crashing. (By kind permission RAF Museum)

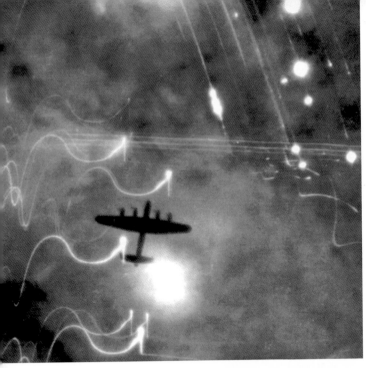

Avro Lancaster over target. Aircraft crashing within the maelstrom of a target would also be severely damaged. (Author's collection)

Another roadside marker, this one to a Polish crew on the Romney Marsh. (Author's collection)

A typical bomber crew. Without painstaking examination, there is very little to tell these men from any of the tens of thousands of other aircrew. (By kind permission RAF Museum)

The German burial of an RAF crew early in the war in Norway. Later, they would be considerably less gallant. (By kind permission RAF Museum, Rideal Collection)

A more typical late war burial site.
(By kind permission RAF Museum)

crew at their stations. In a violent impact, bodies would easily become jumbled and confused.
y kind permission RAF Museum)

Group Captain Eustace Fellowes Hawkins DSO, far right. (By kind permission Flt Lt Myhill)

A typical heavy bomber crash: an Avro Lancaster in Germany. (By kind permission RAF Museum, Rideal Collection)

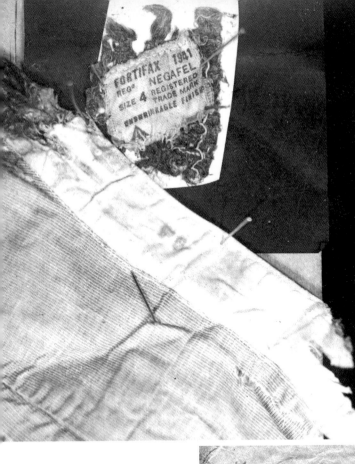

A typical clue: a laundry mark from the collar of a shirt. (By kind permission Mrs. A. Archer)

Letters should not have been carried on operations, but many were. Some, like this one, helped to identify unknown airmen. (By kind permission Mrs. A. Archer)

Bill darling
  I was so glad to get your letter. It was rather late and I was beginning to get anxious about you.
  Seeing that you hint that I have been at the club I won't deny the fact. I have but only in the afternoons because Bertie Gaison gave me a key. We are entirely alone in the afternoons we Muriel + I.
  If you dare to tell my mother that I did not go into town with you I'll never speak to you again. So now you know how to get rid of me if you need to.

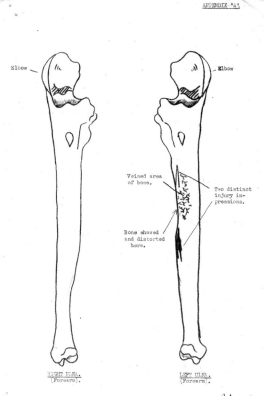

Infra-red photography could bring out added detail in degraded items, in this case a Mae West label. (By kind permission Mrs. A. Archer)

Sometimes more forensic detail was called for. Here two bones are sketched to compare with any known injuries on the suspected airman. (By kind permission Mrs. A. Archer)

The grave of Flight Sergeant William Bracken, who was identified by a spool of reconnaissance film. (Author's Collection)

Exhuming graves in northern France. (By kind permission Mrs. A. Archer)

Using German prisoners to exhume a row of graves in France. (By kind permission Mrs. A. Archer)

Flt Lt 'Cobber' Keen examining wreckage for clues, Germany. (By kind permission Flt Lt Myhill)

Army Graves Registration Unit teams at work, France. (By kind permission Mrs. A. Archer)

EXHUMATION REPORT

Army No. __U/K.__ Rank __U/K__ Name __UNKNOWN__ Unit __R.A.F.__
(If unknown, state "UNKNOWN")

Cemetery or Place of Burial __Vernon Communal Cemetery__ Plot __–__ Row __–__
1/250,000 S GSGS.4042.
__Sheet 7/R.4374.__ Grave No. __12__

(For all SPECIAL cases of exhumation, a pathologist should be present)

1. Height: __5' 9" to 5' 10"__
   (If actual measurements impossible, state "Short", "Medium", "Tall")

2. Build: __Medium (Chest measurement 34" approx).__
   (Thin, Broad, etc.)

3. Colour of hair: __Brown short straight.__
   (also "Straight", "Curly", "Long", "Short")

4. Teeth: 8 7 6 5 4 3 2 1 | 1 2 3 4 5 6 7 8   __See reverse side for complete tooth__
            8 7 6 5 4 3 2 1 | 1 2 3 4 5 6 7 8   __chart.__ (See also Dental Chart overleaf)

5. Fingers and hands: __Bones only.__

6. Nature of wound: __Burning.__
   (or other probable cause of death)

7. Identity discs: __None found.__

8. Documents or other effects on body: __NIL.__)

9. Clothing — details: __NIL.__) __BODY NAKED.__

10. Boots — details: __NIL.__)

11. Equipment (including any Arms) — details: __None.__

12. General Remarks: __This body is believed to be ████████████.__
    __Date of death 7/8. 6.40. Originally buried in Grave 48 in Vernon Cemetery__
    __and concentrated to Grave 12 Military Plot on 12. 2.48.__

Signature of Officer conducting exhumation:

An exhumation report with typically
scant information. Although often fil[led]
in, the dental charts were usually use[d]
due to poor record keeping by the RA[F]
(By kind permission Mrs. A. Archer)

DENTAL CHART

(To be completed when a Pathologist is in attendance)

Abbreviations

Mesial . . . . . M	Labial . . . . . La
Distal . . . . . D	Buccal . . . . . B
Incisal I	Linual Li
	Occusal . . . . . . O

Extraction X	Gold Inlay . . . . . . GI	Bridge . . . . . .
Amalgam . . . . . . A	Porcelain Inlay . . . . PI	Partial Denture . . .
Cement . . . . . . Ce	Gold Crown . . . . . GC	Complete upper .
Synthetic Porcelain . . S	Porcelain Crown . . PC	Complete lower .
Foil . . . . F	Richmond Crown . . RC	
	Jacket Crown . . . . JC	

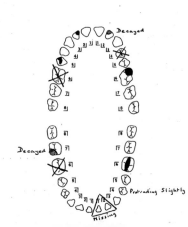

position, hair features, and even a dental description which I noted on the dental chart. The uniform fabric was that of a British airman. The date of burial might not coincide with the date of the crash, but it would help people at MRES HQ, London, to facilitate identification.[179]

In the meantime, while operations were limited, officers could concentrate on the administrative side of the problem, working through the files and planning searches thoroughly and well in advance so as to increase chances of success. They could also relax.

I spent more time sorting out the information coming from mayors of towns and villages in preparation for spring visits. I planned itineraries to several cemeteries for a five-day absence, as soon as weather permitted ... All of the officers frequented one restaurant reserved for officers and the menu was always the same: fish and potatoes. There was an orchestra and fraternization made after-hours life interesting.[180]

With time on their hands, and eventually extra transport too, more extravagant recreations were also possible:

I took two weeks leave in June 1946, when Higginbottom and I fearlessly decided to drive my jeep to the French Riviera. We set off with two spare tyres and two full 20-litre jerry cans. Driving through Brussels and Paris, we refuelled at Allied petrol stations on the way to the Mediterranean. We spent one glorious week at Juan-les-Pins which was nearly deserted. We had our choice of hotels and I bought some souvenirs (terra cotta miniatures of nudes, etc). The jeep was slow and our return trip took a little longer as we stopped to sample local cuisine.[181]

As in France and Belgium the local population and authorities were more than helpful. During the war the Dutch had attended to the crash sites and burials of downed Allied air crew to such an extent that the Germans had begun to bury them on *Luftwaffe* airfields to prevent funerals becoming the focus of anti-German demonstrations. Now they were equally enthusiastic, even to the extent of the Royal Netherlands Navy providing salvage ships to lift wreckage from the beds of inland seas, or from shallow off-shore waters.[182] A very similar situation existed in Norway, as regarding both the use of the navy to retrieve wrecks (including a 235 Squadron Bristol Beaufighter lost just after Christmas 1941 and its crew; one of these was Sergeant Clifford Myhill, whose brother was serving with No. 22 Section No. 4 MREU in Krefeld) and the popular support for recovery and funerals. For example, when Short Stirling LK119 was shot down while dropping arms to the resistance at the end of March 1945, it crashed near Holt in Hegland. After being kept away from the wreck by the Germans for several days a local delegation managed to secure the bodies of the crew and bury them at a secret location in the forest. The local priest was suspected of being a Nazi sympathiser, and so a Methodist minister was brought in from a nearby town to officiate.[183]

Norway had initially been investigated by No. 6 Section from July 1945, but the next month No. 6 had been merged with No. 7 Section, the Danish unit, to form No. 3 MREU. Command was handed to Squadron Leader Mike Shaw DSO, along with promotion to Wing Commander. Shaw had been a pre-war officer, flying ancient Vickers Vildebeest torpedo bombers from 1938 until the end of 1939, and then Bristol Beauforts on anti-shipping strikes in the North Sea until 1941. After a tour as an instructor, he received command of 221 Squadron, operating Vickers Wellingtons from Malta on raids to Italy. In June 1944 he had taken over 69 Squadron, flying initially from England and then from advanced fields in France. In August 1945 he took command of No. 1 Section, then No. 1 Unit. After three years in the field he returned to flying, finally retiring in 1975 as a Group Captain. His long tours on flying, numerous near-death experiences, and finally his work with the MRES led to an interest in spiritualism and, from that, alternative medicine, even setting up cancer support groups. He died in 2002.[184]

It appears that this unit was the lowest in London's list of priorities. Proportionally, it would have contained the least number of cases within its remit, and it was not until January 1946 that, despite problems caused by the winter, operations officially began with sweeps of northern Schleswig-Holstein and southern Denmark. Initially, seven sections were given to Denmark, and one to Norway.

In fact the Norwegian team, essentially still No. 6 Section but now called No. 14 Section, had been hard at it since September. Six Flight Lieutenant search officers gathered under the command of Squadron Leader H. Scott. Until recently Scott had been liaison officer to the British airborne forces who had been dropped into Norway in May 1945 as part of Operation Doomsday, the plan to aid the local Norwegian forces in not only securing the German garrisons, but also deterring the Russians from sending troops into the country.[185] These seven officers had each undertaken a week's duty with Nos 1, 2 or 5 Sections to gain some experience. Even so operations on the ground in Norway were slow to begin. An office needed to be found to work from in Oslo, plus typewriters, filing cabinets, desks, chairs, and other stationary. Transport was to be sent out from England, but after numerous delays alternative arrangements were made with the local RAF units to acquire six Chevrolet Utility cars. This at least made local sweeps and enquiries possible, although longer range journeys were hampered by the lack of infrastructure and increasingly severe weather conditions. It soon became quicker to load teams and vehicles onto trains for transportation as close to the search area as possible. Less orthodox means of transport were also used; in one case a search officer interviewed a lighthouse keeper through a megaphone from a rowing boat, unable to land due to the heavy seas.[186]

From the spring the pace of progress increased. Search teams were posted in from Denmark as and when their own areas had been completed. No. 17 Section arrived first, taking up post at Bergen, to cover western central Norway in May 1946, followed by No. 13 Section to cover northern Norway in June. No. 13 Section would have responsibility for the area around Trondheim, where the German battleship *Tirpitz* had lain for eighteen months. The numerous raids on this area had left a particularly knotty problem for the MRES to unravel, needing as they did to establish which aircraft (mostly of the same types) had been lost on which raid. Norway would arguably see the MRES (as opposed to MRS) at it's most forensic:

> *The actual investigation only concerned five aircraft but the difficulties arose when it was discovered that two similar raids had taken place on the same dates but in consecutive years.*
>
> *The course of the enquiries was to start at the grave of an airman marked 'unknown' and then find out from where the body had come and again more enquiries to ascertain the date on which the crash at that place occurred. One never quite knew if the informant himself was muddled in the year.*
>
> *In these particular crashes careful note was made during exhumations of such things as seaweed on the body or, where twigs were found penetrating limbs, the type of wood so that, as far as possible, a certain grouping of the bodies could be made.*[187]

This attention to detail would prove invaluable in several cases. In the mountainous terrain of Norway, with ever-moving glaciers, spring thaws and mountain streams, a body could be transported some considerable distance after death. Perhaps the most famous case is of Sergeant John Wilkinson of 49 Squadron. Shot down in his Handley Page Hampden (AE421) in April 1942 over the Ijsselmeer in Holland, he was eventually washed up in Norway three months later. By then, plus nearly four years in a grave, only the most determined attention to detail and forensic investigation could have made the mental leap needed to match man to aeroplane and then positively prove identity.[188]

Otherwise matters went increasingly smoothly. Although the Norwegian working day of 9am to 3pm hampered work a little, soon sweeps averaging 3200km (2000 miles) were being undertaken across the country. The high number of British Army units still in the country meant that rations and petrol were easy to come by, while the Norwegian military and civil authorities were more than helpful with supplies, transport (even shipping) and information. The search officers never failed to be amazed by the level of support from the public. In November 1942 two Handley Page Halifaxes had towed two gliders to Norway on Operation Freshman. The gliders had contained the assault teams who were to be used to knock out the German heavy water plant in Telemark. Both gliders and one Halifax had been lost, but the crew of the latter had been located by the MRES 80km (50 miles) south east of Stavanger and the remains taken to the local church at Helleland. A day was spent sorting and identifying the remains and then they were laid out over night in the church. The next day, when the teams returned to re-inter the dead, they found over three hundred Norwegians and an honour guard from the Royal Norwegian Air Force waiting for them.[189]

In July 1946 the most ambitious part of the search began: Operation Polesearch. This trek would take two officers, Squadron Leader Rideal of No. 17 Section and Flight Lieutenant Brooks of No. 13 Section, inside the Arctic Circle for two months. It would be a mentally and physically exhausting task, operating in an area where the sun rarely set and any journey involved severe effort. The working day frequently stretched into the early hours of the morning and a considerable amount of alcohol was consumed. Thankfully, the MRES had chosen their commander well. Squadron Leader Eric 'Chick' Rideal was born in Stockholm in 1920, the son of a Royal Navy officer. He had been to Trinity Hall, Cambridge, and spent a semester at university in Grenoble in 1939. His employment history stretched from post office sorter to deep sea trawler hand, and despite having been in the Officer Training Corp at Cambridge, he had joined the RAF as an other ranks clerk in 1940. Commissioned in 1942, he had spent most of the war working for the Air Ministry. This was an officer of versatile abilities and by no means afraid of hard work.

Again the Norwegians offered every support, with interpreters, food, shelter and transport being supplied, although some problems arose with local authorities. Some officials had been 'Quislings' (collaborators) and had either absconded or been arrested, or were not particularly favourable to the British. Either way, accessing local official records was not always straight forward. British units involved in mine clearance (with German prisoners of war as labour) also lent their aid. Numerous wrecks were investigated, although as often or not these turned out to be either Fleet Air Arm or Russian aircraft. Even so, details were carefully noted and graves recorded for passing to the relevant authorities.

15th July: [Brooks] to Kirkness for motor-boat. Set course myself 09.45hrs. Sleeping bag, petrol, food. Hot day. Lots of dust. Not another car to be seen on the road. Crash report in mountains, 40km away. Interrogate Fisher Lapps. Truck starts going [unserviceable], spitting oil from filter. Press on. Drop off Mine Officer. Get to Vadsoy 17.00hrs. See Police Chief. Mostly Russian aircraft. Mustang in hills, Russian. Also six bodies in mountains.

Fight between Russians and Germans. Two-engined aircraft in harbour. Row out at low tide. Can see fuselage. Find propeller blade. American with Russian letters on same. Visit churchyard. Russian grave, also two SS men. Car packs up. Arrange to borrow German lorry from mine company thirty miles away. Have supper with Chief of Police. Get away at 22.00hrs. See Quisling Lensman. Get him out of bed, not much help. Find Swordfish which ditched. Crew got ashore in rubber dinghy. Made P.O.W.s. Press on. Pass long range heavy guns on mountains above Vardoy; these shelled Murmansk convoys thirty miles out to sea. Names painted on them, Gneisenau, Moltke etc. Midnight sun. Arrived Svartnes breakfast 01.30hrs on top of block house with two German drivers and a Norwegian guard. Lots of mosquitos. Fond farewell. German driver comes from Ost Preussen *'heimatlos'.*[190] *Unroll sleeping bags in sand. Sun very hot, but have to get right inside and zip right up because of mosquitos.*

16th July: Good wash in Arctic Ocean. Ferry should go at 08.00hrs at Vardoy, but cancelled as no Rutebil. Walked to café who brewed some food for us. People waiting for ferry and organise special trip. Ferry arrives and then we cross over to island, long smooth swell. See Chief of Police. Clear up a mystery re Russian aircraft. Also believe find one of missing Hampdens. Crew reported P.O.W.s. Report of American aircraft crash. Walk there. Boston aircraft, but Russian. Find cigarette case. Also Russian helmet. No trace of bodies, probably under wreckage. Talk to U.S. G.R.U. at Vadsoy. Try and clear up mystery of unknown seaman buried [in] cemetery. See barber civilian Red Cross. Cannot help much. Bishop confirms, only one British seaman buried here. Buy postcards. Write them, general distribution. Finish work so sleep. Boat back to Kirkenes delayed. Will not sail before 23.00hrs. Eleven hours late. Try local cinema; appalling film. Jeanette MacDonald in French. General breakdown of electrical supply. Film packs up. Hang around the quay-side and ultimately get aboard. Wangle some food, unroll sleeping bag and kip down on deck.

17th July: 03.00hrs arrived Kirkenes, finding truck waiting. Back to aerodrome. Raining like hell. Roll out sleeping bag and go to sleep again. Wake ten o'clock. Pack, ready for J.U. 52 [transport aircraft] to take us to Banak. 52 does not come. Write out reports. [Brooks] recounts story of Swordfish crews he has found. Also gen on graves in Russia. Afternoon visit Captain Petersen and arrange new truck. Fix naval boat for tomorrow 09.30hrs to see a Lapp called Anti Nitzi at Storefjord. Quiet day.[191]

Shortly after the return of Brooks and Rideal, Norway was declared complete. The search sections were withdrawn and sent down into the American Zone of Occupation in Germany, based out of Karlsruhe. At the end of the year, Denmark was also closed down and the personnel sent south. No. 3 MREU, like Nos 2 and 4, were now based purely in Germany.

CHAPTER EIGHT

No. 5 MREU
Mediterranean and
Middle East

Another week gone by, and we are working at full throttle but I must say,
it is a most disheartening task. The people here just either don't know
anything or won't help us anyway. And, there are no crashes on land apart
from the ones we have already found. When one does find a crash, however,
everything has been stolen and sold; the people who have done the stealing
will not admit to a thing. I have been out two or three times myself and fully
realise what the S.P. Officers are up against. However, we plod on and are
bound to have some luck sooner or later.[192]

Sqdn Ldr A. H. S. Browne, o/c No. 3 Search Party, Greece,
6 January 1947

Missing research in the Mediterranean and Middle East (Med/ ME) was considerably different from that in northern Europe. The unit had been formally established in July 1945, and was commanded directly from the RAF headquarters in Cairo. This was perhaps a strange choice, as the unit arguably had little to do in North Africa. Most air action had occurred along the coastal strip where the Allied and Axis armies had spent several years in a seesaw of attack and retreat. Most aircrew had therefore been discovered and buried as the ground war ebbed and flowed, although many of these graves were subsequently lost again in the shifting sands. Those relatively few who had fallen on either side of the battlefields were lost in either the Mediterranean or the desert seas. Either way there could be little chance of the missing men being found. Therefore the bulk, if not the whole, of the unit itself was established in Italy, with the main tasks of the unit centred around Italy and Sicily, or the Balkans and the Aegean Sea.[193]

Although established the unit did not as yet have any personnel. As a locally raised unit they faced a variety of problems, not least a much smaller pool of candidates from which to find staff. In December 1945 Wing Commander V. G. H. Gee was sent out from the Air Ministry to Cairo to iron some of these out.[194] Firstly there was the question of recruitment. Another issue affecting this had been the policy of only appointing men of Flight Lieutenant rank or higher. This obviously limited even more the choice available, but Gee agreed that it would be appropriate. The terrain and area over which this unit in particular would be operating meant that a higher rank would be needed. Officers would be away from their bases for days or weeks on end, in charge of enlisted men (a search team here would be an officer and two airmen, rather than the one and one of north west Europe) and be responsible for all of their kit and petty cash. There would also be other potentially corrupting influences like extra rations of cigarettes, intended for encouraging locals to be more co-operative, to be looked after. It was identified that in the Mediterranean countries in particular local officials were more likely to respond well to officers of a higher rank. While there Gee also met with the Command accountant to agree on the rules for the use of petty cash, and authorised the establishment of a Med/ME MRES wireless network, although in the end actual use was limited.

Finally on 18 January 1946 Group Captain R. E. Craven, on behalf of the Air Officer Commanding (Administration) for RAF Med/ME, announced that the unit was ready to commence operations,[195] although later MRES internal memorandum would place the date of activation at 1 February.[196] At this point the unit consisted of a headquarters, a records office fulfilling much the same role as P.4 (Cas) and the MRS at a local level, and six sections sharing twenty search parties between them depending on where they were actually needed. Based at Treviso in northern Italy, by the middle of February the unit had completed the bulk of the southern tip of Italy and a 75 mile radius around the big RAF base at Foggia; the teams had then moved north into the Po Valley and had made a start on the eastern part of Sicily.[197] By July the unit had made such progress that a major shift was needed. With the sphere of operations moving ever northward, it was decided to transfer control of the unit from Cairo to London, and bring them under the control of HQ MRES North West Europe, renumbering as No. 5 MREU. This necessitated a major reorganisation and once more an officer was sent out to co-ordinate with the local commanders. Flying Officer Tennison met with Squadron Leader Eddie, of the Base Personnel Office Staff, in order to arrange the standardisation and centralisation of the unit's work. First off would be the rolling loan of the units 15,000 files to London for copying. This was to include files on all missing aircrew, whether they had been found or not, but pains were taken that this would not interfere with active investigations. Any fresh cases or evidence would also be copied to London as and when they appeared.[198]

This unusual arrangement with the paperwork continued until the unit was shut down. Where cases were found in the operational areas of other units related to Italy, they were referred directly to No. 5 MREU rather than the Air Ministry. In May 1948 one of the German-based units was working on a knotty case involving the crews of four bombers found at Ravensbruck (site of the infamous all-female concentration camp), about 80km (50 miles) north of Berlin. Local sources said that they were Canadians and had been on a daylight raid flying from Italy. The same sources also said that the survivors had been murdered. Not many of the details added up. It was unusual to have an RAF raid in daylight so deep into Germany. It was also strange for a raid from Italy to be so far north. As part of the early stages of the investigation the Italian MRES were contacted to see whether they could match the known details to any raid or losses in their files, as were the American authorities in case the 'Canadians' were in fact from American daylight bombers. As the paper trail ends short, they almost certainly were American.[199]

By September 1946 the commander of what was now No. 5 MREU, Squadron Leader S. H. Bell, was able to report on the status and progress of four units to the Air Ministry, and his anticipation of establishing two more.[200] No. 1 Search Party (SP) was 'fully mobile' in central and southern Italy, designated as south of the line from La Spezia to Rimini. This essentially meant the whole of Italy south of where the 'boot' met mainland Europe just north of Florence. Their task was to clear the few remaining outstanding cases in those areas. No. 2 Search Party was reported to be relocating from Vienna to Budapest, with responsibility still for all of the zones of Austria, but with Hungary and Rumania being added as well. The situation for No. 3 SP was less clear. This team was in the process of being formed at HQ No. 5 MREU under Squadron Leader Alfred Browne DFC, with a view of being sent to Greece as soon as possible. Once there, they were to cover Greece, Crete, and the Aegean Islands. The problem was that the Air Officer Commanding the RAF contingent in Greece was unable to offer the MRES any logistical support; transport and supplies were too short for any to be given over to No. 3 SP. Therefore everything that the team may need had to be stockpiled and moved en masse, which led to another problem. Shipping in the Mediterranean was scarce, and long delays were envisaged before suitable arrangements could be made.

In northern Italy No. 4 SP, under Squadron Leader Sidney Linnard DFC was having more luck. Linnard, who had won his DFC commanding the Hurricanes of 274 Squadron over Greece, Syria and Egypt in the early years of the war, was in the process of moving his unit HQ to Milan. Here they would be able to requisition all the supplies, petrol, rations and equipment needed to support the unit as it took responsibility for the whole of Italy north of the La Spezia – Rimini line. The two remaining Search Parties, Nos 5 and 6, had not yet been formed. No. 5 was to cover the Balkans as soon as sufficient personnel became available, and certainly by mid-1947 was active in Yugoslavia. No. 6 was to be sent back south to cover North Africa. It is unclear whether this unit was ever formed. No paper-work appears to survive relating to it, but it was not until June 1948 that HQ No. 5 MREU reported to Group Captain Hawkins at HQ MRES 'Egypt [can be] considered closed unless very exceptional circumstances call for further investigation.'[201] This would imply that a team was operating in the area up to that point.

As can be seen from this one snap-shot, the teams from No. 5 MREU faced some quite different problems from their colleagues further north. Although northern Europe faced transport shortages, it was a relatively easy affair to transfer vehicles between units or find replacements from local sources. In the Mediterranean, stocks of spares and surplus vehicles were even tighter, and moving them between units often meant finding equally scarce air or sea transport space, or relying on a friendly lift from a Royal or allied Navy ship.[202] Long delays were both inevitable and unavoidable. Take the movement of No. 3 SP from Italy to Greece, for example. The advance party, three officers and two other ranks with one jeep and trailer and two motorcycles, left RAF Treviso on 10 October 1946.[203] They arrived at Athens twenty-six days later on the 5 November.[204] The main party, eleven men with seven vehicles and 110 tons of stores, left Treviso eleven days after the advance party,[205] but took nearly three weeks longer than them to reach Athens.[206] Once there, the teams found shortages everywhere. Even with their stockpiling and bulk equipment move, Squadron Leader Browne was to report only the following holdings, illustrating his deficiencies in kit:

Beds:	NIL
Bedding:	Blankets 60
Cutlery:	NIL
Crockery:	NIL
Kitchen Utensils:	Small quantity
Camp kits:	NIL
Bedding rolls:	NIL
Stoves:	20 valor
Mess furniture:	Small quantity tables and chairs
Office furniture:	NIL
Safes:	NIL

Browne pointed out that given the amount of camping and living rough that his men were expected to undertake, he would need more proper camping kit and a comfortable base for them to rest between search operations.[207] These kind of delays and shortages crop up constantly through the reports of No. 3 SP, particularly in the Aegean. Here movement by sea was constricted by the number of mine fields still littered around the islands.[208] Transport of small amounts of men or materiel by air seemed to make little difference, with space on transport aircraft being at even more of a premium. Civilian charter was an option, but could be both expensive and lead to further complications. In December 1947 space was hired from the Denzis Shipping Agency, based in Yugoslavia, for the transport of one officer, two other ranks, two Humber vehicles and thirty-eight cases of supplies from Piraeus to Izmar on board the SS Zuzemberk. Confusion over who was to pay the £160 4s 0d costs led to the Yugoslav Directorate of Shipping getting involved, at a time when relations between the British, and the MRES in particular, and the Yugoslavian government were not exactly smooth.[209]

There were also certain cultural differences to contend with. As we have seen, ranks and bribery were dealt with as early as December 1945. When No. 5 MREU issued its own Search Party Instructions from January 1946, broadly similar to the Standing Orders issued by London, some of these issues were explored further. Small cash payments were authorised to civilians who had been of particular use in searches. 'Search Party Officers are to use their judgement in this matter and act on what they think are fair and just rewards for services rendered.'[210] A further step dealt with criminal activities. Far greater precautions were to be taken against theft in the Mediterranean areas. In northern Europe, vehicles were to be immobilised when left unattended. In the Mediterranean, they were not only to be immobilised when parked, but never left unattended. The driver was to be in attendance at all times.[211] Even so, stolen items were still reported regularly. In March 1947 alone these ranged from a type-writer from the motor transport office at HQ No. 5 MREU[212] at RAF Treviso to complete sets of airmen's kit from a vehicle in Austria.[213] A different approach was also to be taken regarding items taken from wrecks or stolen from bodies. Initially, as in northern Europe, every effort was to be made to retrieve personal items from the local population.[214] This was fairly quickly changed to call for recovery where possible, but not if it jeopardised the positive identification of remains. Locals were to be encouraged to come forward with promises that stolen property would not be forcibly recovered, and that no legal action would be brought against them.[215]

Official procedures also varied, and in some cases were the opposite to the way things were done in the north. As we have seen No. 5 MREU kept its own central casualty enquiry files. In mid-1947 the Army Graves Registration Units were pulled out of Italy, leaving their records (and thus responsibility for any other British soldiers found) with the

MRES. With the Army gone, the MRES also took on responsibility for all exhumation work from all three fighting services in the Mediterranean area.[216]

Most of No. 5 MREU's areas were less than safe. The war had swept away the governments of many of the northern Mediterranean countries, while the Allies had armed countless groups of partisans and guerrillas with diverse political convictions to fight the Germans. Now the entire region had fallen into civil and political strife. These same groups were generally helpful to the RAF and MRES. For example, a case involving a Liberator and crew found in the mountains of Piedmont had been solved when the local partisans had produced a wallet retrieved from one of the bodies, believed to have been the rear gunner. The only useful item within it had been an airgraph[217] from 'Mary and John'. Cross-referencing and discrete enquiries with families had led to the positive identification of one member of the crew, and by default the identification of all of the others too.[218]

The move from Italy was a result of outside pressures. Italy had been in a curious state in the years either side of the end of the Second World War. Having changed sides, and then been liberated, it was in a somewhat hazy legal and political situation. However, from mid-1947 this began to clear. A Republic had been called for by the people in the June 1946 referendum, and subsequent elections voted in a formal government. Italy was returning to self rule, and as part of this was demanding the removal of foreign military personnel. This led to a number of immediate problems. As early as February 1947, with only just over a year of operations completed, No. 5 MREU was being warned that they must be prepared to move, probably to Austria, in May or June.[219] Indeed, movement of teams and equipment to RAF Klagenfurt had already begun[220], even though the eventual destination was not officially confirmed until later. At that time, it was feared that a move to Austria would only lead to a second move shortly after as Austria also reverted to self-rule.[221] In the end, this was not the case.

With the withdrawal of all British and Allied units, the MRES would no longer be able to rely on them for supplies and support. Instead of being able to draw equipment or rations from the nearest base, the teams would now need to carry with them everything that they might need, although petrol would still be available through the Italian Air Force.[222] The situation was eased slightly when a bulk transfer of stores was carried out from 357 Maintenance Unit, who were also pulling out of Italy.[223] Spare parts and kit to last an estimated nine months were secured in one go, and for a short time at least some logistical support would be available through Venice, where the last British military outpost was to be.[224] Even so, Bell, now a Wing Commander, warned his teams that a 'squirrel' attitude now had to be adopted.[225]

In May those families who had come to live with the unit moved to Austria, and all those units who could move joined them. This still left a large number of men in Italy, although these were relocated as soon as possible. The problem remained that British military units were now forbidden to operate within Italy's borders. This issue was neatly side-stepped: the MRES teams still in Italy became members of the British Embassy. As Embassy Assistants (which quite fortuitously carried with it the added bonus of receiving an Embassy Allowance), the officers and men were able to move freely, as long as they did not wear RAF uniform outside the Embassy or official functions.[226] Although the term used was 'civilian dress', standards were expected to be maintained. 'Battledress,' Bell reminded his men, 'without markings and badges of rank becomes "civvies".'[227] New khaki uniforms were to be issued and worn whenever they were outside the Embassy walls.[228] In this way, even though the Royal Air Force had officially withdrawn all units from Italy by the end of 1947[229], in May 1948 a report was being sent to London declaring the Missing Research efforts in Italy to be almost complete.[230]

Operations in Greece, meanwhile, progressed much more slowly. No. 3 Search Party was to cover Greece, Crete and the islands of the Aegean. After being mustered at Treviso the unit was finally sent to Athens, arriving in early November 1946. Here the billets were somewhat basic and the situation was distinctly confused. No. 3 SP was to be based at the RAF station in Athens, although Squadron Leader Browne was quick to establish the independence of the unit with the Air Officer Commanding Greece. Arrangements were made to put out appeals in the press and over the radio across Greece for information on air crashes. However, getting to these sites could be difficult. Although the MRES was issued with passes by the British Police Mission, the area to the north of Athens was thick with bandits, and this central area, plus all roads leading through it to the north of the country, were effectively closed. Although the term 'bandit' is invariably used in the reports, many of these groups were in fact Communist guerrillas, and Greece itself essentially in a state of civil war. Browne reported that:

> If the bandit situation does not improve we will have to write off the whole of central Greece. At the moment there is no Law and Order in the country at all.[231]

By the end of December it was beginning to look as if the constraints placed on travelling by the civil war would not matter. Preliminary searches showed that the behaviour of the general population (not to mention the weather) was leaving the unit completely nonplussed:

We are going ahead with the enquiries but it is very uphill work. The scent is far too cold and the Greeks far too light fingered; they take everything away including the engines. They are also great story-tellers and many miles are being travelled on quite hopeless quests.

The weather has been frightful; pouring with rain, and the roads have been cut all over the place and now have raging torrents pouring across them. This situation does not help us any at all.[232]

On top of this, one of the search officers, while driving under the influence of alcohol, had rolled and badly damaged one of the precious Humber cars. The only positive event to report, in fact, was that Christmas had been a success. The rationing situation that was still pinching teams in Germany was obviously much better here:

We did all the usual waiting on the airmen and got the usual laced beer. However, none of us succumbed in public and the airmen all had a first class dinner consisting of soup, Turkey and Pork, and about fifteen different types of vegetables, then Xmas pudding and compote of oranges. Some of them had two helpings of each Course. I am really amazed as to where they put it all.[233]

In January 1947 the unit began to spread out more. Parties were despatched to Levkas Island (now Lefkada) in western Greece, and to Rhodes and Crete.[234] By the end of the month the SP HQ had moved to Hassani, where much more comfortable quarters could be set up, but the rest of their situation had not improved. Snow now restricted most movement outside Athens, and the transport situation was still grim.[235] A shortage of search officers would follow in February when the Flight Lieutenant who had crashed the Humber in December and been banned from driving, took out another car without permission. Despite having conducted successful searches in the Salonika area (travelling too and from the area by air), it was decided that this officer was not suitable material for the MRES and was to be transferred out as soon as possible.[236]

On a more positive note, work was now underway in the Pelopponese, and preparations in hand to move three search teams to Rhodes (where they would also cover the Dodecanese, a total of 188 estimated cases)[237] and three to Crete (an estimated 219 cases)[238]. Once again, the delay in starting this move was the shortage of sea or air transport,[239] and suitable motor transport for use on arrival. Humber cars would not be suitable for use on the rough roads on Crete in particular, and jeeps would need to be procured. Part of the problem here was administrative; although Crete fell within the area of the AOC Greece, Rhodes and the Dodecanese were outside of it, and so requests for support had to be forwarded to a different and distant headquarters for processing.[240]

Through March the situation took a distinct down turn. Another officer had been arrested for drink driving, and wrecked another Humber in the process. In one way this was beneficial in that it provided a source for spare parts for the other vehicles, all of which were in dire need both within No. 3 SP and RAF Hassani as a whole. The package of spare parts despatched by No. 5 MREU HQ in January had still not been delivered. On the other hand, it meant that staff numbers were almost impossibly low. The Crete party was now just waiting for transport to become available, but sending a party to Rhodes was now deemed impossible with the numbers of officers available, particularly as full scale operations on the Greek mainland were about to begin. The war situation, which had become very serious (one search party had narrowly missed being involved in a large scale battle in Sparta in February)[241], had prompted the Greeks into 'calling up large numbers of reserves and [showing] every intention of being rather rude to the bandits this summer.'[242]

By April things were looking up even more. The two officers who had been convicted of drunk driving both returned in the first week, having been suitably punished. The Crete team was flown out in the middle of the month, and although the Rhodes team was still waiting shipping, it was soon to follow. The north of Greece itself was opening up again as the weather improved and the bandits were suppressed by the Greek Army. The only delay now to getting No. 3 SP operating at 100 per cent was Easter.

We are not doing any work this week as it is Greek Easter. Apparently the Greeks all fast for the last week and our SPs would only get potatoes if they were in the field. Also it is no good trying to get any sense out of people who are not eating … Further our interpreters would all be a bit niggley.[243]

Once operations were fully underway in the early summer of 1947, work progressed quickly everywhere except on Crete.[244] The campaign on the island in 1941 had been short, bloody and confused. Records on where airmen had been buried, or who had been lost over the island, were scant where they existed, but most had been destroyed when the ship carrying them was sunk during the evacuation.[245] To complicate matters, the British had evacuated an unknown number of unnamed wounded air-crew to Athens, which had itself fallen at the end of April 1941. In short, nobody knew who to look for, or where.[246] Therefore, although bodies could be recovered and concentrated on Crete, very few could be identified and by May 1948 there were 178 unknown airmen buried there. Currently, 778 of the 1,502 Commonwealth war dead buried at Suda Cemetery, Crete, are unidentified.[247]

Other islands had fared better, although the six cases on Cyprus had been left to the local RAF garrison units. By May 1948 only forty-three airmen remained unidentified on Rhodes, and forty others through the rest of the Dodecanese. Another 115 airmen were still missing in the Greek Islands, but the evidence for most of these pointed to their being lost at sea. It was therefore decided 'on grounds of economy' to withdraw the outlying units to the mainland.[248] Once there, they could aid those teams in recovering the thirty-six bodies still to be collected from the area around Athens, and possibly the seventy-four which were known to be in the region still largely controlled by Communist forces.[249] Recovery of these men seemed unlikely, until Group Captain Hawkins intervened directly.

A section was organised in Athens of four search officers, with four drivers, and two clerks under the personal command of Group Captian Hawkins.[250] Heading out into the mountains, the convoy ran into a piquet from the local rebel Communist forces. According to later Air Ministry publicity Hawkins, in the lead jeep, calmly ordered the convoy to halt, stepped up to the nearest soldier and quietly commanded him to 'take me to your leader.' The Greeks soldiers, somewhat nonplussed, did so, and the RAF party met a most enthusiastic welcome. After all, the aircrew that Hawkins was seeking had been killed either dropping men and supplies to help these same guerrillas fight the Germans, or had been on offensive operations against the occupiers directly. The Communist leader provided an armed escort, guides and manpower to help with their search, leading to the locating and identification all of the outstanding aircrew.[251]

By the end of July No. 3 Search Party was considered to have completed their task, and were ordered to rejoin No. 5 MREU in Austria. The transport situation dictated that the only way out was by road, and so a convoy was formed in Athens. Leaving on the 29 July[252], they arrived safely at RAF Klagenfurt on the 4 August 1948.[253] As the small team that had been sent to Turkey in December 1947 had already completed its area and returned safely[254], the eastern Mediterranean was now declared as cleared.

Now only the Balkans and Hungary were left within No. 5 MREU's remit. Hungary had been cleared fairly quickly. Although problems had arisen both in gaining permission to enter the country, and the numbers of those who could, the country seems to have been cleared between October 1946 and October 1947.[255] Bulgaria, which like Hungary was falling into the Soviet sphere of influence, was closed completely. There were only two known cases in the country (Handley Page Halifax BB446, lost on 15/16 March 1944, and Vickers Wellington F3479, lost on 11/12 June 1944), but these both had to be written off as inaccessible.[256] Rumania, also now under Soviet control, initially agreed access in September 1947, but revoked this again in December.[257] The eleven cases in this country also had to be given up.[258]

This left Yugoslavia, which would see perhaps the most efficient of all the MRES establishments in action. No. 2 Search Party was operating in Austria in early 1947. Perhaps it was this experience, which involved careful handling of the Soviets in their zone of the country, and frequent problems through bad weather, that prepared them so well for what was to come.[259] In June 1947 the Yugoslavian Government, after considerable diplomatic effort, gave the British and Americans permission to enter graves registration units into their country. Major R. G. Dakin, the GRU representative at the British Embassy in Belgrade who had brokered the deal, reported that Belgrade British Military Cemetery was to be expanded for use and all of the estimated 655 British bodies would be concentrated there. To facilitate this, free rail travel was to be arranged for all recovered bodies, and travel permits for the staff engaged on searches. A strict limit on the numbers of personnel involved was imposed, and the use of wireless sets for communication forbidden, but it was still an overall positive result. Major Dakin concluded that:

After eighteen months of sheer obstruction it would appear that the Jugoslavs [sic] have now done an about face and it is to be hoped that no new inflammatory Churchillian speeches cause them to take further fright.[260]

This last comment was presumably a reference to Winston Churchill's 'Iron Curtain' speech of March 1946 when he heavily criticised Yugoslavian attempted annexation of the Trieste region in north-east Italy.

On 26 August 1947 a mixed unit of RAF and army personnel arrived in Belgrade. After initial delays as identification papers and vehicle registration was organised, and driving tests administered, the teams began work on 12 September.[261] There were enough personnel to establish five search teams, one for the Belgrade area (which would also act as headquarters), two for Croatia, and two for Bosnia. Once these areas were completed the Croatian units were to move on to Slovenia, and the Bosnian to Macedonia and Serbia. Whoever finished these areas first would then clear up the remaining portion of the country in Istria.[262] Although the exact movement of teams worked out a little different to the plan, this arrangement worked remarkably well. By having two teams working in tandem in each area, they could mutually support each other. The Army and RAF staff could lend each other everything from expert knowledge to vehicles or spare parts, saving a lot of time. So successful was it, in fact, that when the Yugoslavian units pulled out they were able to report that they had covered over 43,000km (30,000 miles) on the road without experiencing a single delay due to transport problems, an unheard of situation anywhere else in the MRES organisation.[263] The planning behind the move also benefited the unit. The Army took charge of all administrative aspects of the party, and the RAF all operational control.[264] The mountainous areas were cleared first, so that by the winter the bad weather was no great impediment.[265]

The biggest problem facing the units regarding transport was how to get the remains recovered back to Belgrade as quickly and safely as possible. Although rail travel was convenient for large numbers of bodies, it was also slow. The Yugoslavs themselves provided the answer with three specially fitted out ambulances, complete with airtight coffins, that were made available for use within a practical distance of Belgrade. Driven by civilians, two were ready for use at any given time while the third was being serviced.[266] Road travel was not always practical, however. No. 5 Search Party had been sent to reinforce No. 2 SP in late 1947, and after a brief spell at the end of December 1947 into January 1948 when all the teams were expelled from Yugoslavia[267], they moved into Croatia. Here their remit also covered the Dalmatian Islands, just off the coast in the Adriatic. A Yugoslavian Navy cutter was organised for transport, and the team ferried around the islands. A total of sixty-three bodies were recovered, and piped aboard ship by the Yugoslavs with full military honours. Some of the islands were off limits to foreigners, and the Yugoslavs themselves searched these and recovered a further five bodies. Once back on the mainland, these were moved by rail to Belgrade for burial. The search team itself would record that 'during each operation the co-operation from the Yugoslav Authorities left nothing to be desired.'[268]

This was also true from an American point of view. On 30 January 1948 a mixed American, Yugoslavian and British parade was held to honour the loading of the last of 700 recovered US servicemen onto a train in Belgrade. Again, full military honours were presented by the Yugoslavians.[269]

As of the same date, the British were reporting that their job was virtually complete. A total of 468 personnel from all three services had been collected at Belgrade. Of these, there were 184 positively identified RAF airmen, plus 134 whose identity was awaiting acceptance by the Air Ministry, and twenty-five who were unidentified. It was confidently predicted that twenty-three of those twenty-five could and would have names put to them. The only complaint was that the Air Ministry was taking too long to accept identification of the 134, some of the recommendations dating back to June 1947.[270] Generally, though, progress was good enough for the staff of Nos 2 and 5 SPs to be pulled from the country at the end of February and reassigned.[271]

The final Yugoslavian report, dated 1 March 1948, reported that 633 bodies were currently at Belgrade. Of these, 456 were still waiting acceptance of identification, and twenty-six were officially unknown. The RAF case figures were given as 269 airmen accepted (one of them confirmed as unknown), 102 awaiting acceptance (three of them to be confirmed as lost at sea), sixty-two with known burial sites but not yet recovered, and 135 not yet located. Of these 135, forty-five were thought to have been lost at sea, seven were presumed to be at the bottom of the River Danube, four in the River Mura, and eleven in areas were the firm information had arrived too late for the teams to take any action.[272]

As with most of the other countries in this region, the administration and marking of graves that would result from the final acceptance of identity was now left in the hands of the Air Attaché of the relevant British Embassy. On 10 August 1948 No. 5 MREU was disbanded at RAF Klagenfurt,[273] with the exception of one officer and one driver to liaise with the IWGC and American Graves Service in Rome.[274]

CHAPTER NINE

Germany and Poland

During the war at least 1,577 aircraft were shot down in this area. Many complicated problems have therefore attended the conduct of Missing Research operations. It is so often that many crashes must be considered jointly when endeavouring to get a ruling on one particular incident. The devastation and confusion resulting from frequent large scale air-attacks makes it impossible in many incidents to obtain the true facts of a case without lengthy and detailed investigation work.[275]

Report on work of 20 Section No. 4 MREU, Ruhr area,
by Sqdn Ldr commanding W. H. Armstrong, January 1949

In many ways, in Europe at least, all MRES roads led to Germany. No. 4 Unit had been established there in August 1945, immediately starting work in the British Zone of Occupation, including the Ruhr. This was always going to be the biggest challenge. This was where the bulk of Bomber Command's raids had been, and where the majority of crews had been lost. In the north and east of the country, the Ruhr and Berlin, crashes lay thick across the ground. Reconstructing events, aircraft and crews, and then identifying individuals within them, became one gigantic jigsaw puzzle. To aid them, in September 1946 No. 2 MREU moved their headquarters and most of their staff from Holland and Belgium into the French Zone, based at Diez, and in December 1946 No. 3 MREU transferred from Norway and Denmark to Karlsruhe to cover the American Zone. From the south, No. 5 MREU moved inexorably north through the Mediterranean and Italy and into Austria. From July 1947, bar a few detached searcher parties, the full field strength of the MRES in Europe was concentrated into Greater Germany. By the time the last German unit was shut down eighteen months later, its members were still appealing against the decision because they considered their task unfinished.

Germany presented a number of problems that were rare elsewhere, but which would became the staple of missing research operations. The

101

sheer weight of crashes in certain areas made the research task all the more complicated. Take, for example, when officers from No. 3 MREU investigated the record of fifteen RAF bodies buried at Oberhaching cemetery.[276] In early 1947 these bodies had been relocated by an American Graves Registration unit to Reutti cemetery, and so the MRES had not been able to examine the bodies in their original graves. On 16 June the transported bodies were re-exhumed. It was suspected that the bodies, actually sixteen in number, came from three crews, all of which had been lost in that area and one of whom was entered into the cemetery register. All the crews were lost on operations near Munich across three nights in the autumn of 1943.

It now became a case of matching remains to names. The three suspected crews consisted of:

Halifax V DK233 of 428 Squadron, lost on 31 August/1 September 1943 on operation to Berlin:
   Flight Sergeant John Este RCAF (Pilot)
   Sergeant Sidney Towle RCAF (Air Gunner)
   Sergeant Robert Briggs-Jude RCAF (Air Gunner)
   (Warrant Officers Macaulay RCAF, Dutka RCAF and Haddon and Flight Sergeant Burdoff safe)

Halifax V EB250 of 76 Squadron, lost on 6/7 September 1943 on operation to Munich:
   Flight Sergeant Eoin Little RNZAF (Pilot)
   Flight Sergeant Lumley Gittins (Flight Engineer)
   Sergeant Bruce Phillis (Wireless Operator)
   Sergeant Jack Naylor (Air Gunner)
   Sergeant Ronald Lewis (Air Gunner)
   Sergeant James Arnold (Navigator)
   (Pilot Officer Farrington and Sergeant Broadbent safe)

Lancaster III JA856 of 460 Squadron, lost on 2 October 1943 on operation to Munich:
   Flight Sergeant Frank Lloyd DFM RAAF (Pilot)
   Sergeant Alan Mitchell RAAF (Bomb Aimer)
   Sergeant Raymond Hurrell (Navigator)
   Sergeant Reginald Woodford (Wireless Operator)
   Sergeant George Douglas (Flight Engineer)
   Sergeant Leslie Sim (Air Gunner)
   Flight Sergeant Francis Sheehan RCAF (Air Gunner)

Flight Sergeant Lloyd and Sergeant Mitchell had both been commissioned as Pilot Officers just before the raid, and so could have been wearing either officers or NCOs uniform and insignia.

Exhumations were begun, covering graves numbers from forty-nine through to fifty-eight. This is what was found on the bodies:

49: The remains in a dark blue RAAF battledress tunic with pilot's wings. A name and number found in the shirt confirmed the body as Flight Sergeant Lloyd.

50: Identity disc for Sergeant Hurrell with tunic with matching observer's insignia, and one battledress tunic with flight engineer's brevet. The body was designated as Sergeant Hurrell's.

51: A large quantity of remains, possibly from more than one body, but with no identifying features.

52: Identity disc for Sergeant Woodford.

53: Identity disc for Sergeant Douglas, minus battledress tunic (assumed found in grave 50).

54: Remains of clothing suggestive of an air gunner, with separate RAAF battledress trousers.

55: Remnants of RAAF battledress tunic with bomb aimer brevet and Flight Sergeant rank. Designated as Sergeant Mitchell as only RAAF crewman of that rank and trade.

56:: Tunic with either Pilot Officer or Flying Officer rank insignia.

57: Laundry mark on under-pants of 'Z931'. This number correlated to the last three digits of Sergeant Sim's service number. As a battledress tunic was found with sergeant's chevrons and an air gunner's brevet, this body was positively identified as Sergeant Sim.

58: Remains of an electrically-heated flying suit, suggestive of an air gunner.

This left the search officers with a partially solved problem. All the members of JA856's crew had been found except Flight Sergeant Sheehan. As the bodies had been jumbled to some extent, it was decided to rebury the bodies as a complete crew in Durnbach War Cemetery. This left at least four, and probably more, unidentified bodies. As none were Canadian, this discounted the crew of Halifax DK233. This led to Flying Officer Powell of 17 Section No. 3 MREU returning to Oberhaching a month later. Here, further investigations uncovered that the German documents that had led them to believe that the bodies from DK233 had been taken to Oberhaching, and so to Reutti, were inaccurate. Discussions with the present and previous burgermeisters and their secretary instead indicated that these men had never arrived there. Here the trail went cold, and these three men are today commemorated on the Runnymede

Memorial. The search officers now turned to the missing men from the second Halifax, from 76 Squadron. The evidence collected was deemed sufficient to identify collectively the remaining bodies as Flight Sergeant Little and his crew, and they are now buried under this collective identity, also in Durnbach War Cemetery.

In many ways, this was one of the more successful searches. A significant number of men had been identified either individually or as a crew, without too much difficulty. Sometimes the evidence was much scarcer. In February 1947 another officer of 17 Section No. 3 MREU could only identify the crew of a 101 Squadron Lancaster lost near the end of 1944 by documentary evidence. He was to report that:

> Results were poor as only very scanty remains were found in a small wooden box. No discs or other identifying matter were found.
> It was quite impossible to estimate the numbers of bodies involved as only a portion of a skull, three fingers and a femur were brought to light.

The paper trail alone was deemed sufficient to identify the crew, however, and the remains were buried in a communal grave in Durnbach War Cemetery.[277]

In the above two cases, the search efforts were helped by the fact that whole crews were present, and the officers were piecing together the men's identities within a known framework. This could make the slightest clue sufficient. For example, in a case publicised at the time, in 1947 a team from No. 4 MREU working in the Russian Zone identified an entire crew from a single button. This button had been stamped with the name of a very exclusive Savile Row tailor, and a search of the list of clients cross referenced with a list of missing airmen led to the identification of this one officer, and by extension the rest of the crew.[278] Sometimes the clues were further afield. Local scrap yards were a good source of wreckage and, possibly, engines, which would indicate at the very least the type of aircraft and with any luck the exact air frame. It was not unusual to find sketches of aircraft parts in investigation reports along with transcriptions of maker's plates or other serial numbers. These could then be traced through Air Ministry or manufacturer's records. At least once, the evidence was somewhat more scattered. One case in Munich involved a report that some wreckage had come down in a field during a raid in late April 1945. It appears that the aircraft exploded in the air, and the pieces were fragmented and scattered. What there was had been taken to the local scrap yard. An initial search brought no clues, but a short while later the search officer returned with two drivers to sift through more thoroughly. This time it was discovered that some of the pieces were painted a dull red instead of matt black. Over the course of two days all the red pieces were found and slowly, with much trial and error, fitted together. Eventually the first two letters and last number of a serial number were assembled and parts of the other two numbers tentatively put in place. The serial was run through the Air Ministry records and a match found. Unfortunately, given the nature of the explosion, no associated remains or graves were ever found, and the crew remained listed as missing.[279]

A less common type of case would be where only partial crews were found, thus making it harder to establish a frame of reference. In December 1947 a sweep by No. 4 MREU uncovered three graves scattered quite some distance apart along the banks of the River Elbe. One could be immediately matched to a *Totenliste* entry for Sergeant Frederick Arthur Crawford of 103 Squadron, lost when his Lancaster was shot down during a raid on Hamburg in early August 1943. The second was three miles up river and could, with some slight differences in location, be matched to a German report of the burial of Sergeant Frederick John Swift of the same crew. The third was higher up river still, but the assumption made (given that no other individuals had been found in the area) that he was from the same crew. The question still remained, which one of the five outstanding crew was this? An exhumation was carried out and no distinguishing feature could be found, although the remains of an identity disc was recovered. Although badly degraded, the search officer had it photographed in infra-red. This was a trick picked up from the MRS, and supplied courtesy of the American Graves Registration people, that was often used on faded or obscured fabric items that would pick out the underlying dye (metal items were usually soaked in petrol to clean them). In this case enough could be made out to match the disc to Sergeant Leslie Spurgeon, the crew's flight engineer, and his family informed accordingly.[280]

In the last few months of the war it became less common for the Germans to process wrecks and properly bury the crews. Sometimes, even months or years after the war, the bodies of the crew would still be in the wreckage of their aircraft. These cases could be the hardest to deal with for the search officers, but on an emotional rather than an investigative level:

> In one case in the mountains a Lanc had crashed and, according to the locals, had burned for 22 hours, and when we got into the remains of the cabin there was a little body in the pilot's seat, and this was completely burned and carbonised; that was the pilot less than [two feet tall], sitting in the seat. And you could see all of his little features and his little nose, and we got a cardboard box, and as we'd identified the aircraft and knew who it was, I picked him up to put him in the box and as I picked him up he broke in half. So I put the two halves in the box. It really hurt me, as if I'd got him

in the box in one piece it would have been something, but he broke in half ...
They were the saddest features of it.[281]

One of the most immediate issues facing the MRES teams in Germany was that here they were in many ways operating in enemy territory. Only a matter of months before, these same men (often literally so) had been flying over Germany and bombing her cities. These raids had been designed to cripple the nation's infrastructure and economy, and so well had they achieved this aim that the country was in ruins. Food was scarce, work hard to find, and even basic utilities still out of order. Flight Lieutenant Colin Mitchell, based with No. 4 MREU in Hamburg, would refer to it as 'the chaotic and sometimes hostile environment in which we would work.' He would go on to explain:

A hostile environment was only to be expected. Having had a few thousand tons of bombs rain down on the population it was hardly likely that one would be welcomed with open arms! The mere sight of an officer bearing the insignia of aircrew on his left breast was like red rag to a bull to some and a shout of Terrorfligen *[sic] was some times shouted with venom at some officers during the course of their duties. No doubt there were other epithets when out of ear-shot.*[282]

Sometimes this hostility led to direct confrontation, as this example from Duisburg shows:

One incident comes to mind where the bodies were buried in an allotment, and I arranged for an exhumation to take place and just before the appointed time my interpreter said to me that a lot of the local German people with allotments there were getting rather concerned that they would loose their crops. In view of the severe rationing they could do with the food. Well I said that the British people were experts in the field of rationing, and furthermore I am not going to allow a British airman to lay without a coffin in an unconsecrated grave one moment longer than is necessary.[283]

In this particular case, the crew in question had been shot down over Duisburg on the second raid launched on the town by Bomber Command in 24 hours, not to mention an attack by the USAAF. In all, over 4,000 Allied aircraft were involved in dropping nearly 9,000 tons of bombs on the town over the course of a day and a night.[284] Six of the bodies had been thrown from the wreck, and two remained inside. Witness statements taken after the war showed that the bodies were laid in the street where they had fallen for four or five days until being collected by the German authorities and buried by Russian prisoners of war. Eventually, the whole crew was recovered by Mitchell, and buried in Reichswald

Forest War Cemetery.[285] It was not uncommon for crews to remain in the open for so long after a major raid – the German authorities would have been swamped and it would have taken days to recover all the German dead, let alone the British. It was also not unknown for any British crews to be buried in the mass graves generated by these attacks.

Uncooperative Germans were fairly common. Depending on the rank of the person in question this could pose quite a problem. When the local authorities became difficult, sometimes unusual measures were needed. Flight Lieutenant Kelbrick was serving in Schleswig Holstein. This team also had responsibility for the Frisian Islands, using a tank landing craft with a German crew under a Royal Navy officer to move between them. During one search, they encountered an unhelpful mayor:

This mayor wouldn't cooperate whatsoever, he wouldn't give any infor-mation. I got my senior NCO, along with a Sergeant from the Army [and] two Corporals, to go and call on the mayor with fixed bayonets and all that ... and ordered him down to the shore. [We took him out to an island] and we let the door down on the tank landing craft and told him to walk out up to his waist ... and we told him that they'd lost the war, and we hadn't, and that he was to co-operate ... And that's how we got the information.[286]

Sometimes the ill-feeling ran the other way. During the Christmas party of the headquarters section of No. 2 MREU, held at the Schloss Schaum-burg in Diez, one drunken corporal had to be restrained physically when found with his rifle at the main gate swearing to enter the town and shoot every German he could find.[287]

For the most part, though, relations were relatively good (compared to, say, three years before, and what could be expected). Corporal Douglas Hague was a clerk stationed with HQ No. 4 MREU on the outskirts of Hamburg, which had been devastated in 1943. He found that the locals were best just avoided, which was easy enough in a garrison town like Hamburg, where there were plenty of service clubs.[288] For the search officers it was harder to avoid contact with the general population. For the most part the difficulties that arose were not malicious; if anything they just caused delays:

No matter what strata of society a witness came from or their employ-ment or background, three common factors would emerge. Sooner or later during their questioning they would continue to introduce in their com-ments (1) They never belonged to the Nazi Party. (2) They never voted for Hitler and (3) They never knew or heard anything about concentration camps.[289]

A further delay is often found in investigation reports to have arisen when it was found out that local administrators, who had been Nazis, had absconded. Some interaction was far friendlier, and in fact began the process of healing the divide between the two countries. Although just after the war fraternization with the Germans was forbidden (under pain of fines), with the MRES it was unavoidable, and a certain laxity shown. One night Flight Lieutenant Mitchell and his driver were invited to dinner with a German family, and despite some reservations accepted. It was only at the end of the evening that their hosts explained that their son had been a *Luftwaffe* pilot who was missing and believed killed. By meeting their enemy, and potentially their son's killers, they hoped to gain some closure on his loss.[290]

On occasion this interaction could be on a much grander scale. Squadron Leader Bill Lott had been working for the Control Commission for Germany in Detmold when he had volunteered for the MRES. He had assumed that he would be attached to the Detmold section, particularly as he 'had met and grown very fond of an extremely attractive and interesting German girl, Annegret, who was then employed by the British Army as a highly competent and valued member of staff in their local HQ.' Unfortunately:

To my horror, when my official posting came through it was to No. 2 Missing Research & Enquiry Unit at Diez in the French Zone of Occupation ... Diez was more than 100 miles from Detmold and there was no way in which close contact could be maintained between Annegret and me once I had moved there. There was no immediate solution available and I took up my duties as Search Officer with No. 2 MREU where our quarters were in an old German castle, Schloss Schaumburg, just outside the town.

Close to the castle was a small field used by the local villagers as a sports field. We would occasionally use it for the odd kick-about. On one such occasion, after I had been there some weeks, I was approached by a young German chap who very politely asked if it might be possible to arrange a friendly football game between the RAF unit and youngsters from the local village. He thought it would be good for friendly relationships.

I couldn't see anything objectionable in the idea, asked my compatriots, all thought it OK ... so I got a scratch team together, agreed a Sunday-afternoon date and thought no more about it until our bunch arrived at the venue to find the field surrounded by a couple of hundred Germans! We were dumbfounded: it emerged that the event had received widespread local publicity and given an importance far in excess of anything we had anticipated or intended.

After some hesitation, we decided to go ahead with the game: the Germans took over! It was like an International Championship Final. Each team had to run on to the field from opposite diagonal corners, meet in the centre,

exchange flags (we hadn't brought one), shake hands all round, say 'Hi'
to the referee and linesmen and so on and so on. I can't remember much
about the game or the result but the locals obviously enjoyed it!

The next morning, Squadron Leader Lott was summoned to see his
commanding officer.

I had no idea what might be the cause of so peremptory a summons, but the
C.O. had a face like thunder. I was not invited to 'stand easy' let alone sit
down and this in the days when Service discipline among people like us was
pretty easy-going.

He handed me a sheet of paper, written in French and headed by
an impressive official-looking superscription and concluded with a French
Military Government stamp ... He told me that it was an official complaint
from the French Zone District Commandant that members of the RAF had
grossly violated French Military Government Regulations regarding un-
lawful assembly of German citizens in his area of responsibility. It appeared
that under these regulations, assemblies of more than three Germans were,
without specific prior authority, strictly forbidden and subject to severe
penalties. Our football match had resulted in an 'unauthorised assembly' of
some hundreds of German citizens and an official explanation was invited
from the responsible RAF Commander as to the whys and wherefores
etc., etc.

The situation was serious: I was the principal culprit, having set the
thing up in the first place, but I had not broken any specific RAF rules,
merely caused French Military Government rules to be broken. Handing
me over to the French was not an option, but 'something had to be done'
and quickly. Any reference by the French Governor to British Higher
Authority was to be avoided at all costs! I was dismissed with an order to
concoct some feasible excuse for my behaviour, coupled with an abject
apology and plea in mitigation: I had a 24-hour target.

I had the solution in 10 minutes. My Boss would advise the French
Governor that he had 'torn me off a strip' a yard wide for failing to recognise
that my action might have repercussions of the most serious character, and
to ensure that no future cause for complaint of like nature would occur he
would expedite my transfer out of the French Zone of Occupation without
prospect of return.

My Boss agreed this approach: it got him off the hook and I would achieve
my most fervent wish – to get back to [the British Army on the Rhine], to
Detmold and to Annegret: good show![291]

Not all such gestures were on a grand scale, but every little helped to
improve relations:

I was in the office when our housekeeper came to me and said that two local German ladies were at the door with a 'request'. I invited them in; the birth of Charles, Prince of Wales had been reported in the German press. Did we, perhaps, have English newspapers with pictures of the new Prince and, if so, would we be kind enough to let them have any that we could spare, they would be most grateful! We were, of course, happy to oblige.[292]

Former Pathfinder Squadron Leader Bernard Moorcroft DSO DFC also worked at the headquarters of No. 2 MREU in Schloss Schaumburg. In 1946 he, like many officers, brought his wife across from England, and billeted themselves in the nearby town of Diez. They lived quite comfortably among the local population, employing German domestic staff.

A lot of the interaction with the locals came through the civilian staff employed as grave diggers or interpreters for the search teams in the field, and as household staff, interpreters and clerks at the section and unit headquarters. The unit returns for No. 4 MREU in March 1949 show no less than 148 German civilians on the pay-roll – far more than RAF staff. These included forty-four clerks, twenty-seven grave-diggers, eighteen sign writers (to prepare grave markers), eleven cleaners, eight night watchmen, five cooks and a laundress.[293] For the most part the working relationship was a happy one. Naturally, a few problems arose. Corporal Douglas Hague recalls a certain amount of communication difficulties in his office between the Germans and Leading Aircraftsman Jock Dougherty, who was from Glasgow, but essentially things went smoothly. In fact, a good working relationship was struck up in most areas, and a certain amount of sympathy shown by the RAF staff for their German colleagues.

The years 1945–1948, and particularly that first winter, were harsh ones for the local population. Known later as 'Der Grosse Hunger' (The Great Hunger), between 1 January 1946 and 20 June 1948 some 143,000 Germans (one in three of all registered deaths) died of malnutrition and exhaustion related conditions.[294] The winter of 1945–1946 was especially harsh across Europe, and severe rationing and food shortages were still in effect everywhere. It took longer for this situation to improve in Germany than the neighbouring areas of Belgium, Holland and Denmark, and most of the sections began to procure extra food for their staff, either through the NAAFI or other means. These efforts could make a huge difference to the health of the German staff. Flying Officer Harry Wilson DFM recalls:

It was a happy unit and discipline was lax but not misplaced, and the Wing Commander would reward what work he considered had been well done with the odd 'liaison visit' to 3 MREU in Copenhagen, or 2 MREU in

Brussels. The Copenhagen 'jolly' allowed us to bring back extra rations of eggs and bacon. Wing Commander Morgan approved of this because of an unhappy event which happened when one of our young 16 year old German typists fell off a tramcar and broke her leg which should have been just an unfortunate accident, but she died of malnutrition. This upset all of us when we considered the standard to which we were living. The CO subsequently said that every member of staff would have a hot meal every day. We paid for vegetables to be bought and hot soup was served to the staff each day. The rations from Copenhagen helped greatly there.[295]

The means used for gathering the required food was not always particularly legitimate. Food brought in from Belgium or Holland was sometimes smuggled across the border to avoid complications with the local customs authorities, and a certain amount of black market dealing was known to go on. One MRES officer was even court martialled and dismissed from the service for dealing in this way, albeit for the best of reasons.[296] These activities certainly had a considerable effect on head-quarters life. Once the worst of the food shortages had lifted, according to Flight Lieutenant Myhill it was even quite a high life:

We had some good times as well, with our staff. We had a lot of female staff, and we all used to go swimming, or all have parties, and there were a lot of affairs going on. I think a lot of the barriers broke down because of the work we were doing.

The women were plentiful and the alcohol was cheap because we could buy the army duty-free stuff, so we lived a full life in that respect, but then it took our minds off the sadness of the job we were doing ....[297]

Some officers, like Squadron Leader Bill Lott, Squadron Leader Tommy Thompson, and Flight Lieutenant Ron Myhill even ended up marrying local girls.

Such activities were not always looked upon too kindly. Lieutenant Duncan Torrance was an officer with an Army Graves Concentration Unit, attached to No. 3 MREU in the American Zone of Germany in 1947. At the time he would write that he:

was ashamed of [the] conduct [of the MRES] as occupiers of enemy territory. Probably the worst behaved was the Squadron Leader in charge. He lay himself open daily to serious charges. He was entertaining German women on the mess rations, using [War Department] vehicles to transport them, and holding drunken orgies in the mess which lasted until between eight and ten the next morning. He used to break his own speed limit with his jeep coming down the drive to the mess. One Sunday afternoon he took a jeep into the town at two o'clock. He was wearing pyjamas, the officer with him was wearing civvies. They brought two German girls, back to the mess. Another night I caught him in my headlamps, sitting on a bridge in the town, with a German girl and a bottle of gin. Many of these women slept regularly in the mess.

Sixty years later Lieutenant Torrence would modify his remarks somewhat:

Those are the words I wrote in 1947. They are true. They are absolutely true. That's why I feel I must not now expunge them. But I must intrude my judgement of to-day. These were wonderfully brave men. . . . . They were like the crews we had to re-bury. Now, of the MRES officers I served amongst, and the few who behaved badly, the years convert initial emotion to a more balanced judgement. In the American Zone we had twenty or so MRES, ex-aircrew. Many may have been suffering from post traumatic stress syndrome, a condition unrecognised then.[298]

Stress was certainly a factor. These were very young men, who had already been through a harrowing experience as aircrew. Quite apart from any previous experiences, they were now performing a very hard job. Most teams worked at least a six-day week. Leave seems to be left up to each section to arrange for themselves. For some, it was set at a fortnight every six months[299] and for others it was simply whenever it was felt that the men needed it.[300] The working day was long, and although the day of rest could be spent in the various pleasurable pursuits already detailed by Flight Lieutenant Myhill (or, according to the Operations Record Book of No. 4 MREU, in the forests shooting stag and boars)[301] the work was still physically and mentally draining.

Take for example, 'G' Section No. 4 MREU. Their task was to clear the north coast of the British Zone of Germany, including the Frisian Islands, a total of 30,000 square kilometres (19,000 square miles). Four search officers operated from G Section, under the command of Squadron Leader William Armstrong: Flight Lieutenants Taylor, Saager and McIntyre, and Flying Officer Harry Wilson DFM. In the month of April 1947, their work consisted of[302]:

Week ending 5th April
  Flight Lieutenant Taylor: Investigated two cases, and conducted a sweep (Operation X), locating one case involving seven bodies.
  Flight Lieutenant Saager: Investigated one case and carried out twenty-three exhumations at Wittmund.
  Flight Lieutenant McIntyre: Investigated seven cases.
  Flying Officer Wilson: On leave.

Week ending 12th April:
>   Flight Lieutenant Taylor: Operation X in Hamburg area, locating two cases involving ten bodies.
>   Flight Lieutenant Saager: Carried out fifty-nine exhumations at Wittmund.
>   Flight Lieutenant McIntyre: Operation X, locating two cases.
>   Flying Officer Wilson: On leave.

Week ending 19th April:
>   Flight Lieutenant Taylor: On detached liaison duties with HQ RCAF.
>   Flight Lieutenant Saager: Investigated seven cases (concerning twenty-eight bodies) and carried out thirty-seven exhumations at Lueneburg.
>   Flight Lieutenant McIntyre: Operation X, and exhumed sixteen bodies at Rendsburg.
>   Flying Officer Wilson: Conducting final sweep of the islands, exhuming forty-eight bodies from Norderney.

Week ending 26th April:
>   Flight Lieutenant Taylor: Operation X in Hamburg area, investigated one case and carried out eight exhumations at Lueneburg.
>   Flight Lieutenant Saager: Investigated six cases involving forty-one bodies before proceeding to the UK on leave.
>   Flight Lieutenant McIntyre: Exhumed twenty bodies in the Heide area.
>   Flying Officer Wilson: Completed Norderney with seven exhumations, commenced final sweep of Juist, exhuming twenty-two bodies.

Week ending 30th April:
>   Flight Lieutenant Taylor: Completed exhumations at Lueneburg, with five bodies.
>   Flight Lieutenant Saager: On leave.
>   Flight Lieutenant McIntyre: On Operation X sweep in Rendsburg area.
>   Flying Officer Wilson: Exhumed fifty-seven bodies on Juist.

These tasks led to a varied and busy existence. Operation X sweeps meant a lot of time on the road, talking to locals and physically searching large areas. Exhumations were physically and mentally hard work. The work on the islands could be even harder work, especially as there were strict deadlines to meet. Flying Officer Harry Wilson recalls:

A priority for work was given by the army for the island of Norderney where a great number of bodies had been washed up. There was to be an

Officers Club Leave Centre due to be opened in April and they didn't want bodies being transported through the town at that time. As hundreds of bodies had been washed up on the six German Frisian Islands from Borkum to Wangerooge we decided to base ourselves in Norderney. Captain Patterson, ex-Gurkha Rifles officer with 74 GCU and myself decided to requisition premises nearby and clear all the islands. We were there for about four months, returning to Oldenburg with the bodies. We had a German fishing boat which took the bodies from the islands to Norden on the mainland and then by truck to the cemetery.

The islands work wasn't straightforward. The island of Juist, for example, had its pier washed away in the winter storms, so the only means we had to get to the island was to get as close as the draught of our boat would allow and then transfer onto a horse and cart to take us on to the island, and the same way back with the bodies. All this had to be arranged with the burgomeister, and we also had to arrange hotel accommodation for ourselves and the civilian workers who were doing the grave digging.

Lying between Juist and the mainland is a sand dune known as the Memmert Sands which is uninhabited, but had two RAF bodies buried there. The only way we could retrieve them was to bring our boat in as close as possible, then Captain Patterson and myself transferred to a dinghy and paddled to the shoreline, dug up the bodies, transferred them to the dinghy and swam back to the boat pulling the dinghy behind us.[303]

Somewhat pricklier neighbours to work with were the Soviet authorities who controlled half of No. 4 MREU's area of operations: Eastern Germany, East Berlin and Poland. Teams operated to a small extent in the Soviets Zones in late 1945, but all unaccompanied access was soon halted in the Russian Zone of Germany. In Berlin itself the rules seem to have been more relaxed, at least until 21 October 1947 when Squadron Leader Eric 'Chick' Rideal and Flight Lieutenant John Hughes of the Berlin Detachment, No. 4 MREU, were arrested by Russian soldiers while investigating bomber wreckage beside a railway embankment just north of Biesdorf. They were detained for fours hours and questioned separately by non-uniformed Russian officials on their work, their pay and working conditions, and also the sources they used for their work. Rideal recorded in his report on the matter that he was careful to mention the German and Air Ministry files that they used, but not to give any mention of information being supplied by the local population.[304]

In October 1946 the border was reopened with strict limitations.[305] Search teams were allowed to enter the Russian Zone, but only under escort and with detailed, and approved, itineraries. Access to entire areas was forbidden at certain times, and everything subject to sudden changes by the Soviet authorities. Essentially, everything possible was done by the Soviets to limit any intelligence benefits that the British may

EXHUMATION REPORT. (R.A.F.)

Number: Rank: Name: Service: **R.A.F.**

Cemetery or Place of Burial: **HAUCOURT COMMUNAL.**   Map Ref: **B5/N5994.**

                Plot: **M1.**   Row: Grave: **2.**

DESCRIPTION OF BODY: **SKULL SMASHED. REMAINS BURNT. EVIDENCE 2 SKULLS.**

HEIGHT:

BUILD:

HAIR: **STRAIGHT, LONG, BROWN.**

TEETH: **LOWER LEFT JAW ONLY.**

FINGERS AND HANDS:

IDENTITY DISCS:

DOCUMENTS OR LETTERS OR RELICS:

CLOTHING:

        TUNIC: **F/S.TUNIC OTHER RANK (HOOK FOUND). SGT's STRIPES. F/O BRAID.**

        TROUSERS:

        SHIRT: **OFFICER TYPE FRAGMENTS.**

        UNDERWEAR:

        SWEATER:

        SOCKS:

        BOOTS: **FLYING LEATHER SIZE 9.**

        MISCELLANEOUS: **CIVILIAN TYPE BRACES. R.A.F. TIE.**

EQUIPMENT: **SCRAPS MAE WEST, PARACHUTE.**

DATE OF DEATH: **24. 5. 40.**
                                    ICI
CROSS SHOWS: **AVIATEUR ANGLAIS.   3 AVIATEURS   AVIATEUR ANGLAIS.**
               MAI 1940.   ANGLAIS.   MAI 1940.
CEMETERY RECORDS SHOW:

REMARKS: **THERE ARE THREE CROSSES ERECTED OVER THE TWO COFFINS.**

DATE EXHUMED: **16. 4. 47.**   EXHUMATION DONE BY: **CAPT. HILLIER.**

CASE REFERS TO: **F.857s.**   RAF WITNESSING OFFICER: **F/LT. R. GOLDSTEIN.**
                                              No. 1 M. R. & E. U.,
                                              Royal Air Force.

Another exhumation form, this time with a physical description of the body recovered. (By kind permission Mrs. A. Archer)

A

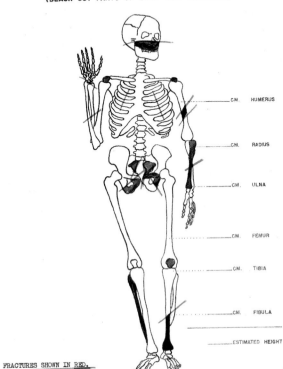

SKELETAL CHART
(BLACK OUT PARTS OF BODY NOT RECEIVED)

.....CM.   HUMERUS

.....CM.   RADIUS

.....CM.   ULNA

.....CM.   FEMUR

.....CM.   TIBIA

.....CM.   FIBULA

_____ESTIMATED HEIGHT

FRACTURES SHOWN IN RED.

PROCESSED BY:

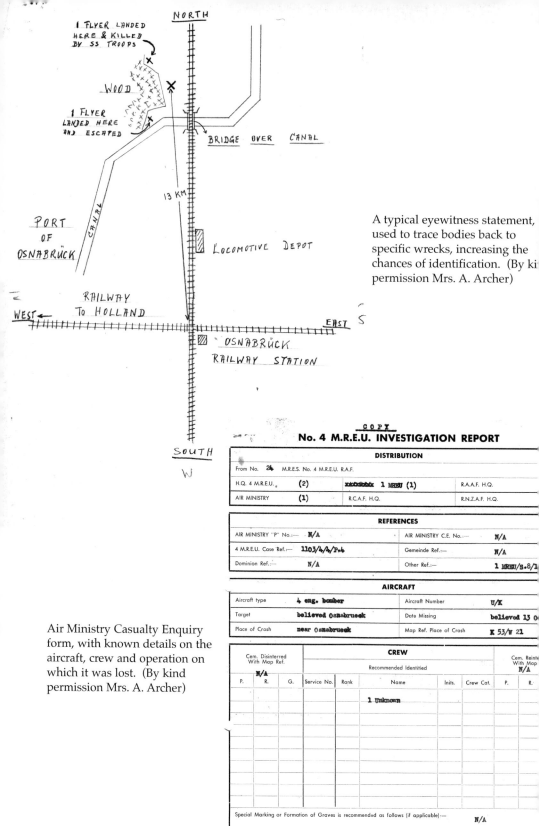

A typical eyewitness statement, used to trace bodies back to specific wrecks, increasing the chances of identification. (By ki permission Mrs. A. Archer)

Air Ministry Casualty Enquiry form, with known details on the aircraft, crew and operation on which it was lost. (By kind permission Mrs. A. Archer)

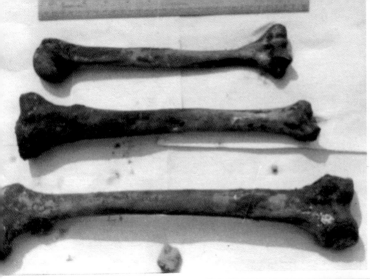

Sometimes expert advice was called for. These bones were photographed for analysis by a pathology laboratory in Canada, leading to the identification of the airman. (By kind permission Sqdn Ldr Lott)

Off duty: Flt Lt Ron Myhill and some of the German staff relaxing in Krefeld, a good way to shake off the weight of their daily work. (By kind permission Flt Lt Myhill)

The unofficial MRES crest, encapsulating the spirit of the work and workers. (By kind permission Flt Lt Myhill)

Flt Lt Noel Archer recording a grave in France. (By kind permission Mrs. A. Archer)

Supermarine Spitfires over France. Many crashes along the northern coast were fighters, making the wreckage smaller and harder to locate, but crews easier to identify. (By kind permission RAF Museum)

GRAVES REGISTRATION REPORT FORM   F.W. 3372

F3155   3204

Place of Burial :   **CAPPELLE COMM. CEMETERY**
           NORD B2/H2280

Series 1

Department & Map Reference :   Date :   **22.3.48**

The following are buried here : –

Number	Rank.	Name and Initials.	CE No.	Date of Death	How Marked	Plot, Row Grave
202	ADJUDANT	R. PORCHON (F.F.A.F.)	F. 315	19.11.44	"Hier Ruht ein Unbekannter Alliierter Pilot der am 19.11.44 Hier Abgesturzt ist"	see sketch

This cancels our AFW.3372 ser. No. 2868 dated 28.11.47

W/O. PORCHON

Monument

NCE

O.D. G.R.E.
S. 14 CAS
DASCAN
R.A.A.F.
R.N.Z.A.F.
I.W.G.C.

R.A.F. L.O.   91 G.C.U.

Investigating Officer: **F/LT. ARCHER**
       P.425605/S.7 CAS.C.7

Authority :
dated :   **28.11.47**

Squadron Leader, Commanding
France Detachment M.R.& E.S.
ROYAL   AIR   FORCE

Map compiled by Flt Lt Archer of the burial place of Free French pilot Adjt Rene Porchon.
(By kind permission Mrs. A. Archer)

A successful case. MRES officers (Flt Lt Archer front right pallbearer, Flt Lt Laronde front left pallbearer) bury an airmen, with full military honours supplied by the French. (By kind permission Mrs. A. Archer)

Noel Archer marrying civilian interpreter Anne Marie Hamon-Dubreuil, May 1947. (By kind permission Mrs. A. Archer)

Telegram ordering Flt Lt Archer to transfer his operations from France to Belgium. (By kind permission Mrs. A. Archer)

HQ No. 2 MREU, 23 Rue de la Toison d'Or, Brussels. (By kind permission Wg Cdr Moorcroft)

ALLIED SERVICES FRONTIER PASS № 17355

(in lieu of Leave or Duty Movement Order Pass)

name _Archer_ Christian Name(s) _Robert Noel_ Rank or Grade _F/Lt._
ne Vorname(n) Rang oder Dienstgrad

No 4 MREU Personal/Passport No _184638_
heit Ausweis- oder Paßnummer

uthorised to proceed from _Paris_ To _Sundern & Return._
berechtigt. von nach

the purpose of (give detailed reasons) _Duty_
reisen, zwecks (genaue Einzelheiten angeben)

s Pass is valid for travel via the Service Personnel Road/Rail Frontier Crossing Point at _Aachen & Return_
ser Paß ist gültig für den Grenzübertritt in _____ per 'Service Personnel' Fahrzeug oder Bahn

) Entry to	(a) ~~zur Einreise in die~~	
) ~~Exit from~~	(b) ~~zur Ausreise aus der~~	Delete whichever is
) ~~One Return journey to~~	(c) für eine Rückreise in die	applicable
) One Return journey from	(d) ~~für eine Rückreise aus der~~	
) ~~Repeated journeys to and from~~	(e) ~~zu wiederholten Reisen in die und aus der~~	Nichtzutreffendes
~~the British Zone of Germany~~	~~Britischen Zone Deutschlands.~~	durchstreichen

f Issue _30th Sept 49_ Date of Expiry _10th Oct '49_
llungsdatum Verfallsdatum

s Pass is only valid when used in conjunction with a Services Identity Document or, in the case of CCG (BE) Civilians, UNRRA, e
d National Passport and Military Entry/Exit Permit.
ser Paß ist nur dann gültig, wenn er in Verbindung mit Dienstausweispapieren benutzt wird, oder, falls Zivilangestellte der Kont
mission oder der UNRRA usw. betroffen sind, in Verbindung mit einem gültigen Nationalpaß und einer militärischen Einreise/
sreisegenehmigung.

s Pass does not exempt the holder from compliance with the requirements of the Customs Laws of Denmark. Holland/Belgium
British Zone.
ser Paß schließt seinen Inhaber nicht davon aus, die Zollgesetze Dänemarks, Hollands, Belgiens oder der Britischen Zone zu
gen und ihren Ansprüchen zu genügen.

me, Rank and Unit of Issuing Officer (IN BLOCK LETTERS) _D. McCartan ST_
me, Rang und Einheit des ausstellenden Offiziers (in Druckschrift) _RAF Movs Paris_

RAF MOVES
AIR ATTACHE Signature of Issuing Officer
mpel der Dienststelle Unterschrift des ausstellenden Offiziers
PARIS

POSTE CONTROLE
TULLE
30 SEP 194-
SORTIE

Frontier pass for Flt Lt Archer, for travel from France to Germany, 1949. (By kind permission Mrs. A. Archer)

o. 1 MREU, St Omer, March 1947. Standing: Goldstein, "Brother" Simon, Noel Archer; sitting: Ullward (?), Ralph Laronde, and a surgical glove. (By kind permission Mrs. A. Archer)

COPY

Tel: SLOane 0751

JKMcN/PS

IMPERIAL WAR GRAVES COMMISSION
32, Gosvenor Gardens,
London, S.W.1.

Ref. A/53/3   20th January 1949

Sir,

        I am directed by the Imperial War Graves Commission
to refer to Air Ministry letter No P.362304/41/S.14.Cas/408
                              T.14132/45/S.14.Cas/408
of 8th December., on the subject of the grave of 61927 Pilot
Officer T.P. McGerty.

        In reply I am to say that in accordance with
documents handed over to the Commission by the War Office this
officer is recorded as being buried in Bergen General Cemetery,
Holland. No information as to the removal of this grave has
reached the Commission from the North West European District, and
enquiries are being instituted.

        With regard to para. 5 of your letter I am to say
that no decisions have been made which in any way differentiate
the treatment of Americans serving in the Royal Air Force
from other members of the R.A.F. and Dominions Air Forces so
long as their graves remain in the custody of the Commission.
It has, however, now been agreed with the United States
Government that the graves of American citizens who served with any
of the British Commonwealth Forces may be transferred under
American regulations to American territory upon the request of the
next-of-kin residing in American territory, such request being
duly certified by the competent American Authorities.   No such
request has yet been received in the case of Pilot Officer
McGerty.

                I am, Sir,
                   Your obedient Servant,
                        (Signed) J.KINNEAR.
                           for Secretary.

The Under Secretary of State,
Air Ministry,
2, Seville Street,
London. S.W.1.

Letter clarifying who should deal with the case of Pilot Officer McGerty, an American in the RAF, and whether his body should go to the IWGC or the American authorities. (By kind permission Mrs. A. Archer)

No. 1 MREU, relaxing at Vieux Boucau in the south of France, June 1947. Left to right: Goldstein, Anne-Marie Archer, Ralph Laronde, Noel Archer, Stephenson. (By kind permission Mrs. A. Archer)

No. 3 MREU demonstrating extraordinary dedication and perseverance in Norway. (By kind permission RAF Museum, Rideal Collection)

No. 3 MREU preparing for a 'sweep' in Norway, 1946. (By kind permission RAF Museum, Rideal Collection)

The Polish expedition at a camp site, 1947. (By kind permission RAF Museum, Rideal Collection)

Cologne 1945. It could be expected that RAF teams operating on the ground would meet some hostility from the population. (Author's collection)

HQ No. 22 Section staff, Krefe[ld] Flt Lt Myhill second from left. (By kind permission Flt Lt Myhill)

Inside HQ No. 22 Section, Krefeld, with paper files being translated onto area wall map. Flt Lt Myhill seated. (By kind permission Flt Lt Myhill)

Wall plaque from another section office in Germany. (By kind permission Sqdn Ldr Lott)

Bomber crash site in Germany, where a mid-air explosion had scattered wreckage over several square acres. (By kind permission RAF Museum, Rideal Collection)

An exhumation in progress, somewhere in the Ruhr. (By kind permission Flt Lt Myhill)

On the road with No. 22 Section, Germany. (By kind permission Flt Lt Myhill)

A far from uncommon scene: MT trouble in Norway. (By kind permission RAF Museum, Rideal Collection)

Staff from 74 GCU on a sweep of the Frisian Islands, 1947. Fg Off Harry Wilson far left. (By kind permission Flt Lt Wilson)

Officers of 74 GCU, northern Germany, 1947. Fg Off Harry Wilson front right. (By kind permission Lt Wilson)

RAF and German drivers, clerks and interpreters relaxing Detmold Section, N 4 MREU. (By kind permission Sqdn L Lott)

gain from having officers moving around in their forward defence zones. They need not have been concerned. In a tense meeting in November 1946, Air Marshal Sir Thomas Elmhirst, Assistant Chief of Air Staff (Intelligence), informed the Director of Military Intelligence (DMI) and Joint Intelligence Committee (JIC) that their request to attach intelligence officers to the MRES teams beyond the Iron Curtain was denied. Elmhirst was to report back to the Air Member for Personnel, Air Chief Marshal Sir John Slessor:

I told my Foreign Office and Military colleagues on J.I.C. of your ruling, and that in my personal opinion the ruling was the right one. D.M.I. (General Templer) was almost in tears!

To help him, I said that in due course I would approach you and ask if you saw any objection to these teams being 'briefed' to keep their eyes open when on tour and being 'debriefed' on return to the British zone. Anything they saw to be kept in their heads and on no account to be put on paper.

D.M.I. jumped at this suggestion. I feel myself that this is a reasonable proposition and that it is part of the normal duty of an RAF officer in a foreign country to keep his eyes open and report anything noteworthy on his return to his own country.[306]

It appears that the risk of being caught and the MRES teams being banned from operating in Soviet areas was too great. The task of locating and identifying missing aircrew was too important to risk.

For the most part the actual task on the ground in the Soviet areas was less intense. Apart from Berlin, few of the major targets were this far east. One exception was the northern town of Peenemünde on the island of Usedom on the Baltic coast, which had been the main research, testing and development site of the V-1 and V-2 rocket systems. On the night of 17/18 August 1943 Bomber Command main force paid a visit and destroyed large parts of the facilities, loosing forty heavy bombers in the process. A majority of these fell around Peenemünde itself, either on the island or off-shore. Four had come down in Denmark or on the German side of Danish border, and in a further four cases the entire crews were deemed lost at sea. Dozens of individual members of other crews were also officially accepted as lost at sea. The rest were cleared by men from the Berlin Detachment, No. 4 MREU, and concentrated into the Berlin Military Cemetery in January 1949.[307]

A few crewmembers had been washed up on the Polish side of the border not far Peenemünde. Access to Poland was even more restricted, and involved lengthy diplomatic negotiation. As early as July 1947 Group Captain Hawkins was briefing Squadron Leader Rideal, at that point working in No. 3 MREU in the American Zone of Germany, to prepare for a Polish expedition.[308] He selected Leading Aircraftsman Ashman as his driver. Several trips to Berlin (to be used as forward base) and London to compile information in readiness followed. Time was going to be strictly limited, and so the utmost in ground work needed to be completed before hand. With no particular progress being made with the Soviet authorities, in January 1948 Rideal returned to his normal duties, and when No. 3 MREU was closed down in March he and Ashman were transferred to the Berlin Detachment of No. 4 MREU. Here they acquired the use of a Humber car and had it thoroughly overhauled for the coming journey. Finally, permission came through from the Poles for the search to begin.

In early April Rideal made several trips to Warsaw by air to consult with the authorities regarding final arrangements. In mid-April Rideal and Ashman arrived by air to begin the search. Because of limitations with the aircraft, instead of their Humber they had to bring in a jeep. Here they conducted some final negotiations with the Polish authorities. The MRES would accompany an Army GCU that was currently crossing Czechoslovakia. Vehicles would be supplied by the British, but the drivers were to be Polish. All British staff were to be carefully vetted and the convoy would be accompanied by Polish representatives at all times. British bodies would be collected, identified, and then buried in three centralised cemeteries.

Finally, on 25 June the convoy, after a few last minute complications, crossed the border into Poland. On the 26 June, Squadron Leader Rideal returned to Berlin to collect another vehicle and receive final instructions. Two days earlier, the Soviets had officially shut all access to and from the British, American and French Zones of Berlin, beginning a blockade that would last until May 1949. On the day that Rideal arrived the first RAF and USAAF flights of what would become the Berlin Airlift were landing. Having completed his business, Rideal then managed to leave Berlin by road (claiming later to be the last British vehicle to do so), giving two Russian officers a lift on the way.

After taking the long route back through the Allied Zones of Germany Rideal rejoined the Polish expedition, now operating around Kraków. About a dozen cases were investigated here, mostly aircraft lost on supply dropping operations to Warsaw during the uprising of late 1944, plus some scattered prisoner of war graves. Most of these were from Stalag VIIIB, but included one at Auschwitz concentration camp. All the bodies were concentrated into Kraków Rakowicki Cemetery. In early October work moved to the Stettin (Szczecin) area and 65 bodies recovered were from mass graves. At this point the Polish authorities shortened the deadline to 1 December, and the work immediately took on a more urgent pace. Exhumations now continued far into the evenings, digging by light of the headlights of the contingent's vehicles. In early November the group moved again up towards Danzig (Gdańsk), covering the north of the country and the Baltic coast. Here bodies were to be concentrated into Marlbork (formerly Marienburg) Cemetery, just south-east of Danzig.

Earlier the Polish Government had forbidden them to visit the cemetery at Sagan, where several prisoner of war camps had been situated, but now Rideal was allowed access. There was one outstanding crew (which was successfully located) as well as the bodies of men who had died in captivity. More famously, there was the memorial holding the ashes of the fifty officers from Stalag Luft III shot by the Germans after the Great Escape. A few of the urns were found to be broken or missing, but most were successfully collected and, with the rest of the recovered bodies, taken to Poznan Old Garrison Cemetery. Men from Stalag VIIIC, Stalag XXIB, Stalag XXID and Oflag XXIB were also concentrated here.

On 29 November Rideal and Ashman returned north to rendezvous with the rest of the British team. After a brief meeting with the British Consul, the convoy returned to Warsaw with only a day or two to spare from the deadline. They remained in Czechoslovakia until 6 December, by which time a consignment of marker crosses had been flown in from Berlin (despite the air traffic limitations) and a lorry-full sent to Krakow to complete the marking of the graves there.

Rideal and Ashman arrived back in the American Zone of Germany on the evening of the 9 December, having covered approximately 2,500 miles (4,000km). Over a period of six months seventy-two cases involving 417 airmen had been successfully investigated, with only four cases, involving eleven airmen, still outstanding.

At the end of September 1947 No. 2 MREU was shut down, followed by No. 3 Unit in February 1948. As the numbers of outstanding cases dwindled for each unit's operational area, so it became harder for the Air Ministry to justify the expense of maintaining them to the accountants. Eventually even No. 4 MREU was shut down. Advance warning arrived in mid-August 1949. Files were to be handed to relevant organisations – the Imperial War Graves Commission, the new Missing Research and Graves Registration sections, or back to the Air Ministry – and offices closed down. Civilian staff were to be handed notice for termination of employment on 30 September.[309]

Operational correspondence was to cease on the 31 August, halting the arrival of further casualty enquiries, and, allowing a suitable period to tidy up outstanding cases, all search teams were to end their work on the 15 September. From mid-September RAF staff also began to be posted out, with many of the remaining men being posted to the Missing Research and Graves Registration (MRGS) teams, who were being left behind to oversee the final concentration and marking of graves.[310]

By the end of September 1949 a total of 22,975 of the 41,881 personnel listed as missing since the end of the war had been accounted for, and either identified or buried as unknown airmen. Around two-thirds of this number had been accounted for in Germany.[311]

CHAPTER TEN

The Far East

Later, the team was sent up to Mandalay to operate over all North Burma. Two short trips to Mogok and the area South of Sagaing were successfully completed. The team's main task was to tackle the area along the Chindwin River and the Indo-Burma Frontier. Two trips of just over four weeks duration each were made before the team was recalled in early June. The roads in this area were by no means good and towards the middle of May, when the Monsoon commenced, travelling was made slow and many hardships encountered. LAC Shannon is to be congratulated on his expert driving and hard work that enabled the team to carry on as it did.[312]

Fg Off A. C. Carrott, i/c No. 3 Search Party.

Missing research in the Far East was in many ways very different from the rest of the world. Although the basic problems remained, it was all a question of scale and extent. In the west, the onus had been very much on identification. Particularly in north-west Europe, and most especially in Germany and Holland, the main problem facing the search teams was not so much finding wrecks and graves, but telling them apart and identifying them from among all the others. Finding remains was easy enough with the help of locals who had the same cultural outlook and frames of reference on language and dates. Usually substantial signs of a crash still existed on the ground. The high concentration of crash sites and human remains meant that filtering the evidence and differentiating between potential candidates took up the bulk of the MRES's work.

In the Far East it was not as easy. For a start the search area was much bigger, stretching from eastern India through Burma, Siam and French Indo-China, down through the Netherlands East Indies and Malaya, and on across the Philippines to the northern coast of Australia. The number of crashes in these areas was also less, making them further apart and harder to locate. Accurate maps and logistical support would be hard to procure. Leaving aside the question of how much of this area was open

119

water, the jungles and mountains that covered most of these regions would make operations very difficult indeed. Centres of population of any sort were fewer and more spread out, and travel and communications between them correspondingly harder. Crashes were likely to be in the middle of nowhere, and there was less likely to be firm intelligence on the exact location or any witnesses to a crash. If there were witnesses there would be all sorts of difficulties in obtaining usable information from them, apart from languages. As the teams in the south Pacific in particular found, some cultures were very literally minded and only a narrow and specific question would elicit a straight answer.[313]

Underlying all of these issues would be the implicitly hostile nature of the country. There was the jungle that covered most areas, and all of the poisonous or disease-ridden elements that nature chose to populate it with, or the vast tracts of semi-desert, plus there were the more human problems to deal with. The war had led to a breakdown in law and order and a plentiful supply of weapons across South East Asia. Dacoits (bandits) were a constant threat, while Burma, French Indo-China, Malaya and the Netherlands East Indies were all undergoing political strife and popular uprisings against the returning colonial rulers. As we shall see, some areas were designated as too dangerous for search teams to enter.

The search in the northern half of the Far East area of operations can be readily split into three stages, each roughly representing one calendar year, whereas the southern Pacific searches should really be dealt with as a separate entity. The first of the northern phases began even as the war ended. As we have seen in a previous chapter, one of the major issues facing the Allied powers in the Far East was the absence of information on the numbers and identities of their personnel held prisoner by the Japanese. A majority of the prisoners had been held since Japan's early victories in Malaya, Java and the Philippines in 1941 and 1942, including nearly 7,000 RAF personnel. Since then a steady trickle of aircrew had been going missing over enemy-held territory. It simply was not known how many of these men had fallen into Japanese hands, nor, considering the known tendency of the enemy to mistreat their prisoners, how many had survived the experience.

It was known, however, that a significant number of prisoners had been concentrated along a fairly narrow stretch of territory to construct the Burma-Siam Railway. Being a known quantity in terms of terrain and parameters, this must have seemed a good place to start the search for the missing men. As the survivors of the workforce of the railway were brought into Bangkok for processing and evacuation, some brought with them records and musters from their camps and maps of their camp cemeteries. Others provided information on similar documents that had been sealed and buried at cemeteries along the route. All of this information was collected and collated, and it was decided to form a Graves Commission to retrace the route of the railway, logging the exact locations of the cemeteries or isolated graves before the jungle reclaimed them. The obvious candidates for such an operation would be the ex-prisoners themselves:

Then came the appeal, 'who will volunteer to go back along the Railway line to show the Graves commission the positions of the cemeteries?' It was necessary to have fit men and those who knew the areas concerned. A party of thirteen ex-prisoners volunteered in spite of the fact that they could hear the aeroplanes engines roaring which were taking their fellow ex-prisoners home.[314]

The author of the above passage did not count himself, and the volunteers were joined by two members of the 26th Australian War Graves Unit, bringing the total to sixteen men.[315] They were a mixed group: an officer from each of the British and Dutch armies, one from the Federated Malay States Volunteer Force, and two officers from the Australian Army; seven Australian other ranks, including a signaller and a medical orderly; three Royal Australian Air Force airmen; and finally a British Army padre.

The team mustered at the Oriental Hotel, Bangkok, and set out on the 22 September 1945 to trace the line of the railway. Eighteen days and 400km (250 miles) later they reached the limit of the railway. The intervening time must have been a strange one for those on the search, and several left accounts of their remarkable journey. Perhaps best is the diary compiled by Major Joseph Eldridge of the South Lancashire Regiment and Padre Babb. They give a daily journal of their efforts, aided and escorted by detachments of their erstwhile captors. Moving primarily by rail or by foot, living in their carriages or with the Japanese garrisons, they travelled back along the line that had been the setting for years of untold suffering, and the deaths of thousands of their comrades. Along the way they logged 144 cemeteries. The conditions varied greatly. Some cemeteries had been maintained by the Japanese who were waiting to be rounded up and sent to their own prison camps. More had been maintained by the local population. However well the burial grounds were kept the problem of the lack of resources available to the prisoners remained. Few graves had any form of marker, most being a simple mound of earth, with just a communal cross to represent all who were buried there. Records kept by the prisoners at the time were for the most part buried by the communal monument when the camp population was moved on to the next section of construction, being sealed as far as possible against the elements in bottles or tins. Inevitably damp and rot had got to some and destroyed any record of which grave was which.

Just as inevitably, some cemeteries and isolated burial plots had been reclaimed by the jungle. Even so, of the 10,549 graves which they knew to exist, the team positively found 10,397 of them.[316]

Even while this extraordinary little party completed this small but significant corner of the war, the Air Ministry was preparing to extend their search efforts into the Far East theatres of operations. A priority was establishing the scope of the missing problem. The efforts of the team along the railway, and of the units which were working to repatriate the inmates of the numerous prisoner of war camps around the region, were whittling down the numbers still outstanding. By February 1946 the Air Ministry was confidently stating that all of those men who were going to turn up alive had done so, and there were 894 men still missing in South East Asia. Of these, thirty-two were known to have been prisoners at some time, and there were indications that 102 more were definitely dead. That total would, like that in Europe, also later be nudged upwards.

It was decided that search units would be raised and controlled locally, but there was still some disagreement about the number of teams and how they should be organised. There would be few similarities with the European teams. The chain of command and communications would run from P.4 (Cas) to a co-ordinating office, referred to as a 'Clearing Unit',[317] at HQ Air Command South East Asia (HQ ACSEA), consisting of one Squadron Leader and one clerk. From there it became slightly disjointed. There would be eleven teams operating across the region: three in Burma, two in each of India and Malaya, and one each in Siam, French Indo-China, Sumatra and Java. Each team would consist of a Flight Lieutenant from the Intelligence Branch (the implication being that these men would have local language skills), a senior non-commissioned officer and an airman equipped with a jeep and a trailer. However, direction for these teams, along with logistical and administrative support, would come from the local Air Head Quarters rather than HQ ACSEA.[318] Here a further Flight Lieutenant would co-ordinate efforts and channel the paperwork. For the most part the search teams would be acting semi-independently with a remarkable level of freedom. This would be one reason for the stipulation that team commanding officers would have to be of Flight Lieutenant rank.

Recruitment was carried out in a much less voluntary way in the Far East. There was a smaller pool of potential members and so the tendency was for personnel simply to be posted to the search teams. The problem was decreased when the decision was made to reduce the number of teams to five. Sumatra, Java and Malaya were deemed too dangerous at the moment as widespread rebellions gripped them. India was left to locally raised teams from the permanent garrisons, who would be more familiar with the area. An additional decision saw the Siam and French Indo-China teams being combined, but an extra team being raised in

Burma. This would bring the Burmese total up to four, which perhaps seems a lot. Consider, however, that this was a country roughly the same size as France and Belgium, but with virtually no internal infrastructure. The geography ran mostly north-south, with the rivers Chindwin, Irrawaddy, Sittang and Salween slicing the country in long slithers. The Arakan mountain range, with peaks averaging between 914m (3,000ft) and 1,524m (5,000ft), ran down the western border with India and then down the west coast. The Shan Plateau stretched down from China to cover much of the north, east and central regions. In between was the dry belt, a largely arid area of semi-desert. Bridges over the rivers and tracks, let alone roads, were scarce, with few suitable for mechanical transport. Almost none ran east-west.

Even though only around thirty men were needed there were problems in staffing the organisation, and work for the second phase of operations, beginning in February 1946, was patchy.

The teams that were set up received minimal training, nothing really stretching beyond a general briefing on the task ahead and the unit's objectives. A few specific points were covered. Good relations were essential with both the local colonial authorities and the native population. In the current political climate of anti-Colonialism this could potentially be quite a tight-rope walk. In case of trouble, and as a defence against the bandits and dacoits who were an increasing threat, weapons were to be carried and guards mounted when stationary. However, in order to discourage pilfering and to avoid scaring friendly locals, the weapons were to be kept hidden as much as possible. Generally there were no problems. The population of the average Burmese village were still fiercely loyal to the British:

We always hired a couple of coolies at whichever village we came to. The headmen were always very helpful. If you presented the headman with a large five rupee piece, he wouldn't spend it anyway, wouldn't realise it was meant to be spent, but if he put a little hole in the top and put a ribbon through it, he had a nice medal from the King-Emperor. Very proud.[319]

Weekly reports were to be sent to the controlling Air Head Quarters. With these regular communiqués the search officers could include details of locals whom they believed had provided significant aid to downed Allied pilots during the war. This information would potentially lead to financial rewards.[320]

The first team to become operational was No. 3 Search Team, under Flight Lieutenant A. C. Carrott. The inaugural expedition for the Far East MRES organisation was an eleven day sweep through the Karenni Hills, including a six day trek on foot to Biya, which located three crashes.[321] Next they moved to Mandalay, from where they would be responsible for northern Burma. This area had seen heavy air traffic throughout the war, primarily through American, plus some RAF, shuttle flights taking supplies from India to Chiang Kai-shek's Chinese armies. Carrott, who knew the area well and was fluent in Burmese, led his team of Flight Sergeant Watson and Leading Aircraftsman Shannon in two long expeditions lasting over four weeks each along the upper Chindwin close to the border with India. Operations here were far from easy. Supplies had to be collected and transported from Mandalay, over 500km (300 miles) away over rapidly deteriorating roads. By May the monsoon was setting in, making conditions even worse and slowing progress drastically. In early June Flight Sergeant Watson was posted away, and Carrott and Shannon carried on alone to Chauk, about 90km (56 miles) south of where the Chindwin joined the Irrawaddy. This operation came to an abrupt halt following a motor accident on Mount Popa. Soon afterwards, Carrott was also posted out, although Shannon remained in the area attached to No. 2 Search Team.

No. 2 Search Team had been set up in March 1946, although they only became active in early April. Their area of operations, under Flight Lieutenant K. C. Rose, was to be the mid-section of Burma. Initially the team covered an area east of the Irrawaddy and north of Toungoo, in the dry belt. Of the twenty-two crashes in the area, sixteen were located and identified, five could not be found, and the last one, in the Shan Hills, was deemed 'impossible to approach ... so it can be regarded as closed.'[322] From the end of July the team moved north, further towards Mandalay. This was the centre of Burma's plains country, where water and shelter was limited and far between. The area had seen heavy fighting during 14th Army's rapid and stunningly successful advance of 1945, under the indomitable Lieutenant General Bill Slim. Slim is widely accepted as having invented true combined operations, with the headquarters of 221 Group, under Air Vice-Marshal Vincent, being all but merged with his own. No. 221 Group, plus the rest of the Third Tactical Air Force, provided not only extensive close air support in a ground attack role but also an armada of transport aircraft to keep Slim's scattered and fast-moving divisions supplied. Considering the complexities of this operation (for example, the religiously and culturally diverse 14th Army contained troops requiring around thirty different ration scales)[323] it proved remarkably successful, although of course it was not without its losses. This area overlapped to some extent with No. 3 Team's, so only nine crashes were found to be outstanding. Of these, just one could not be located, perhaps because there was little left to find. Rose reported:

The main difficulty encountered in the Mandalay area was the lack of aircraft parts due to looting by the Burmese but it is quite understandable

*that as the aircraft have been lying in villages and fields for several years,
the Burmese could not resist the temptation of using the aluminium for
making cooking and other household utensils.*[324]

In October the team moved on again, this time crossing the Irrawaddy
and taking over from the now defunct No. 3 Search Team. In November
the deteriorating weather conditions led to this team too being closed
down, although not until after their non-commissioned officer had been
posted away.

The next team to be established was No. 4, raised in Bangkok in March,
with a remit for Siam (Thailand) and French Indo-China (Vietnam). The
team was commanded by Flight Lieutenant Geoffrey Ellis, who had spent
the war at the School of Oriental Studies, and was fluent in Mandarin
Chinese. Perhaps to compensate for Ellis's lack of practical experience in
the field, and due to the large distances involved, his senior NCO was
James Kingham, who had spent the last year of the war as a navigator on
Bristol Beaufighters with 27 Squadron over most of South East Asia.
Again, getting operations underway was a slow process. There should
have been a jeep and trailer waiting for the team, but instead it took
a week for transport to become available. When it did it was less than
inspiring. Ellis would record, in the third person, in his final report:

*When it was finally handed over to the officer i/c the team, it had no hood,
no windscreen, no spare wheel, no four-wheel drive, u/s battery and hand
brake, and required the joint efforts of four people pushing to start it. The
trailer provided was a home made one of less than half the capacity of a
normal trailer and approximately four times the weight, and was equipped
with two Morris wheels for which there were no spares and whose tyres
both had a minimum of three major gashes, bulging at the weight of the
trailer alone.*[325]

Considering that this team had perhaps the longest journey to undertake,
and would need to carry adequate fuel and provisions with them, this
situation was far from satisfactory. For unknown reasons, nothing could
be done about this in Bangkok, and it would not be until May that
matters would be put right by a friendly French Foreign Legion unit
outside Saigon.

With only the barest of briefing and information, the team set about
searching Siam. For the most part the information on each crash consisted of the aircraft details, crew list, operational target and usually at
least a rough longitude and latitude. Warrant Officer Kingham was often
able to work out more detailed locations based upon local knowledge
and navigational calculations. Once in the general vicinity, the team

would question the locals, and usually the local police or other colonial authorities.

> *The Thais particularly were very friendly, except in one respect. They had some bandits, Dacoits, who on the road out to Don Wang airfield one night put a wire out across the road, the idea I think to decapitate the people in the jeep and then rob them. But otherwise they were very friendly.*[326]

After this incident, a vertical bar with a blade was attached to the bonnet of the jeep to cut any further wires.

By mid-May Siam was completed. After working mainly in the Bangkok area, travelling out to sites each day and returning to base by night, the team had located every missing aircraft in the country. Now came the long haul through to Indo-China. Food en-route was purchased locally and all other supplies carried with them. Locations were much more vague in Indo-China, although again the local population and authorities proved very helpful. Despite the growing unrest in the country, which would break into open conflict at the end of 1946, the team faced no direct hostility or opposition. The only problems caused by the locals were indirect:

> *We didn't find any scraps of the aircraft. The locals were very good at making use of anything they could find.*[327]

Despite this lack of both documentary and physical evidence, the team located and recovered the bodies from two of the four wrecks in Indo-China, and positive information was collected on the third. In June Warrant Officer Kingham was posted back to the UK, and the following month Flight Lieutenant Ellis was transferred to AHQ Burma to act as the co-ordinating officer. The previous incumbent, Flight Lieutenant Wade, had been returned to the UK some months previously. This left only the driver until No. 1 Team was reassigned to wrap up the remaining cases.

No. 1 Team had been set up in February 1946, although it did not become fully operational until March. Under Flight Lieutenant I. L. Puttock they began in the Moulmein area, on the opposite side of the Gulf of Martaban to Rangoon and next to the Siam border. After clearing down this thin sliver of land they moved to the area north of Rangoon, at the mouth of the Sittang River. When the monsoon made this area inaccessible they began moving up the river towards Toungoo. They carried on clearing the Rangoon-Toungoo road and its environs until July, when they were reassigned to Saigon. In September Flight Lieutenant Puttock was posted back to the UK for release, with the rest of his team following shortly after.[328]

The final unit in phase two of the operations – the search season of 1946 – was No. 5 Search Team. This unit was not activated until April, by which time it had been decided to give their original area of operations, French Indo-China, to No. 4 Team. Instead Flight Lieutenant C. J. Durrant and his men were diverted to Burma to cover the southern portion of the Arakan mountain range. At this point this particularly steep and inaccessible range formed a peninsula parallel to the coast along the Bay of Bengal. However, as this area was usually affected by the monsoons in India across the Bay, which arrive five or six months earlier than those in Burma, the further decision was taken to post them again, this time to a sector south of the other Burma teams. This covered the lower reaches of the Irrawaddy, and, to the east of it, the area north of Rangoon and the coast along the Andaman Sea. This area was cleared by June, at which time Flight Lieutenant Durrant was admitted to hospital, and the rest of his team were posted to make up deficiencies in other teams.[329]

This is the only illness mentioned in the reports from the Far East teams. Considering the climate, this is nothing less than remarkable. Only two years before the 14th Army had suffered terribly across the whole of Burma, with an annual malaria rate alone of 84 per cent of troops; Slim would later write that 'for every man evacuated with wounds we have one hundred and twenty evacuated sick'.[330]

In August Durrant was released and, by assigning a senior NCO but no driver due to staff shortages, No. 5 Team re-formed. This time they did make it to the Arakan, working out of Akyab. Due to the extremely rugged nature of the country a lot of work was carried out by boat along the chaungs, or creeks, but work was again hampered by the monsoon. By now the early stages of the Burma monsoon were swelling the rivers and in September work had to be halted for a fortnight due to the conditions. In early October Durrant was posted back to the UK for release and his senior NCO, unable to carry out the task by himself, returned to Rangoon.

The shortages of personnel were crippling the search efforts across the region. By October 1946 only one team was still in the field, although a few stray members of the organisation were still in or near their areas of operations and simply unable to proceed alone. After much persuasion, two officers, Flight Lieutenant's T. P. J. Hewitt and Westcott, were obtained by AHQ Burma as replacements at the end of October. Westcott only lasted a day before being recalled for repatriation and release, but Hewitt remained and became an increasingly effective search officer. In November 1946 he was sent with two NCOs, presumably one of them the surviving member of the old No. 5 Team, back into the Arakan, where a large number of cases were still outstanding. This area had been heavily fought over both during the protracted First Arakan Campaign of December 1942 to March 1943, and then again in the Second

Campaign of January to February 1944. This second action had seen the first heavy and effective use by the Allies of airpower, in not only ground attack roles but perhaps more importantly to airlift supplies in and casualties out of the various defensive 'boxes' that had been set up to resist the Japanese. This battle would see the first major defeat inflicted on a Japanese land army by the Allied powers. In December the search members in the area were joined by a second officer, Flight Lieutenant Sharrock, but once again he was recalled for demobilisation before he could have any effect on operations. Soon Hewitt was also notified that he was to return home for release, but he opted for an extension to his tour to remain with the MRES.[331]

By the end of the second phase of operations it was clear that the single issue that could make or break operations in the Far East was personnel. It was also clear that another season of searching at least was needed to complete the job, and so this time proper preparations were put into place. Group Captain Burges, Inspector of Missing Research, had visited the Command in November 1946 and talked to the officers involved.[332] After hearing their concerns, he had pulled strings at the Air Ministry to change some of the ways that things were done in the Far East. The footing of expenses by search officers and later reimbursement was first to go. Instead of having to pay for food and transportation out of their own pockets and then attempting to claim the money back, officers were now allowed a 500 rupee expenses fund.[333] Perhaps most important among these changes was that the men who were recruited from across Air Command South East Asia were this time gathered together at RAF Mingaladon, a station on the northern outskirts of Rangoon, which had become AHQ Burma on 1 January 1947.[334] Here the officers, NCOs and airmen underwent at least a few days if not a few weeks training under Flight Lieutenant Hunter of the RAF Regiment.[335] Personnel were issued, like their predecessors, with jungle green uniforms and 'those cute little floppy green hats like the Americans used'[336], and then subjected to various types of training including survival but focusing on driving skills.[337] This allowed the men to get to know one another as well as gain a better idea of the task that was facing them. With one exception, and unlike the 1946 set, each team that went out into the field in 1947 knew at least something about each other, and had formed an idea on how they would work together.

The one exception was No. 5 Team. As the only team still active from the previous year it was decided to reinforce them and let them keep operating under the same title. To avoid confusion, each of the other teams would receive a new number, from 6–9, even if they were covering areas that other units had already been operating in. As it was, Sergeant David Harrap, Sergeant Theobald, and Aircraftman 2nd Class Jock Frame (as driver) were sent to join Hewitt, who had now been operating for some time on his own, at RAF Akyab. Hewitt was nothing if not committed to his task:

> I think that Hewitt probably did better than anybody in getting his area cleared up. He took a real passionate interest; it was important to him, didn't matter how bloody difficult it was, if there was a crashed aircraft there he wanted to find it, and if there was a bloke there to bring him back.[338]

However, there were frictions with his team almost immediately. For one thing, they were somewhat surprised to find him dressed in a longyi, the Burmese equivalent of a sarong. He had recently based himself at Rathedaung, a village actually on the coast of the mainland opposite the Arakan peninsula that had seen heavy fighting during the First Arakan Campaign, and the team left by river steamer almost immediately to return to Hewitt's field headquarters. Here he had created firm links with the local police commissioner who was able to provide help not only in the form of information, but also on occasion the loan of the police launch to travel to crash sites. When the police launch was not available, a local vessel would be hired. There were essentially no roads in the region, and the team did not even have a jeep and trailer issued, so the chaungs were the only means to navigate the region. Sergeant Harrap recalls:

> Everything we did was by boat, up and down the chaungs. [We used] whatever Hewitt could hire ... We would get as close as we could by boat and then look for the local village headman ... Sometimes they would take you to where the aircraft had crashed. Sometimes there wasn't a great deal left anyway. Sometimes of course what to us was a 16 cylinder engine was sixteen cooking pots: aluminium, and very nice too. And if you [asked where the pilot was] they pointed towards India, and that meant he'd got away.[339]

The team set to work, but within a few days Sergeant Theobald had decided that he could not work with the team and requested a transfer out. Jock Frame found the work to be different to his expectations as well. For one thing, this driver had nothing to drive, and so he spent most of his time travelling to and from RAF Akyab with reports and supplies. Part of the reason for this was that Hewitt was proving difficult to get on with, a situation not helped by the circumstances:

> When you have three people thrown together for a long time in difficult circumstances sparks do tend to fly, and tempers do get lost, but he made more people than Frame and me angry.[340]

The terrain was far from easy to work in. The land was not only over-grown, but tended to be marshy and waterlogged, which presented its own problems in trying to recover aircraft or their crews. Sergeant Harrap would write home with an example of a day's work:

> This morning Hewitt, two coolies and I set off. The aircraft had crashed in a mangrove swamp and we had to tramp through about 400 yards of this. We had to go through thick squelchy mud, where every step meant going in up to the thighs or wading waist deep through the various grey and swirling streams which intersected the area. The kite hadn't sunk but was upside down and nose in, so we couldn't get the engine number and any idea of which aircraft it had originally been. That the pilot this time hadn't escaped was more than obvious, as after rooting about for a bit I found a hip bone. (In fact I trod on the bloke's pelvic girdle and cut my foot ...) A rotten place to leave your bones, in the middle of a dense, steaming, oozing and a watery mango swamp.[341]

Despite these problems, though, 'most jobs we got cleared up within a day. Hewitt, as horrible as he was, was bloody efficient.'[342]

The trips into the field would last for anything up to a fortnight, living on the hired boats. Conditions were seldom ideal, with vermin and cock-roaches sharing their lodgings, a state of affairs not made any easier when there were bodies on board. As in Europe, the MRES teams were not supposed to exhume bodies, but were to leave it to the Army. Unlike Europe, the men who accompanied Army parties to oversee exhumations did not receive a special allowance. However, given the circumstances Hewitt's team took a different view:

> We weren't supposed to bring them in. Our job was to find them [and identify them] ... But it seemed silly to send three people ... and then send an Army expedition at vast expense to bring back the bodies, so we brought back the bodies too.[343]

Limited space meant that often the canvas wrapped remains would share accommodation with the team. For all of that, though, the boat remained a haven amid the humid and unfriendly jungle:

> You'd be surprised how you can fall in love with an ancient motor boat, when it's not merely got your bedding in it, and you know you're going to have a good night's sleep, but you've also got a bottle of beer which has been on a string hanging in the river all day long, and there's fags, and a few creature comforts.[344]

The beer ration, acquired through the stores of the local deputy commissioner, seems to have been a definite highlight in the day; a much needed relief from the climate and workload.

Sometimes the team would be accompanied on these trips with men from 47 Graves Concentration Unit, under Major Dobbin, even if only a single soldier to help guard against Dacoits. (Only once was a serious risk encountered, when their boat nosed up to the quay of a village. Firing could be heard on the far side of the village, and as soon as Hewitt became aware of it a hasty retreat was called.) These joint expeditions made a lot of sense in saving time and repeated effort, and the two units got along well together. In fact, in Sergeant Harrap's view, the Army were friendlier and more helpful to the team than the RAF were. Perhaps due to Hewitt's peculiar behaviour, the authorities at RAF Akyab were not overly hospitable to the team, and when the team made their periodic returns to Akyab:

> the RAF didn't want us, so we ended up living in the bashas of 47 GCU, which had been laid out in the garden of a family of Anglo-Indians ... Considering what we had been doing, the level of help from the RAF was appalling.[345]

Hewitt was even moved to note this lack of support in his final report in May 1947 when the team was stood down.[346] Over the last six months, they had located and examined sixty-two wrecks, and concentrated the remains of twenty-two missing men.

The other teams experienced less success in their efforts. No. 6 Search Team had been sent to Prome (now Pyay), about 160km (100 miles) north of Rangoon, on 24 February. Commanded by Flight Lieutenant G. Gough, this team was one of two that had been experimentally equipped with wireless sets. They left this set with its operator at Prome, and then carried on still further north to Allannyo and Magwe in the mid-regions of the Irrawaddy River. In March the team's NCO, Warrant Officer Whiteman was recalled for repatriation and release, and Sergeant Theobald, late of Flight Lieutenant Hewitt's No. 5 Team, was sent to replace him.[347] They achieved a moderate success rate, but were forced to abandon some areas on the west bank of the Irrawaddy due to flooding, and were warned off the northern tip of their area by the Army because of increased Dacoit activity. With their operations curtailed, the team returned to Rangoon on 22 April.[348]

No. 7 Search Team was sent to Mandalay on 8 February 1947 under Flight Lieutenant H. Pollock. From Mandalay they proceeded 110km (70 miles) north into the Shwebo area. Theirs was probably the toughest assignment of the year, as this was an inhospitable, largely inaccessible district of the country. This had been where the second Chindit expedition,

Operation Thursday, had taken place from March 1944. Most of the 12,000 men involved had to be airlifted into place by the Third Tactical Air Force, and then supplied solely by air. After locating three out of the four crashes around Shwebo, the team went still further north. A search for a missing aircraft along the border with China proved fruitless, and so the team moved again, this time to the Fort Hertz area. Fort Hertz was a British Army outpost deemed too remote by the Japanese to attack. During the war it had served as a navigation point and emergency landing ground for Allied flights to and from China, and several aircraft were believed to have crashed in the vicinity. The jungle here was virtually impenetrable, however. One case investigated was of Flight Sergeant Alexander Campbell, 81 Squadron, who had been killed in a Supermarine Spitfire on 13 March 1944. Campbell had been shot down directly over his aerodrome, code-named Broadway, and had crashed only a matter of yards away. However, ground and aerial searches at the time had failed to show any sign of the wreckage.[349] Despite sterling efforts Flight Lieutenant Pollock's team were forced to give up, returning to Mandalay in May.[350] Campbell's body has never been recovered, and today he is remembered on the Singapore Memorial.

A much easier task was given to No. 8 Team, under Flight Lieutenant R. Stewart. Based at Rangoon, they were given the task of clearing up the rump of the searches in central Burma that remained from the previous year's efforts. They broadly succeeded in their task, although, again, interpersonal problems caused difficulties. Stewart had stood out as a cut above the rest of the officers in January at Mingaladon, but the reality in the field apparently was less successful:

In January we all thought he was wonderful – very good looking, fit and full of fun. When his team came back in May or June, they agreed he was the biggest ******* they had ever met.[351]

The final team was, like No. 5, essentially a continuation from the previous year. No. 9 Search Team covered basically the same region as No. 3 Team had covered in 1946. The team included Flight Lieutenant A. C. Carrott and Leading Aircraftsman Shannon, who had both been on No. 3 Team. In January 1947 they were sent up the Chindwin almost as far as the Indian border. A large part of their work centred around Kohima and Imphal, where in the spring of 1944 the Fourteenth Army had finally stopped the invading Japanese forces, before turning them around and pushing them out of Burma. Their efforts were severally hampered not only by the area having been heavily fought over, but the thickly wooded hills and the fact that most of the indigenous population had fled to escape the fighting. In early May, with the monsoons hampering the work of this as with every other team, they were recalled.

By the end of May search operations in Burma had ceased. Not including the preliminary searches around the Burma-Siam Railway and other prisoner of war camps, two seasons of searching had located and retrieved 236 of the 1,032 airmen missing in the Burmese theatre.[352]

This still left the rest of the Far East to deal with. Siam and French Indo-China had been cleared as far as possible. The Netherlands East Indies were deemed to be too dangerous and essentially off limits:

> With the uncertain conditions prevailing at present it is not advisable to allow RAF Search Teams to operate anywhere in the country. Moreover, the risks run by these teams would be greatly out of proportion to the possible gains in information.[353]

In fact, in April 1946 a mixed group of British and Australian officers from various war crimes investigation or prisoner of war contact and enquiry teams had been ambushed in the village of Tjaringin, Java, by nationalist guerrillas. Squadron Leader Frederick 'Bob' Birchall RAAF, Flight Lieutenant Hector McDonald RAAF, and Captain Alistaire Mackenzie, Australian Army, had been killed, and Captain James Collins, Royal Artillery, had been wounded.[354] There were RAF units in the country, albeit gradually handing over their responsibilities to the Royal Netherlands Air Force, and these were sustaining steadily increasing casualties in ambushes and attacks on convoys and stations.[355] Instead, the Dutch authorities undertook to carry out basic search and concentration tasks for the RAF.

Malaya was a different prospect. Although just as hostile, this was a British colonial province and so there was no escaping from sending teams into the area. In November 1945 two search parties had been formed to work with the War Crimes Investigation Teams in Malaya, but the unsettled state of the country and a lack of information had seen these withdrawn in January 1946. In May 1947 volunteers were called for from the returning Burma teams, and two more units put together. They arrived in Singapore on 26 May and underwent several weeks of briefing and familiarisation work before proceeding up-country to RAF Kuala Lumpur on 13 June 1947. Questionnaires similar to those used in Europe were circulated to local authorities and figures of authority to gather information.[356] Work over the next few months was severely hampered, though. Documentary evidence was scarce and the five years since the incidents had obliterated most of the physical evidence. Despite this:

> With complete disregard of personal discomfort, the teams for long periods lived under the most abominable conditions, during monsoon periods were wet for days on end, trekked through thick jungle and swamp, over mountain and valley completely cut off from white civilisation.[357]

Despite lack of information and support, staffing problems, and all the many and varied difficulties thrown up by the terrain and climate, the efforts of the MRES in the Far East meant that 1,868 of the 4,858 RAF casualties listed as killed or missing in the war against Japan were buried in identified graves.[358]

The Pacific was dealt with somewhat differently than the land masses of South East Asia. The vast stretches of open water made the job all the harder, as did the countless small, usually mountainous and densely wooded islands. Many were uninhabited, whilst others had tribes who had had little if any contact with the outside world. A further complication was the lack of information on exactly who or even how many persons were potentially alive and awaiting rescue in the area. The war in the Pacific had seen large areas of Japanese held territory bypassed and cut off, and so the priority in late 1945 was to find these isolated garrisons and secure any prisoners who may be held by them. There was also a possibility that some of the missing aircrew were alive and well and living with the local inhabitants on some of these islands.

A majority of the missing persons in the Pacific were Australian, American or Dutch. On these grounds, the Air Ministry and Royal Australian Air Force came to an arrangement; just as RAAF personnel in Europe, the Middle East and South East Asia were left to the RAF search efforts (albeit with RAAF input initially), so the RAF personnel in the Pacific were left to the RAAF search teams. Three were formed under the title of the Contact and Enquiry Service and one as a designated Searcher Party, travelling the region contacting Japanese garrisons and local tribes, gathering information on missing persons. The Contact and Enquiry Units laid their emphasis on the living; the Searcher Party on the dead. The Americans had a similar organisation, while the Dutch had the less optimistically titled Death Investigation Service. This came under the Netherlands Department of Justice, and so presumably also covered the thousands of Dutch civilians who had been swept up in the Japanese campaigns. Each of these nations also had extensive organisations of war crimes investigation and graves registration units, working in mutual support with their search parties and each other.

Perhaps the closest unit to the MRES was the RAAF Searcher Party, under the redoubtable Squadron Leader Keith Rundle. A charismatic, capable and deeply committed officer, Rundle commanded the unit from its inception in late-1945 until it's disbandment in 1948. Their main area of operations was in the South West Pacific, principally the islands of and around New Guinea. Searches were usually carried out from motor launches, either Rundle's own *Merrygum* in the central zone of operations, or Launch 06-16 under Flight Lieutenant Martin O'Shea who cleared the western zone, recovering eighty-five Australian, Dutch or American servicemen over the course of four months in late 1946.[359] However, the nature of the job meant that land operations were also needed. For the most part these meant anything from a few hours to a few days hike from the coast and the launch, but on occasion a much grander effort was needed. Between August and November 1946 Flying Officer Lloyd Cogswell trekked across the interior Papua New Guinea, an environment among the most impenetrable and hostile on earth. While covering 1,965km (1,219 miles), 1,000km (600 miles) of them on foot, Cogswell found and identified ten wrecks and the fates of their crews.[360]

By the time Rundle's unit was wound up in 1948, they had accounted for 147 aircraft (almost half of those missing in the South West Pacific, including those lost at sea) and recovered the remains of more than 300 of the 915 RAAF or RAF aircrew missing in the area, plus dozens of Americans and Dutchmen.[361] However, the search efforts did not stop there, and wrecks would continue to be found and recovered by the RAAF, often under Rundle's watchful eye, for decades to come.

CHAPTER ELEVEN

Missing Research and Graves Registration Service

The task of graves registration is naturally dependent on and subsequent to that of the investigating officers, who provide the graves registration officers with the material on which to work. It includes the concentration of bodies and their regrouping, where necessary, for collective registration, followed by photographing. If investigating officers ceased to operate and the source of supply dried up, graves registration could be completed in a few weeks. As it is, work is up to schedule.[362]

Memo on Royal Air Force Graves Service,
by Sqdn Ldr Sinkinson, 30 January 1950.

Tracing the missing had only been half of the task allotted to the Missing Research and Enquiry Service, albeit the half that would take the most time and effort, and been the most rewarding. Although the early debates on the establishment of the Service had focused on elucidating the fate of missing men (as indeed enshrined in the titles of both the MRS and MRES), it had been implicit that this would include confirming the known details on crews who had been accounted for through information supplied by the Germans or the International Red Cross. Initially these two tasks had involved visiting crash and burial sites to examine the evidence and confirm identities. From 1946 onwards, and particularly from the middle of 1947, this also involved physically moving the remains to prepared plots where the Imperial War Graves Commission (IWGC) could take them under their care; this process was known as concentration.

Graves concentration increasingly bit into MRES time. The Army had established specialised Graves Concentration Units (GCUs) to undertake this task, but in the RAF units this was simply added in to the schedules of administration and field trips that made up the daily routine, albeit with GCU help. In March 1947, a conference at headquarters, Army

136

Graves Registration Directorate (Western Europe) heard that 20 per cent of GCU field team time was spent on secondment to the MRES.[363] This system, they noted, had 'not always been very satisfactory', and they had proposed a system that was later adopted across North West Europe whereby MRES liaison officers were attached to GCU units on a permanent basis. RAF work was now incorporated into the working day, rather than requiring a special effort.

One element that had been conspicuous by its absence so far had been the IWGC. Formed in 1917 to take care of British and Dominion war graves around the world, the IWGC had established a pattern after the Armistice. Graves were gathered together into designated plots and received uniform headstones. Men who had fallen on enemy ground (for example, Gallipoli) stayed there. Partly it was due to the expense that would have been involved in moving them, but also as a symbolic gesture. Their task had been mammoth, and only completed just before the outbreak of the Second World War. During this conflict, a lot of the overseas plots had been neglected. Some, such as the Australian cemetery and monument at Villers-Bretonneux or the cemetery at Blighty Valley, both on the Somme, had been badly damaged by enemy action. All were overgrown and becoming dilapidated. The staff who had maintained these sites had dispersed during the war – the British back to the UK, and the local staff on to other jobs. Enticing them back was difficult, particularly as IWGC pay could not keep up with the rate of inflation in Europe. Until March 1946, IWGC employees and their families received food parcels through the Red Cross, and other support from the British Army.[364] This meant that in 1945–46, the IWGC had been preoccupied with getting their existing commitments into shape, without taking on the 350,000 new cases that the last six years had created.

From 1946 onwards, the IWGC began to devote resources to the new war. Although there were less bodies, they were spread over a greater area and for the time being the focus became Europe and North Africa. Operations on grave concentration began in France in February 1946, and Holland by November, although operations in both countries dragged on into the mid-1950s. The first cemetery in Italy was completed in 1949, although four years later only nineteen of the forty-two sites in that country had been completed. Burma was not even begun until 1950.[365] These sites were initially very temporary. Although laid out formally markers were rough, and the replacement programme did not see the first permanent headstones begin arriving on the Continent until 1948. Once headstones were in place, landscaping began to bring the plots up to IWGC standards.

Where new dead were near existing First World War plots, they were interred on these. However, in most cases new plots were established, as the majority of the fighting had occurred away from the battlefields of the First World War. This was particularly true for the Royal Air Force, with large numbers of airmen now lying in Germany. After some debate over whether these men should lie in enemy territory (the New Zealand government in particular was not keen on this idea), it was decided to establish local plots as had been done in France. In the Ruhr, where the bulk of airmen were, these would predominantly take the form of two massive plots, one in the Reichswald Forest and the other at Rheinberg.

Not every airman would be concentrated, however. Some villages and towns had taken a very possessive stance towards the men buried in their cemeteries, and lobbied the IWGC to keep custody of 'their' graves. Where the IWGC could be assured that the graves would be properly cared for, this was not a problem. Probably the best known case of this is the graves of Wing Commander Guy Gibson VC DSO DFC and his navigator, Squadron Leader John Warwick DFC. The pair, from 627 Squadron, had been killed when their de Havilland Mosquito had crashed into a hillside in Holland in September 1944. Their remains had been recovered and identified by the Germans, and laid to rest in Steenbergen cemetery. The IWGC agreed that the people of Steenbergen could retain these graves, although an MRES team was dispatched to confirm the identities of the two men. An exhumation in February 1948 uncovered a battledress tunic marked with Wing Commander Gibson's name, and personal effects that could be traced to Squadron Leader Warwick.

Even with these exceptions, this still left tens of thousands of exhumations to be carried out, identities to be confirmed, and bodies to be transported and re-interred in correctly marked graves. To cope with this very specific task, two new subsidiary units were formed in November 1948: Nos 2 and 3 Missing Research Graves Service (MRGS). No. 2 MRGS was based on an old airfield at Rotenburg, close to Reichswald. No. 3 was formed from No. 20 Section No. 4 MREU, and was based at 69 Rheinstrasse, Rheinberg. Both had an establishment of four officers, with drivers and clerical staff. With the disbandment of the MRES, the MRGS remained as a stand-alone unit, named the RAF Graves Service, directly controlled by the Air Ministry.

The RAF Graves Service had five principal tasks: Graves registration in Germany; graves registration in France; liaison with the IWGC to finalise the schedules of cemeteries; photography of graves, and; continued investigation of open cases.[366] In many ways these should have been straightforward, albeit taxing and exact, tasks. Concentration and registration meant moving bodies *en masse*, while keeping track of each and making sure each coffin or blanket-wrapped bundle retained the correct identification, and the scheduling and compiling of a final list of the exact location by cemetery, row and plot of each person. The photographing of graves had a twofold purpose: to furnish each family with a visual record of the grave of their lost relative, and to double-check their details. If mistakes appeared in the naming of a serviceman (all too possible when working from often handwritten records), the family were invited to contact the Air Ministry to rectify the problem. A lot of mistakes were identified and corrected through this system.[367]

However, these tasks were to be complicated from the start. As soon as two weeks after the independence of the units, problems were arising. A meeting of the MRGS was held at Rheinberg to assess the situation, and it became clear the location of the units, although very close to the main cemeteries, was ill suited for other reasons. The accommodation at Rheinberg was suitable and comfortable, but a long way from the unit's supporting services. Daily trips had to be made to Viersen, 62km (38 miles) away, for rations and to Krefeld, 37km (23 miles) away, to collect the mail, including reports to and from London. Krefeld was also the closest place that medical care or petrol could be obtained. There were no recreational facilities in Rheinberg and so airmen and officers had to travel further afield to enjoy their time off. To have money to spend when they did reach somewhere where it could be spent, pay had to be collected from Wahn, a journey of 120km (75 miles). All of this required transport that was already fully committed to the core duties of the unit, and was an added strain on already tired vehicles. Servicing of motor transport could only be done 265km (165 miles) away.[368] A second meeting in mid-November reported that some steps were being taken to relieve these pressures on time and transport, but already the proposed deadline of 1 April 1950 for the completion of work was being pushed back into May.[369]

Despite these problems work did forge ahead. In the first six months of operations (April to September 1949), No. 3 MRGS completed the investigations into 450 cases, involving 2,048 airmen. This left ninety-six cases on their books, of which fifty-six were the rump left by No. 4 MREU and could probably be assumed to be almost impossible. The unit commander, Squadron Leader Bill Lott, was willing to try, but had to emphasise that if the other core tasks allotted to his men were to be completed, all investigative activities would need to be stopped immediately.[370] This would be difficult. Between November 1949 and January 1950 approximately fifty 'new' bodies were found in Germany, and an officer had to be despatched to Denmark to deal with a new find there.[371] On top of this, with the closure of the Directorate of Army Graves Registration in March 1949, the MRGS was now responsible for British Army casualties, too. Incidentally, as proof of the work load, of the seven officers then serving in the MRGS in Germany, none of the six who were eligible for the 28 days End of War Leave authorised in August 1945 had yet to take this time off.[372] This also speaks volumes about the commitment to their task felt by the officers as well.

While these new investigations were opened and old ones closed, the main thrust of MRGS activities remained the collection and concentration of graves from across the British, American and French Zones of Germany. Despite every precaution, mix-ups were perhaps inevitable. When a body was lost, special investigations were immediately launched and every effort made to trace it. Sometimes identities had simply become confused among a consignment of bodies. Less often a body would physically go missing, for example when the body of Pilot Officer James Willing was misplaced during a move from his original burial site at Wilhelmshaven to Oldenburg. After a lengthy search the grave was located and correctly dealt with.[373]

Once in the correct place, the airmen were laid out in specific ways. Where individuals had been identified they were marked with their own headstone, properly spaced. Where the bodies had been identified as a specific crew, several actions could be taken based on the condition of the bodies, each with the headstones grouped closer together. Where none of the individual crew members had been identified, headstones were set out in alphabetical order. Where some of the crew members had been identified, they were given their own markers, with the rest of the names being on individual markers laid out in alphabetical order. If the bodies of one crew were inseparable, they would be buried under shared headstones. Some dispute was caused when the IWGC announced that once in one of their plots, bodies could not be moved as it would interfere with the landscaping of the sites. This meant that where a crew were already buried but were not lying together, they could not be moved to form one row. In the cases where not every member was identified, the scattered headstones would be named in alphabetical order from the top right-hand side of the cemetery, but marked 'Buried near this spot'.[374]

In April 1950 the life span of the MRGS was again extended. The pace of work had shown no sign of abating, with the cemetery building progressing at a steady pace. In the late summer a rash of new cases also came to light when an intensive salvage drive by the German authorities turned up several new bodies still lodged in wreckage.[375] A new closure date of 21 October had been set, which was met in all areas except Berlin. It was therefore decided to retain a Berlin Detachment, but to let the two MRGS units close. As of that date, No. 2 MRGS, with a remit that included Berlin, Hamburg and Kield, had handled the reburial of 8,035 airmen, only 591 (7 per cent) of whom were still unidentified. No. 3 MRGS, meanwhile, who covered Rheinberg, Reichswald Forest and Cologne, had dealt with 9,536. Of these, just 223 (2.3 per cent) remained as unknown airmen.[376]

The Berlin Detachment consisted of a driver, a clerk and a sign-writer under the command of Flight Lieutenant John Rhys Hughes DFM and bar, the man who had been arrested by the Russians with Squadron

Leader Rideal in October 1947. Hughes had been a Flight Engineer and later Bomb Aimer with 582 Pathfinder Squadron, often flying as Master Bomber on the sixty-seven operations he completed in 1944 and 1945. As well a co-operating with the IWGC to complete the scheduling of cemeteries, the detachment was expected to deal with new cases that arose. For the most part, these came from the Russian Zone. In some cases Hughes was asked to look directly into a particular case. For example, from February through to April 1950, a flurry of paperwork flew between S.14 (Cas), the Chief of the Air Staff, the Air Member for Personnel and the Provost Marshal concerning Flying Officer Sir Chandos Hoskyns. MI5 had picked up rumours in Vienna that Hoskyns, who had been posted missing from 190 Squadron in April 1945 while on resupply operations to front line troops in Germany, was alive and being held by the Russians in Kiev. No evidence to support this rumour was found and Hoskyns is now recorded on the Runnymede Memorial.[377] The majority of the case load, though, came from bodies recovered by the Germans.

In April 1950 an organisation known as the German Board for the Registration of War Dead had held discussions with Hughes about the possibilities of bringing British bodies back from the East. The Board had received permission to travel to the Russian Zones of Berlin and Germany to retrieve the bodies of German civilians on behalf of their relatives in the West. Hughes had agreed that if the Germans could, very quietly, pick up British bodies, the MRGS would cover the costs. It would need to be kept very quiet as the Cold War was now truly underway and Anglo-Soviet relations were gradually deteriorating. It could not be guaranteed that the Soviet authorities would approve of the scheme, probably quite the opposite. In fact, even the IWGC were not informed of any such arrangement until after operations had ceased nearly two years later, leading them to refer to it as 'all this "cloak and dagger" stuff' with more than a hint of annoyance.[378]

The first trip was made on 12 June, a fortnight before the Korean War broke out and East-West relations took another down-turn. In the first month of operations twenty RAF airmen, from five crews, were recovered, and preliminary sweeps suggested that as many as 500 more were within reach.[379] This number was later halved, but it was still going to take a considerable time to bring all of these men back home. Schedules for the work were not helped by Soviet hindrance. Although the Board had already received all the necessary permissions to operate behind the Iron Curtain, problems still arose. On 29 September 1950 Bernard Senf, a Board employee, was arrested while arranging for two bodies to be exhumed from a cemetery inside the perimeter of a Soviet airfield. After questioning he was released, only to be arrested again on 3 October. This time he was held in a Soviet prison, in fairly horrendous conditions, under suspicion of espionage for two weeks before finally being released back into West Berlin.[380] Most operations ran smoothly, however, and by the time Senf had been arrested a total of twenty Board expeditions had returned with forty-five RAF, fifteen British Army and three USAAF bodies.[381] Sweeps fell into a routine, roughly three in a two month period, but the results gradually grew less and less. As with MRES work, the easy cases had tended to be solved the quickest, leaving the more difficult for last. These included sites in the middle of Soviet training grounds where access was difficult and severely restricted[382], or cemeteries that had been obliterated by the advancing Russian forces in 1945.[383]

A further difficulty had arisen in February 1951 by the reorganisation of the Board. The German government had decided to merge the Board with the *Deutsch Dienstelle für die Benachtrichtung der nächsten Angehörigen von Gefallen der ehemaligen deutsche Wermacht* (German Service for Information of the next of kin of the former Wehrmacht), or WAST for short. The principal problem with this was that the WAST was based in the French Zone of Berlin. The French, as the British had been, were unsure how the Soviets would react to hearing of British military involvement in German civilian operations in the East, and were unwilling to find out. They applied pressure to end all MRGS involvement in the WAST. After lengthy negotiations between Hughes, the French and the WAST, a compromise was reached. A small detachment of the Board would remain independent for the next six months, under Herr Friedrich. Friedrich, who had been in charge of the section of the Board that dealt with the MRGS, set up offices in the British Zone of Berlin, establishing plausible deniability for the French while making his team available to work for the MRGS. Once the six months expired, an extension was negotiated until the end of December 1951. At that point, the French demanded the detachment rejoin the WAST, illustrating the point by sacking Friedrich.[384]

On 1 February 1952, Flight Lieutenant Hughes presented himself to the Air Ministry in person to report that the Berlin Detachment, Royal Air Force Missing Research Graves Service, had been formally shut down and all operations had ceased. After a week's debriefing, during which time he volunteered to return to Berlin to carry on with his work, he was sent home to begin six weeks of the leave he had accumulated over the previous seven years service in Germany.[385] With his departure, the Royal Air Force's missing research efforts officially ceased.

CHAPTER TWELVE

Last Resting Place

When you go home, tell them of us and say
For your tomorrow, we gave our today.

Kohima Memorial

The story of the search for missing aircrew does not simply end in 1952. The MRES may have found tens of thousands of the personnel listed as missing seven years previously, and confirmed the fates of as many more, but tens of thousands more remained unaccounted for. The search carried on through the second half of that century, and into the beginning of this, and interest in the subject shows little sign of abating.

Most will never be found: it is estimated that some 16,000 were lost at sea. The Battles for both the Atlantic and the Mediterranean cost the RAF thousands of aircraft, as did anti-shipping strikes against enemy supply lines in the North Sea and the Pacific. Off the coast of the UK alone there are countless wrecks of crippled bombers and fighters who never quite made it home from operations over enemy territory. The resources and technology to find and recover these aircraft are still beyond current means. However, some progress has been made on the other side of the Channel where extraordinary circumstances have prevailed.

Since the 1950s the Dutch have been gradually draining the Isjlemeer, the massive (approximately 1,000km/620 mile) inland sea better known to RAF airmen as the Zuider Zee, that almost cuts Holland in half. Beneath the surface, they have found hundreds of aeroplanes. Some are civilian, a few even military from the First World War, but the majority are from the Second World War. The Royal Netherlands Air Force established a unit specifically to excavate these wrecks, with Netherlands Army support to make them safe, and then recover any bodies that they may contain. In the quarter of century between 1960 and 1985, 167 wrecks were discovered in drainage operations. Of these, eighty were RAF aircraft from the war years, eleven of which contained human remains.[386]

The Royal Australian Air Force has also maintained search efforts. Their post-war Searcher Party had kept up ad hoc operations even after disbandment. Right up until his retirement in 1967, Wing Commander Keith Rundle was investigating crash sites and recovering missing aircrew. Some of these were in the rugged, inaccessible mountains of Papau New Guinea, where the jungle could swallow up wreckage for ever. In 1964 a commercial aeroplane spotted the wreckage of an Avro Anson on Mt Kenevi. A joint expedition of RAAF and American recovery teams, including Rundle, spent several months combing the area on foot. In early 1965 the remains of the two crew members were formally identified as Group Captain Frederick Wight and Wing Commander Walter Hammond. These two men had been missing since January 1944, and numerous search efforts at the time and since had failed to locate the wreck. As it was, the site had been one of eleven wrecks discovered during nearly 100 sorties to try and discover the fate of a Papuan Air Transport Piaggio that had been lost in the area. The Piaggio was never found.[387]

Some wrecks were found even closer to home. In February 1945 an USAAF Consolidated B-24 Liberator 'Beautiful Betsy' had taken off from Darwin with six American crewmen and two RAF pilots under transit to Brisbane. They were never heard of again, despite search efforts both at the time, and again (under Rundle) in 1966–67. In July 1994 Beautiful Betsy and her crew were found by a park ranger in the Kroombit Tops National Park, Queensland.[388] Between 1987 and 1997, the RAAF dealt with six Second World War wrecks.[389] Two, both Bristol Beauforts, in Papua New Guinea; a Consolidated Catalina and a Bristol Beaufighter in the South Pacific, and; Beautiful Betsy and a Royal Netherlands Air Force Douglas Dakota, both in Queensland. Discoveries continue to be made. In 2000 commercial divers discovered wreckage from an aircraft off Kawa Island. In early 2001 an RAAF team surveyed the site and identified the aircraft as a Bristol Beaufort from 8 Squadron, lost on operations in November 1943. All four crew members were recovered and identified.[390]

More recently still, in 2007 a veterans group called Operation Aussies Home recovered two of the six Australian servicemen missing from the Vietnam War. Lance Corporal Richard Parker and Private Peter Gillson, of 1st Battalion, Royal Australian Regiment, had been posted as missing in November 1965 in Dong Nai province, north-east of what was then Saigon. The bodies were located with the aid of former-Viet Cong personnel, and repatriated to Australia in June that year.[391]

In north-west Europe hundreds more crew members have been recovered. As we have seen, since the late 1960s a trickle of aircrew have been recovered in the UK as the result of the work of aviation archaeologists. Research into the Battle of Britain has recovered the most, although others have come through less systematic events. In July 1987 a body was uncovered by workers harvesting peat just east of what had been RAF Lindholme, Yorkshire. The police were called, and the resulting murder investigation quickly dissolved as the body was examined, and found to be wearing Second World War flying clothing. Instead the investigation changed tack, and one of the officers involved, Detective Constable Andrew Greenslade, took on the burden of trying to establish the dead man's identity. Despite extensive ground work at the Ministry of Defence, through the station records and those of the squadrons based there, and at the Royal Air Force Museum, he met with no luck. Even with the aid of a strictly limited list of units, and the full benefits of computers and databases, in short every advantage that the MRS and MRES had not had, the man could not be identified. Eventually he was buried as an unknown airman in the Commonwealth War Graves Commission plot St Oswalds Churchyard.[392]

Detailed research has also recovered personnel overseas. In late 2002 it was announced that the crash site of one of the more famous missing men, Wing Commander Adrian Warburton, had been discovered near the village of Egling an der Paar, outside Munich. Warburton was famous for his low level reconnaissance work in the Mediterranean, particularly in preparation for the devastating British strike against the Italian fleet at Taranto in 1940. He had been lost in April 1944 while photographing German airfields, and remained missing without a trace until the meticulous work of researcher Frank Dorber traced his crash through German records. In May 2003 he was laid to rest in Durnbach Military Cemetery. Such fates are not just reserved for the famous, although sheer chance has played a heavy role. Between July 2005 and July 2007, six lost bombers with over thirty aircrew have been found on building sites or by farmers or researchers in Germany and Poland. These are just the ones that have been reported in the national press.

This has not only applied to the RAF. Perhaps the most famous missing aircraft found since the end of the Second World War is the Lady Be Good, a Consolidated Liberator from the 514th Squadron, USAAF.[393] The Lady Be Good went missing, with all nine crewmembers, in April 1943 when returning to her base in Libya after a raid on Naples. The crew, on their first operation, had become disorientated at night and lost their way, ultimately mistaking the broad expanse of desert for the Mediterranean. An extensive search at the time had failed to find any trace of them, and the crew were listed as missing. The wreckage was not found until 1958, by an aerial survey party scouting for an oil company about 650km (400 miles) south of Tobruk. It was not until the next year that a ground party reached the wreckage and collected the necessary evidence to identify it positively as the Lady Be Good. A team from what was then the US Army Mortuary Service was despatched to the site in March 1959, but an extensive search found no trace of the crew. Even when helicopters were flown in and the search area expanded, nothing was found after three months combing the desert.

In February 1960 another oil survey party passing through the area found human remains near their campsite. Again the authorities were called in, and five skeletons uncovered with evidence to confirm their identities as members of the missing crew. This site was in the middle of the area searched the previous year. A further search was then launched, but again it was an oil survey team that found two more bodies about 40km (25 miles) north of the main group. Shortly after the official search was called off for a second time, another survey party found an eighth body further north still. The ninth crewmember remains missing. If nothing else, this demonstrates why very little systematic effort had been put into searching the desert by No. 5 MREU. In the sand-blown wastelands of North Africa, you literally have to be standing on a body to find it.

In fairness, most American search efforts have achieved more success. In 1973 the US Army established the Central Identification Laboratory in Hawaii with the specific task of identifying human remains and linking unknown bodies to names on the list of missing men. This had been partly in response to public pressure over the Vietnam War. The war was not a popular one in America, partly because of the spiralling casualty rates. At the end of the war 2,583 American service personnel were still listed only as missing in action, and calls were increasing for every effort to be made to account for these men, often by positively identifying unknown remains. Such is the momentum of this movement that even the Unknown Soldier from the Vietnam War, one of the four symbolic service personnel from America's twentieth-century wars laid in the designated Tomb in Arlington Cemetery, has been identified, and his space now lies empty.

Expeditions were also mounted into the field to visit sites, but these were strictly limited given the political climate of the time. Little more could be done until 1992 when the Joint Task Force – Full Accounting (JTFFA) was set up. This organisation, like the MRES before them, was tasked with recovering specific missing personnel from the field of battle, and with a remit that covered the entire twentieth-century. In 2003 the two units were combined into the Joint POW/MIA Accounting Command (JPAC). Each year field teams from the JTFFA and JPAC visit and excavate sites in Vietnam, Laos, Cambodia, France, Germany, the Philippines and numerous other countries where American service personnel have given their lives, recovering and identifying hundreds of bodies over the years.[394]

Efforts to recover missing personnel in recent years just go to prove that the issue is far from forgotten. The continued interest in war graves, and in memorials, also proves this. In April and May 2007 the Estonian

einberg War Cemetery, Germany, contains 3,326 servicemen, almost all RAF. (Author's collection)

ichswald Forest War Cemetery, Germany, contains 7,594 servicemen, almost all RAF. (Author's llection)

The altar and Cross of Sacrifice at Rheinberg. (Author's collection)

One of the unlucky ones: an unknown airman at Rheinberg. (Author's collection)

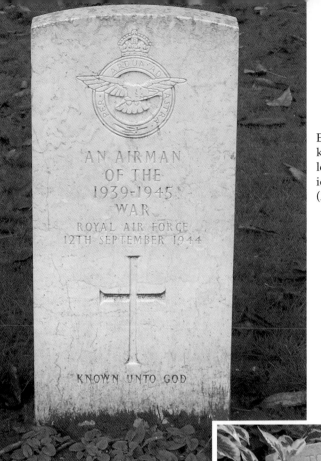

Even with the date of death known, so many men could be lost on the same day that identification was impossible. (Author's collection)

Commemorated at Rheinberg, but his original grave was lost, probably destroyed by Allied bombing. (Author's collection)

A collective grave at Reichswald: the crew had been identified, but they could not be individually separated and identified. (Author's collection)

A myriad of nationalities and religions lying together at Rheinberg, all RAF. (Author's collection)

tish, Canadians, Christians and Jews all resting together as an RAF crew at Reichswald. (Author's lection)

tish, Polish and Czechoslovakian members of RAF aircrew at Reichswald. (Author's collection)

Czechoslovakian members of RAF aircrew at Reichswald. (Author's collection)

Unidentified airmen laying at Reichswald. (Author's collection)

e silent rows of RAF aircrew at Reichswald Forest War Cemetery. (Author's collection)

Belgian, British, Canadian, Australian and New Zealand aircrew in Reichswald Forest War Cemetery (Author's collection)

Wg Cdr Guy Gibson, who lays with his navigator still at their original burial site. (Author's collection)

Wreck recovery in Norway, 1970's style. This Handley Page Halifax, the most complete original extant, is now on display in the RAF Museum.
(By kind permission RAF Museum)

Menu from the MRES reunion, 1958.
(By kind permission RAF Museum)

THE CORONET RESTAURANT
9 SOHO ST. W.1

SATURDAY, OCTOBER 25TH 1958

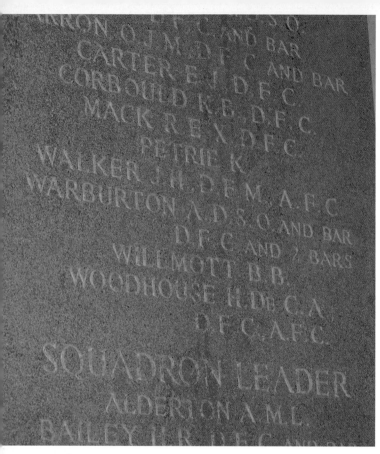

The Runnymede listing for Wg Cdr Adrian Warburton, whose body was recovered in 2002. (Author's collection)

The Air Forces Memorial, Runnymede. A beautiful site. (Author's collection)

e cloister at Runnymede, with the seemingly endless lists of the missing. (Author's collection)

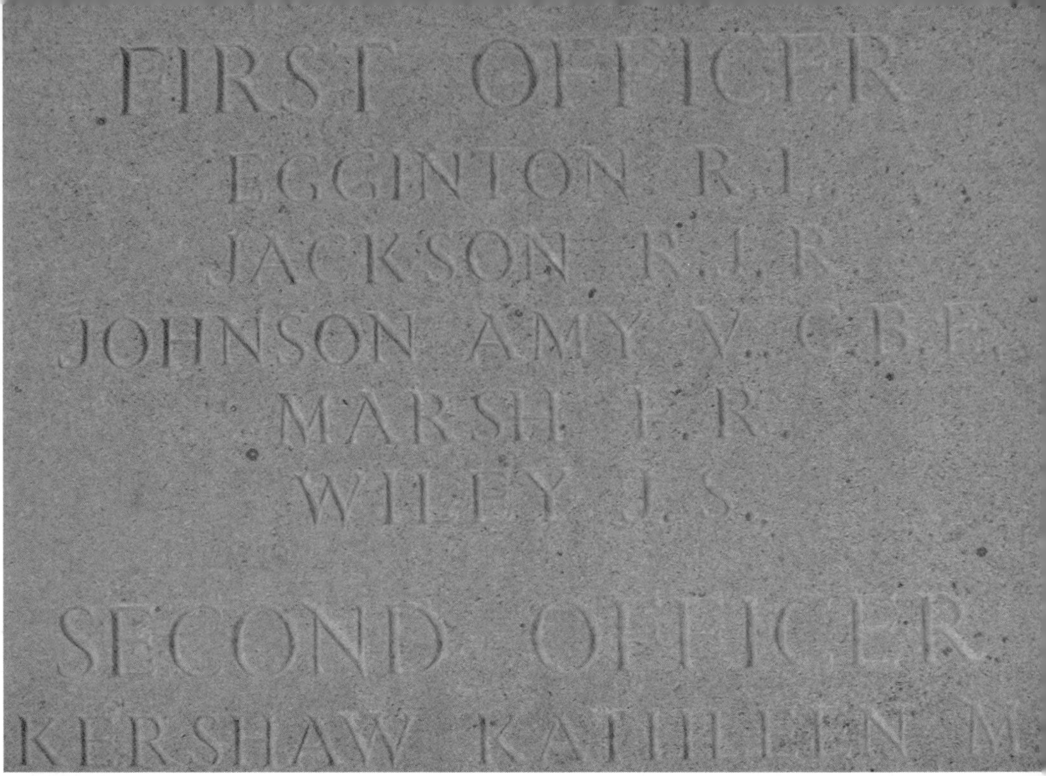

FIRST OFFICER
EGGINTON R.J.
JACKSON R.L.R.
JOHNSON AMY V. C.B.E.
MARSH F.R.
WILEY J.S.

SECOND OFFICER
KERSHAW KATHLEEN M.

Runnymede covers all the support organisations of the RAF too. Amy Johnson went missing with the Air Transport Auxiliary in 1941. (Author's collection)

The Runnymede listing for Inayat-Noor Khan, a WAAF with the SOE who was murdered and her body destroyed by the Germans. (Author's collection)

WOMEN'S AUXILIARY
AIR FORCE
SECTION OFFICER
INAYAT-KHAN N., G.C.
ROWDEN D.H.
UNTERNAHRER Y.E.M.

ROYAL CANADIAN
AIR FORCE

The Fleet Air Arm chose to have a separate memorial, on the Embankment, London.
(Author's collection)

In perpetual memory: The awe-inspiring RAF cemetery at Reichswald Forest, German (Author's collection)

A simpler memorial erected by the locals at Arnhem, to commemorate the RAF crews killed during Operation Market Garden, September 1944. (Author's collection)

e Battle of Britain Memorial, Capel-le-Ferne, opened in 1993 and touching in its simplicity.
thor's collection)

ir memory lives on. The annual memorial service at the Battle of Britain Memorial, Capel-le-Ferne,
7. (Author's collection)

Two of the hundreds of unit, station or personal memorials that continue to sprout up all across the
(Author's collection)

capital of Tallinn saw extensive protests, resulting in rioting, over the future of a Russian memorial in the city. The so-called Bronze Soldier of Tallinn commemorated the Russian ejection of the German garrison of the city in 1944, and included the war graves of about a dozen Russian soldiers. The removal of the memorial and graves to a cemetery elsewhere in the city led to violence between Estonian nationalists and Russian minorities in the country.

The situation regarding memorials for the RAF was shaped from very early on to ensure continued interest. Even before the end of the war the Air Council, the ruling committee of the Air Ministry, was discussing plans for the perpetual memorialisation of the Royal and Dominion Air Forces. This was partially at least for political reasons. Then, as now, the future of the RAF as an independent element of the British armed forces was far from guaranteed. This was still a young service which had, since 1917, worked hard to gain and (from April 1918) maintain its existence. After the First World War they had put considerable effort, under the capable guidance of Marshal of the Royal Air Force Sir Hugh Trenchard, to build an identity, role and ethos. A curious hybrid attitude was developed. On the one hand, the infrastructure of the RAF, both airfields and the training academies, had been deliberately designed architecturally to look old and established. On the other hand, much was done to highlight the younger and more vigorous nature of the air arm. Principal among these were the air displays, most famously those at RAF Hendon which, through its close proximity to central London, drew huge crowds and had the highest profile. In these extravaganzas daring displays of aerobatics, aerial bombing and parachuting promoted the glamour and innovation of the new service in the public eye. Even so, politicking had taken its toll. In 1937 the decision had been taken to pass the Fleet Air Arm back to the Royal Navy. Although the front line squadrons remained under RAF control until 1939, and much of the administrative and logistical direction continued to be throughout the war, it was still a blow.

After the Second World War many of the same issues were still being discussed in Whitehall. In some ways the RAF was a victim of its own success. The close co-operation achieved with the Navy during the Battle of the Atlantic, and even more so that which was developed with the Army in the Far East, Middle East and during the liberation of north west Europe, lent weight to the suggestion that perhaps the relevant parts of the air force were better off being incorporated back into the parent services. One of the counter-measures deployed by the RAF and Air Ministry was a renewed effort to raise and maintain their profile in the public eye. A natural part of this would be memorials, which would have a dual role of honouring the dead and emphasising the immense contribution made by the air force in the recent victory.

The memorials would take several forms. Already a Battle of Britain Chapel had been established in Westminster Abbey, the nation's principal church, and yearly thanksgiving services held on 15 September since 1943. After the end of the war this had been supplemented by a flypast over central London, in some ways taking on the mantle of the old Hendon air displays. Essentially an extensive aerial exhibition straight through the centre of the capital, combining historic types of aircraft with the very latest, cutting edge jets, this emphasised both the importance of the Battle and the identity of the RAF. A more permanent record was also sought in the heart of London, and in April 1945 the idea was put forward for the restoration of the bombed-out church of St Clement Danes as a memorial to both the dead in general and those who still had no known grave.[395]

Concerns were raised at the same meeting, and continued to be, that the dedication of a church as a memorial was inappropriate. Although it could be consecrated as multi-denominational, it would still only cater for Christians. This left a significant minority unrepresented. For all that the 14th Army in Burma is always held up as the last of the great armies of the British Empire, encapsulating races and religions from four continents and almost every country of the Commonwealth, the RAF if anything went further. In the 14th Army they served in their own units as part of the greater whole. In the RAF, over a million men and women who had flocked from every corner of the world served together, frequently in the same units and crews, with very little distinction. Not only was the Commonwealth well represented, but most of the countries of occupied Europe, parts of South America, and even countries which had fought long and hard to gain their independence from British rule such as Ireland and the United States of America. Naturally, such a force brought together a host of religious beliefs, all of whom deserved recognition.

The conclusion of the argument led to the Air Forces Memorial at Runnymede. As early as that first discussion in April 1945, the Chief of the Air Staff, Marshal of the Royal Air Force Viscount Portal of Hungerford, had advocated such a structure, arguing that:

> there was general support for the idea of a Garden of Memory as the central RAF War Memorial. This might be situated on high ground within reach of London. A site of, say, 50 acres, might be devoted to a shrine in which the names of the dead and the badges of squadrons would be reproduced. It would be important to have the scheme superbly done.[396]

After much continued debate, and the decision was made in March 1948 to bring the memorial more in line with the proposed Army and Navy memorials (which were never built) by listing only those with no known grave[397], the idea was placed before the Imperial War Graves Commission for final approval. A suitable plot of land was donated in October 1949 by Sir Eugen and Lady Effie Millington-Drake. A better place could not have been chosen. On Cooper's Hill, the site was just outside London and looked down on both Windsor and Runnymede. This latter distinction was particularly fitting. In 1215 Runnymede had been the site of the signing of the Magna Carta. Originally known as the Charter of Liberties, this was the first document in British history to lay out in clear terms the ideals of common and incorruptible liberty and equality before the law. Centuries later it had formed the basis of the American Declaration of Independence. In short, this plot of land was closely linked with everything that separated Britain, and indeed Western Civilisation, from Nazism, and symbolised the very ideals and cause for which the Royal Air Force had fought. The first IWGC guide book to the memorial pointed this out, calling it:

> *This haunt of the spirit of liberty, of the fair and happy way of dealing between men and men in orderly society ... The brave spirits whom it signifies in their turn accomplished in defence of an ideal, maintaining a great freedom for after-comers in a world of doubts and failures, such as indeed the grandest compassion implicit in this name and scene of Runnymede.*[398]

The Air Forces Memorial was opened in October 1953, and it was indeed superbly done. As it stands today, Runnymede is a beautiful site. Allusions have been made that the main tower, containing the shrine, and which can be climbed to obtain views over half of London and, on a clear day, seven counties, is reminiscent of an airfield control tower, but this is in the eye of the beholder. Approach the memorial and you see a simple, understated building that flows into the hillside and the trees. There is none of monolithic grandeur of the First World War memorials at Thiepval or even the Menin Gate. This does not dominate the landscape or impress the visitor with its grandeur. Instead, the presentation is understated yet undoubtedly dedicated, one could almost say reflecting the ethos of the men and women it represents.

Simple inscriptions by the doors explain the purpose of the monument, as do the RAF wings and motto above the doors themselves. There is no need physically to overwhelm with the scale of the loss. Around the interior cloister, and out along both wings to the look-out points at each extremity, the lists of the missing line the walls, interspersed with slit-windows. The arrangement gives the impression of opened stone books, recording the names for eternity. Above them, on the ceilings of the cloisters, are emblazoned the arms of the Commonwealth countries whose dead are recorded here. In the open space in the centre of the cloister the simple altar standard to all Commonwealth War Graves Commission plots stands. Such simple imagery imbues the whole memorial. From the tower, the figures of Justice, Victory and Courage look down on the altar. Above them, the Royal Air Force Astral crown tops the vane on the tower. At the foot of each window appears the clam shell, the traditional symbol of pilgrimage. On each half door are three lions, the heraldic symbol of Britain. Around each are four rosettes: a leek, a shamrock, a thistle and a rose.

For the most part, the symbolism is subtle and understated. There is no need to crush the visitor with symbols of loss or sacrifice. The lists on the walls say all that needs to be said. Nearly three hundred panels, listed by date, force, rank and name, contain over 20,000 names of those who never came back from Europe alone. Other monuments hold the names of more; at Northolt, the memorial to the Polish Air Force; at Karachi, for those lost in India and Burma; at Ottawa, for those lost in training in Canada and America; at El Alamein, for those lost in the Mediterranean and Middle East, and; in Singapore, for those lost in the Pacific.

These are of course not the only places where RAF dead are commemorated. Virtually every town and village in the country had a memorial for the dead of the First World War. Most now added the dead of the Second World War to that list. Other dedicated memorials sprang up, and in fact continue to do so. In 2003 an Australian and a Commonwealth war memorial were opened around Marble Arch, London, followed by a New Zealand memorial in 2006. In 2005 the National Monument to the Women of World War Two opened in White-hall, close to the Cenotaph. Almost parallel on the Victoria Embankment a new Battle of Britain memorial was unveiled a few months later; this being in addition to the Battle of Britain memorial opened in July 1993 at Capel-Le-Ferne, Kent.

The Battle of Britain figures large as a symbol of the RAF contribution. As we have seen, it was quickly identified as the one, complete air victory that no-one could tarnish, despite recent attempts by revisionists. Memorials to Fighter Command and the Battle of Britain abound, at Capel-le-Ferne, on the Victorian Embankment, in Westminster Cathedral and St Pauls Cathedral. The RAF's official day of remembrance and celebration is Battle of Britain Day, 15 September. Although the air action on this day in 1940 was not especially different, more successful or more intense than previous or subsequent weeks, this is the day that both sides acknowledge beginning to feel the balance of the battle shift. The first Battle of Britain Day celebration was in 1943, and after the war the Air Ministry was careful to keep cultivating the day and the Battle to keep them in the public eye. Even perhaps the most public and high profile of all of Britain's war memorials is named for it: the Battle of Britain Memorial Flight (BBMF). At any major, and many minor, ceremonies of remembrance or celebration since 1957, their Spitfires and Hurricanes have appeared as absolute symbols of victory. Ironically, though, its centrepiece is from Bomber Command. Despite its obvious contribution to the war effort, this force was seen as being politically dubious even during the war, and had been instantly dropped by the political leadership of the country virtually the minute that peace had been declared. The only statue that even touches on Bomber Command, that of Sir Arthur Harris, outside the RAF Church of St Clement Danes, is frequently defiled. Despite this, it is the BBMF's Avro Lancaster that most frequently appears as the symbol of sacrifice and remembrance.

The fact is, war dead are and will continue to be a contentious and emotive issue. The reasons are complicated. Partly it is the scale of loss, partly the unproportional number of young among the dead, and partly the fact that, however hollow it may be for later generations, these people died for a cause. 'The conviction that war on such a scale must have a meaning on the same grand scale has been doggedly clung to by many.'[399] These concepts are usually summarised into one word on memorials: sacrifice. At the end of the day no-one can deny that the men and women of the Royal, Dominion and Allied Air Forces who died during the Second World War did so for a worthy ideal. No matter how revisionist historians or politicians twist the actions of the RAF it cannot be denied that their contribution played a significant role in thwarting a great evil. As usual, it takes one who has been there to cut through the post-war politicking. In 1988 the then Archbishop of Canterbury, the Most Rev'd and Rt Hon Robert Runcie, was asked to comment on the question: can war ever be justified? Runcie had spent his early years commanding a tank in the Scots Guards, driving from Normandy to Belsen, and winning the Military Cross along the way. As far as he was concerned, the Second World War:

> produced no heroic poetry, many of my friends died in it. I do not believe that they died in vain and I do not believe they would think so either. A war which closed down Belsen and Buchenwald was worth fighting.[400]

Perhaps this idea fed into the passion of the MRES, or perhaps not. Talk to any veteran of the unit, or read anything they write, and you cannot miss the deep sense of purpose towards their chosen task, or mistake their pride in their work. This was a generation who did not have the luxury of being able to sit and talk about emotions and feelings, but these still come through in their words. These were young men doing an unimaginable job, but one they deeply felt was worth doing. Long hours, physically hard labour, and constant reminders of death formed their working day, but then they had done ever since enlistment. They were going to find their friends and comrades, a military bond which few who have not served will ever truly grasp. This bond even spread through the organisation itself. Amazingly, for such a small and loosely based unit, an MRES old comrades association was set up. Their first meeting was as early as 1949, while some teams were even still in the field, and annual dinners would carry on for at least the next twenty years. At their first meeting they adopted the motto: Around the world I search for thee.

In the age before computer databases, DNA testing, or any form of effective biometric records, the Air Ministry went out to search for 70,000 needles in an unimaginably large haystack. More incredibly still, for the most part they found them.

APPENDIX A

Casualty Statistics

One of the problems facing the MRES was the lack of accurate information on the exact numbers of personnel that they were looking for. This severely inhibited their ability to plan ahead, or set meaningful goals. In 1945, both Europe and the Far East were in chaos. Displaced persons wandered in their millions. Many prisoners of war had been moved from their established camps, where the international authorities had been able to monitor them, as the Allies had got closer. In Germany this had sparked the Long March over the winter of 1944–5, where extreme weather conditions, lack of adequate supplies, German reprisals and even Allied air actions had all taken their toll in lives. The Allies now had no idea where these men were, or what their status was. In Europe many were behind Russians lines, who were proving reticent in listing and returning those that they held. It would take months to sort out which prisoners were alive and who had died in the moves and confusion, or whether aircrew lost in the final weeks of the war had been taken prisoner at all.

On the same day, 9 August 1945, Air Marshal Sir John Slessor, Air Member for Personnel, wrote two letters. The first, to Air Marshal Sir G. Johnson at HQ RCAF, estimated the missing toll to be 20,000 men.[401] In the second, to Sholto Douglas, commander of the British Air Forces of Occupation in Germany, estimated it at 30,000.[402] A year later, and the situation was no better. The Air Member for Personnel was now estimating 31,000 missing, of whom 7,000 had been traced. Half of those left, it was stated, were probably 'out of reach', presumably meaning lost either at sea or in similarly inaccessible areas.[403]

The break down of missing personnel in proportions, which influenced the initial make of the MRES units was:[404]

RAF	69 per cent
RAAF	7 per cent
RCAF	17 per cent
RNZAF	3 per cent
Allied[405]	4 per cent

Perhaps because of the distances involved, the Far East was usually counted separately. In February 1946, the situation was stated as:[406]

	Officers	Airmen	Total
Missing no news:	203	557	760
Missing believed killed:	41	61	102
PoW – not accounted for:	4	28	32
Totals	248	646	894

Only in late 1947 did clear figures begin to emerge. By now the vast majority of prisoners of war had been accounted for and brought home, and the list of the missing solidified. In October, Squadron Leader Sinkinson of the MRS reported to the Air Minister for Personnel that there were 42,000 personnel missing in all theatres, 37,000 of them in Europe. So far 16,000 had been traced in all theatres (15,200 in Europe) and 17,000 (40 per cent) were now presumed lost at sea. This left a nominal 9,000 still either unidentified or not yet found, of whom 8,400 were in Europe.[407] In the next four months, 3,000 more were found, of whom 80 per cent were identified. By now it was thought that at least 1,250, and possibly as many as 3,000 personnel were on the Russian side of the Iron Curtain.[408]

By 1949 the figures had been agreed upon. The final accepted number of RAF personnel missing at the end of the Second World War was 41,881 world-wide.[409] By January 1951, when the Air Ministry's search operations were scaling down and grinding to a halt, the figures stood at:

Missing at cessation of hostilities	41,881
Accounted for (known burials)	23,881
Formally lost at sea	9,281
No information	6,745[410]

This somehow left 1,974 personnel totally unaccounted for in the statistics, possibly bodies buried as 'unknown airmen', but they still stand as the most complete set extant to symbolise the achievements of the MRES.

In 1953 the Runneymede Memorial was opened to commemorate those RAF airmen and women who had no known graves. The list was not comprehensive, the Polish Air Force having its own memorial at Northolt, and further memorials for the missing of different theatres built elsewhere. Also, it has not been kept up to date. Even while it was being built, nine of the listed missing were found. Many more have been found since, although no accurate record of how many has been kept. The following list shows a breakdown of those listed:

RAF	15,462
WAAF	10
RCAF	3,050
RAAF	1,397
RNZAF	576
SAAF	17
RIAF	7
ATC	4
ATA	8
BOAC	7
Ferry Command	9
Total	20,547

Chronology and Organisation of Units

Original Search Sections:

Unit	Date	Event
No. 1 Section	December 1944	Established by Casualty Branch Air Ministry, and sent to France (Paris).
No. 2 Section	May 1945	Established in Belgium (Brussels).
No. 3 (Mobile) Section	June 1945	Established to sweep France.
No. 4 (Mobile) Section	June 1945	Established to sweep France.
No. 5 Section	July 1945	Established in Holland (The Hague).
No. 6 Section	July 1945	Established in Norway (Oslo).
No. 7 Section	August 1945	Established in Denmark (Esbjerg).
No. 8 Section	August 1945	Established in Germany (Bunde).

15th July: Decided to reorganise (SD155/1945/2044) under 28 Group, Technical Training Command as:

Unit	Date	Areas
1 MREU	August 1945	France and Luxembourg. HQ Le Mans. Task: Search Dunkerque to Brest, inc. all Departments.
	15 December 1945	All Sections in the field, although some delayed by mine clearance problems around the coast.
	August 1946	Coast complete. HQ move to Chantilly, a section detached to Luxembourg.
	31 July 1947	Disbanded at Chantilly, leaving a detachment in Paris.

156

Unit	Date	Areas
2 MREU	August 1945	Belgium, Holland, Czechoslovakia, French Zone of Germany. HQ Brussels. Initial search Belgium and Holland.
	September 1946	Search of Belgium complete, Holland bogged down with bad weather. HQ moves to Schloss Schaumberg, Diez, Germany, leaving a section in Holland.
	Winter 1946/47	Severe winter hampers operations.
	30 September 1947	Begin disbandment.
	14 October 1947	Disbanded.
3 MREU	August 1945	Norway, Denmark, American Zone of Germany. HQ Esbjerg (Denmark).
	January 1946	Arrives in Denmark, begins sweeps of north Schleswig-Holstein and south Denmark. Hampered by weather. Four sections in Jutland, a section in Funen, two in Zealand, a section in Norway.
	September 1946	Norway complete.
	December 1946	Denmark complete. HQ moves to Karlsruhe, US Zone (same building as HQ American Army Graves Service).
	29 February 1948	Disbanded in Germany.
4 MREU	August 1945	British and Russian Zones of Germany, Poland. HQ Hamburg. Search from north to south, with HQ moving through Wesendorf for central & south eastern areas, and Sudern (nr. Gotesloh) for south western (inc. Ruhr).
	October 1946	A section allowed into Russian Zone, HQ Berlin.
	1947	This section spawns Berlin Detachment, directly under HQ MRES.
	April 1948	A section begins operations in Poland.
	1 September 1948	All liaison officers, Motor transport & staff of MRES transferred to 4 MREU at Sundern.
	December 1948	Polish section returns to HQ 4 MREU.
	30 September 1949	With HQ MRES, disbanded.

Unit	Date	Areas
5 MREU	27 July 1945	Created as Med/ME MRES
	1 July 1946	Renumbered 5 MRES, under HQ MRES NWE
	1 July 1947	HQ moves from Treviso, Italy, to RAF Klagenfurt, Austria. To come under Operation Control of OC MRES NWE, and Administrative Control of AHQ Austria.
		Two sections left in Italy and Sicily.
	10 August 1948	Disbanded at RAF Klagenfurt.

Official Establishment:[411]

Headquarters, RAF Missing Research and Enquiry Service, North West Europe:

1 Group Captain:	Officer Commanding MRES, North West Europe
1 Squadron Leader:	Administration Officer
1 Flight Lieutenant:	Asst Administration Officer
1 Clerk:	General Duties
1 Driver:	Motor Transport
1 Car, passenger utility.	

Missing Research and Enquiry Unit: (HQ + eight Search Sections)

1 Wing Commander:	Officer Commanding MREU
1 Squadron Leader:	Second in command
1 Flying Officer:	Adjutant
5 Squadron Leaders:	Officers Commanding Search Sections
35 Flight Lieutenants:	Search Officers
40 Drivers:	Motor Transport
35 Airmen:	General Duties (clerks)
1 Car, passenger heavy:	For Officer Commanding Unit
40 Cars, passenger utility:	For Search Officers
1 Cycle, motor:	For Dispatch Riders
2 Vans, 15 cwt:	Attached to HQ
1 Tender, 3 ton:	Attached to HQ

Search Section:

1 Squadron Leader:	Officer Commanding Search Section
4 Flight Lieutenants:	Search Officers
5 Drivers:	Motor Transport
5 Cars, passenger utility:	For Search Officers

History of P.4 (Cas)

As early as 1937 the Air Ministry was becoming aware of the problems that the coming war, which they had been preparing for in an half-hearted way since 1934, would bring to their peacetime establishment. Up until then virtually everything that came under the broad heading of 'personnel' came under section S.7 of the Department of the Air Member of Personnel. Postings came under S.3, along with the establishments of stations and units (i.e. how many people and in which roles), but casualties, insurance, personnel records, courts martial, and all manner of other issues were the domain of S.7. In March 1937 S.7 was split into two: S.7 (R) to deal with the regular air force, and S.7 (W) to deal with the blossoming non-regular (Auxiliary and Volunteer Reserve) forces and all matters pertaining to warfare, including casualties under S.7 (Cas).[412] With only thirty staff, S.7 (W) would be hard pressed when war came.

On 5 September 1939 the first news of RAF casualties arrived at the Air Ministry: Blenheim crews from 2 Group, Bomber Command on a raid to Wilhelmshaven the day before. Almost immediately, the system broke down.[413] Almost all of S.7 (Cas)'s information was being gleaned from the BBC and other media sources. For more than three weeks the Air Ministry was frozen from lack of information, until details began to arrive from the families of survivors, contacting them from prisoner of war camps in Germany. Clearly, this situation was unacceptable, but the Air Ministry moved fast to reform the system. S.7 contacted the International Red Cross Committee to ask for their advice, and with their help a proper mechanism was established whereby lists of casualties could be exchanged as promptly as possible through Geneva. The Germans quite bluntly called these *Totenlisten*: 'Death lists'. The first one arrived on the 14 October 1939.

Meanwhile the Permanent Under Secretary of State for Air, Sir Arthur Street MC, had been busy restructuring the internal structure of the Ministry. On 16 October he announced the formation of a new Branch, P.4 (Cas) of the Directorate of Personal Services. Under the command of Commander R. Burges RN (Retired), with the honorary rank of Wing

Commander, P.4 (Cas) now took on sole responsibility of dealing with officer casualties and the main responsibility of dealing with other ranks, with some areas such as the updating of records, processing of accounts and allowances to families, and the handling of personal effects being retained by S.7 working out of their Records Office in Gloucester.

The system stabilised into one aimed at processing casualty information as quickly and, vitally, as accurately as possible.[414] This was not easy. With so many different circumstances in which a member of the RAF or WAAF could die or be injured across the entire globe, with means of communications severely limited by war time constrictions, this was no easy matter. The first step would be to recognise that someone had become a casualty. Perhaps the most straightforward situation for this would be aircrew lost on operations. Daylight operations usually, although by no means always, involved witnesses, be they other aircrew or Allied troops or ships. Even if there were no witnesses, as would be the case at night, it was a simple case of the aircraft not returning home. It was not uncommon for aircrew to land at a base other than their own, through either being lost or battle damaged. It was also fairly common for aircrew to bale out and be picked up by ground or naval forces. In these cases a signal would be sent from the unit or station to the aircrew's home base to confirm their survival and/or status.

If the aircraft crashed, or an airman or airwoman died while separated from their unit – in a road traffic accident, for example – the parent unit would be notified immediately. In the case of the casualty being on detached duty, for example a rigger or fitter attending a course at one of the Technical Training Schools, then that unit would be informed. The authority dealing with the case would inform the parent unit as soon as identity and origin had been established. If the parent unit could not be identified, then the process would move directly onto the next step.

Four standard forms were used according to the situation. The first covered aircrew losses, and came in two variants. The first was for a confirmed death, and the second for a failure to return from operations. In each case the type and serial number of the aircraft, and in the case of missing aircraft only the serial numbers of the engines, were noted first. Unlike names, these details were unique and would avoid confusion from the start. Next would be the unit designation and either the place name and map reference if known, or the target. This would include an approximate time, and a code word to indicate time of day or night and the phase of the moon if applicable. Essentially, this was meant to indicate visibility at the time of the loss.

Only then would come the names, ranks and service numbers of those involved. The location of the personnel or their bodies, if known, followed, and then any details on explosive munitions or specialist equipment carried by the aircraft. Then came the apparent cause of the loss or accident. The next two items confirmed the condition of the wreckage if relevant, and the number and designation of the salvage or maintenance unit detailed to deal with it. The last item was only used when the signal originated from the parent unit of the casualty, and was a one word code: either 'KINFORMED' if the next of kin had been informed, or 'KINNOT' if they had not. If they had, the signal received an 'Important' priority. If they had not, it received a higher 'Immediate' rating. Even if an aircraft was overdue by only one hour, the parent unit was required to send a copy of this form to the Air Ministry.

The second message form applied to non-flying casualties caused by enemy action. Without an aircraft being involved, the details were simpler. The place, date and time of the casualty headed the form, followed by the name, rank and number of the casualties. Each person would have their status noted: killed; wounded or injured either danger-ously, seriously or lightly, with a note on the nature of the injuries; if they died of their injuries or wounds with the date and time of death; various grades of missing – believed killed, believed interned or believed prisoner of war; or, if nothing else was known, simply missing. After the names came the nature and cause of the incident, followed by their location if known. Again, the final line recorded whether the next of kin had been informed or not.

The third form was simpler, and covered natural death or illness. The title would specify death, serious illness or dangerous illness. Next would be the name, rank and number. After that the cause of death or nature of illness, followed by the location of the hospital or medical unit the person had been sent to. Lastly was the standard notation of KINFORMED or KINNOT.

The fourth form was for death or injury through either accidental or self inflicted injuries. Once more the title specified straight off whether the subject had been killed, injured, or had died of their injuries, and whether they were accidental or self inflicted. Then came the name, rank and number. Following this was the nature and cause of the accident, and then the date and place in which it occurred. Penultimate was the name of the hospital, medical centre or morgue where the person or corpse had been sent, and finally the familiar status of notification.

Between them, these forms presented the facts of any given casualty in as succinct and comprehensive means as possible. Perhaps most important, in the case of missing aircrew, were the minutia on the serial numbers of the aircraft and engines, which would provide valuable clues after the war.

If the casualties occurred in the UK, copies were to be sent to various authorities. In every case the Air Ministry was the priority, but in the case of other ranks only then the RAF Records Office in Gloucester also had to be informed. In the case of aircrew losses in the air (the first form) the parent Command or Group HQ or parent unit would also be sent a copy, as would HQ 43 (Salvage) Group if wreckage needed to be cleared up. In the case of overseas commands, copies would be sent to the theatre Air Headquarters and to the parent unit. They would then be responsible for informing the Air Ministry and the RAF Records Officer.

Taking second place by only a narrow margin to informing the Air Ministry was the duty of informing the next of kin. It should be mentioned that the next of kin did not always simply include the closest family member. On enlisting, the recruit was given the option of nominating one other person, related or not, to be informed upon death or injury. Both of these names and addresses would be recorded on their permanent Records of Service. If the casualty occurred in the UK, or while the person was stationed with an unit based in the UK, then the onus lay on the commanding officers to see that a telegram was sent. This was also the case with overseas units if the next of kin was living in the country where the person died, for example an RCAF pilot killed while training in Canada. If it was not possible for the commanding officer to attend to this, or if the casualty was serving outside both the UK and their next of kin's homeland, the matter would be passed to the Air Ministry. Casualties from the other services who were killed while serving with or attached to the RAF would also be initially processed by the Air Ministry, albeit with copies of all paperwork being forwarded to the War Office or Admiralty as well.

The initial telegram would be blunt and to the point, almost brutal. In the case of death from accident or enemy action, the specified form read:

Deeply regret to inform you that your [relationship] [rank] [full name, with surname in block capitals] lost [his/her] life on [day, month, year] as a result of [air operations/an aircraft accident/enemy action/other causes]. Letter follows. Please accept my profound sympathy.

If a person was missing, the tone of the telegram would be downgraded to simply 'Regret to inform you', and that the casualty was either 'missing' or 'missing and believed to have lost his life'.

In cases of death through illness, the telegram differed in format and included more detail. The person would be listed as dangerously or seriously ill, wounded or injured, and the Air Ministry would specify whether the incident had been flying or non-flying. Depending on which, there would also be basic details on the situation (air operations/aircraft accident, or enemy action/road accident/name of illness/etc.). There would follow the name and address of the hospital or medical centre to which they had been admitted. If the patient was *dangerously* (but not if *seriously*) ill, and the next of kin was resident in the UK, they would be authorised to present the telegram at the nearest police station, where they would receive a rail warrant for two persons to visit the patient.

Following swiftly on the heels of the official telegram came a letter of sympathy, and de facto of confirmation, from the casualty's commanding officer. It fell to the station commander to make sure that a letter was sent 18–24 hours after the initial telegram, to make sure that the former had arrived. If, as sometimes would happen, operational pressures or the number of letters to be sent prevented the commanding officer from dealing with all the cases arising, the station commander would pick up the deficit. The Air Ministry was both plain and insistent on the point that these letters 'should be signed personally and not relegated to junior officers'.[415] Equally strict were the rules on content. They should be couched in the same terms as the telegram, include as much personal detail as possible, and give away no information on the circumstances, not even the type or role of the aircraft being flown at the time. Printed forms were enclosed not only explaining why this was necessary for security reasons, but also ordering that any death notices that the family may wish to publish should not include the date, circumstances or any unit details. Within a few days of this letter would follow a second communiqué from the Air Ministry, confirming the original information, and including details on funerals, disposal of personal effects, and allowances open to the families in the case of missing persons.

If a person was killed in the UK on active service, while serving with their parent unit, then it would fall to the unit or station commander to issue a death certificate to the local authorities. If the casualty was on detached duties, or on leave, then it would come down to the local authorities to process the body. In the case of an accident or death from natural causes, the case would be handed over to the local coroner to decide whether or not to hold an inquest. If the body were held by the local authorities, it would fall to them to contact the next of kin to make the funeral arrangements. Unless an inquest was deemed necessary, they had 48 hours grace before being required to bury the body in the local cemetery. If the body was still in RAF hands, the family would be contacted whenever possible (not always the case for families of personnel from the Allied Air Forces) to decide on how to dispose of it. If in the UK, the parent unit was responsible for this through the nearest RAF station. It would be up to them to arrange for a coffin and then follow the family's wishes. This could follow two courses.

Firstly, the family could claim the body. In this case, the RAF would arrange for the transportation of the body to their home town. The regulations were insistent that coffins should never be transported in an open, freight, or cattle car. The schedule for movement would be communicated to the family before hand, and all costs would be met by the RAF. Further allowances would be made for the plot and other expenses: the families of other ranks would receive £7 10s regardless of cause of death. If the cost of the coffin exceeded £3 10s, although by no more than an extra £2 10s, this would be met by the RAF and later deducted from the deceased final accounts. Officers would receive £7 10s if the RAF were handling the funeral if they had been killed in an aeroplane either on active service or in an accident, or £14 if private arrangements were being made. Any other cause of death would not receive any funds.

Secondly, the body could be buried at an approved RAF cemetery close to the parent station. Two rail warrants would be provided for the family, and an RAF Chaplain and all service honours laid on at no charge. Other ranks would receive a free coffin and plot, although the families of officers would have to pay for these. This option was usually taken in the case of Allied or Dominion personnel.

A representative from the parent unit or station was to be sent wherever possible to accompany the body and attend the funeral. Units were also strongly encouraged to provide flowers or a wreath, although these could not be purchased with public funds. This representative would also be responsible for the Union Jack, or national flag of Allied personnel, that would cover the coffin in transit and at the funeral. These had to be retrieved and returned to the unit after use. Being an Ensign, it was against protocol to use the RAF's own flag at a funeral

The effects of the deceased were to be carefully collected and catalogued by the unit adjutant, or other designated officer. Public property, that is issued kit, had to be returned to stores, and any items that were missing or damaged would be charged to the deceased's account. Any money would be handed to the Accounts officer for crediting against their account. Once all of their kit had been accounted for, their mess, funeral or laundry bills paid, and any pay arrears collected, the account would be closed and a cheque sent to the family. Personal items were to be packed up and carefully inventoried, and then sent to the RAF Central Depository at RAF Colnbrook. If the casualty was confirmed as dead, the items could then be claimed by and sent to the next of kin. If they were wounded or missing, they were held until their status or final destination was confirmed. Log books would be retained at Colnbrook until further notice due to security consideration. All of this did not include large items, such as cars, pedal or motorbikes, wireless sets or furniture. The family would need to be contacted about these to arrange for disposal. All of this needed to be processed within 14 days of the casualty being reported.

Obviously, the procedure was different if the casualty was overseas. Funerals would be arranged locally, with no option for the body to be sent home. Effects would be sent to the local Air Headquarters to be held until such a time as they could be sent home.

This system remained broadly unchanged for the rest of the war, although the mechanism that handled it changed again in April 1943 when P.4 (Cas) and the remaining casualty section of S.7 merged. This was mainly to streamline the system, which up until then had been spread out between London and Gloucester. As the war gradually picked up tempo around the world, though particularly through the bomber offensive in Europe, the pressure on these two departments had increased, as did the number of cases (under the system whereby entire crews were filed together) that spanned both departments. However, the straw that broke their back would come from the Far East (see Chapter 3).

The Far East project made it clear that it would make much more sense if the two separate branches were combined. A time and motion study by the Secretarial (Organisation and Manning) branch in December 1942 confirmed this. Their report[416] highlighted that the way files were raised and the departments of the branch organised led to considerable loss of time. The various departments worked on a task-basis, i.e. Telegrams, Air Council Letters, Death Certificates, etc., which meant that if one department developed a backlog, all the subsequent departments in line would also run them up. Similarly, when it came time to review old cases for the purposes of assuming death, while the Presumptions department was looking at the file the Missing department may be wasting time trying to find it to add new information. The physical distance between London and Gloucester did nothing to help this situation.

Over the winter of 1941 and into the spring of 1942 Japanese forces swept through Singapore, Java and Malaya. By the end of March 1942, nearly 7,000 RAF personnel had disappeared and were unaccounted for. In London, the Air Ministry decided to wait for the Japanese to provide an equivalent of the *Totenlisten*, confirming who was a prisoner at least, before contacting the families of the missing.[417] As time dragged and still nothing was heard from the Japanese, the Air Ministry decided to follow the War Office's lead and declare their men as 'unaccounted for', and therefore outside the established system. By September there had still been no official news but questions were being asked in Parliament[418], and pressure was being applied by the Australian government regarding those members of the RAAF who had been captured in the Far East. In a memo of 30 September 1942 Wing Commander Burges was reporting that 'the pushful and persistent methods' of the Casualty Section of the RAAF Overseas Headquarters had created all sorts of problems in his department.[419] His staff had been dropping other work to give Australian cases precedent, causing him to step in several times, and two RAAF airmen had been perhaps prematurely declared as dead. Certainly, the presumption process had been artificially accelerated, leaving them open to being proven wrong. (Incidentally, Burges reported that to date only one airman had been wrongly reported as killed. This was a Pole who had been reported as killed by the rest of his crew, but had later turned up as a prisoner. As he had no family in Britain to inform, no distress to anyone had been caused by the mistake.)

With pressure mounting the Air Ministry set up a team to investigate the matter. Although the members were formed from P.4 (Cas), their work was mainly completed at the Records Office in Gloucester as that is where the bulk of the records (i.e. those for the 6,500 other ranks) were held. From this process a list was compiled, and an appeal published in the Air Ministry Orders 15 October 1942 for information on the missing men.

The decision was taken to bring the section from Gloucester under the wing of P.4 (Cas) and move them both into bigger offices at 73/77 Oxford Street, London, where departments would be able to share office space and everything could be much more tightly knit and co-ordinated. This initially led to some fears from staff members on several issues, such as what would happen if the new combined offices were bombed[420], and whether the area would be safe for female members of staff on their way too or from their night shifts (WAAF staff were to be billeted in what had been luxury flats in Bentick Close, some distance away). After a long period of planning the arrangement came into force on Monday 19 April 1943. Over the weekend before six Women's Auxiliary Air Force (WAAF) corporals with sixty-six Aircraftswomen (ACW) travelled to London from Gloucester, bringing the various files to be transferred with them. To bring the numbers more into proportion to deal with the administration of the lower ranks, three of the WAAF corporals were promoted to sergeant rank: Corporal Elliott in Air Council Letters, Corporal Sheppard in Missing, and Corporal Quinn in Presumptions. They then took over charge of not only the duties of the WAAFs (mainly proof reading drafts and letters, but also answering public enquiries and keeping the records in order) but also responsibility for their discipline, administration and welfare. This of course left a corresponding gap in the lower ranks, and Burges was faced with yet another area for constant bickering with S.1, in charge of secretarial manning and establishments, over the need for more staff.

The Branch was split across twelve departments, each with a specific role:

- Air Council Letters: Responsible for confirmation letters to next of kin, and subsequent enquiries from the families.

- Telegrams: Responsible for the initial telegrams to next of kin.

- Presumptions: Responsible for deciding when the presumption of death should be declared. Cases would be reviewed after four, six and twelve months as to what new evidence had been received.

- Kits: Responsible for liaising with the RAF Central Depositary, RAF Colnbrook, and Accounts over the settling of accounts and disposal of personal effects.

- Accidents: Responsible for processing all casualties resulting from accidents.

- Prisoners of War: Responsible for dealing all with prisoner of war paperwork.

- Death Certificates: Responsible for overseeing the issue of death certificates.

- Transit: Responsible for the supervising the movement of bodies.

- Interviewing Officers: Responsible for dealing with members of the public who visited P.4 (Cas).

- Missing: The Missing Research Section responsible for following up leads on resolving cases of missing personnel.

- General: Responsible for general correspondence and duties.

- Sick: A new section taking over responsibility for dealing with cases of illness or wounds.

Also present was the Canadian Casualty Section, of about forty-five personnel, on the top floor of the building, and the special Far East Section whose establishment had contributed to the merger originally.

Despite the streamlining and reorganisation of the branch, the backlogs continued to pile up. This was clearly unacceptable. Tens of thousands of families were waiting in desperate hope for accurate information on their loved ones, and mistakes simply could not be tolerated. Delays, though, were sadly unavoidable. Part of the reason for this was caused by the activities of the Far East Section. On 22 February 1943 the War Office informed Burges that the 250 Army officers and 5,200 other ranks still missing from the Japanese victories the year before were to be declared as officially missing as of the 1st of that month.[421] This had various practical repercussions, particularly regarding the pay and allowances still being forwarded to the families of the missing. On the 26th Burges passed the news onto his superiors, recommending that the Air Ministry follow suit.[422] Unfortunately this stirred up a hornet's nest. The late date meant that the Air Ministry would not have time to stop that month's salaries going to the families of the officers, who were paid by standing order into bank accounts (money to other ranks came in cash through pay parades, and so was easier to stop). If the Ministry waited until the next month, it would mean that the missing RAF personnel would receive an extra month's full salaries than the Army personnel, which was obviously not fair. An added issue would be what rate to pay them at.

Families received a portion of the normal wage, in the case of wives two-sevenths, but of course the pay rate depended on what rank the person was. While 'unaccounted for' officers received automatic promotions due to seniority, officers listed as 'missing' did not.

This led to a series of issues to be resolved as quickly and fairly as possible.[423] It also led to an enormous number of casualties needing to be processed at once. In the end it was decided that the change of status would be actioned on the 1 March, at the ranks held as of the 31 January 1943. The Accounts Branch would share some of the work load with P.4 (Cas), processing and sending some of the paperwork along with their own to the next of kin. Even so, coupled with the increased workloads from the absorption of the airmen's records from Gloucester and the Far East Section, plus the increasing casualty rates across the board, meant that work began to back up to an unacceptable degree.

In June 1943 Mr Beckess of S.1 Secretarial further criticised P.4 (Cas) and their efficiency, and the Assistant Under Secretary of State (Personnel) Mr R. C. Richards, stepped in to mediate between the two. Although defending his people as much as possible, he upheld two of the criticisms from personal experience. Firstly, that the Air Council Letters, that it was his duty to sign before being sent, were growing sloppy in composition and content. They were clearly being rushed through and errors were creeping in. The second was that, despite the process being artificially sped up, it was now taking 2–3 weeks for the letters to be sent, instead of the 2–3 days that was laid down in the Air Ministry guidelines.[424] One of the causes of this was the desire to give some news as to the circumstances of the loss or casualty. Waiting for this news to arrive from the stations or units slowed things down. He did not offer any solutions, admitting that he did not have enough experience of the Branch to offer practical advice, but stated himself to be open to 'some desperate remedy' if appropriate.

Burges was on leave when the two reports arrived, but on his return in July he rallied to his Branch's defence.[425] He did admit there were problems. Air Council Letters were behind schedule, although he believed this was not as big a problem as Beckess and Richards would argue. Burges explained that bald, newsless letters could be expected to lead to at least a 50% rise in correspondence as relatives wrote back asking for those details. Better to delay slightly, he believed, to avoid this increase in work, although he agreed that the backlog was too much and a target of 7–10 days should be met. Burges attributed most of the problems in this Section to too many inexperienced staff working in an area that needed a lot of practice and attention to detail, and confidently predicted a gradual improvement in their efficiency. The principal problem across the Branch was staff. Throughout the war so far, even not including the two recent major projects, there had been a steady and fairly rapid increase in the number of casualties being processed. For example, more RAF personnel were lost during the single Bomber Command raid on Nuremberg on 30/31 March 1944, than during the entire Battle of Britain.[426] Because of the way the system worked, new staff only ever arrived after these rises occurred, leaving the Branch in a constant state of trying to catch up with their work. Apart from anything, this has a serious effect on the morale of the staff who were already carrying out a fairly grim job:

> Later on we got some from the Far East, and these were quite distressing because [if the crew] got out and managed to land, the Japanese simply beheaded them, which of course ... I found it very upsetting.[427]

As at the date of writing, Burges reported, the backlog of the Branch stood at:

Far East Section: Approximately 3,000 cases outstanding.

Death Presumption Section: In proportion to Air Council Letters.

General Correspondence: Ditto, largely due to families writing for news.

Accidents Section: 'Serious congestion' mainly from cases inherited from Gloucester.

Telegrams Section: Suffering due to an increase in the RAF casualty rate, but recruitment and training of extra staff in hand.

Sick Duty: Same situation as the Telegrams Section, with the growth of numbers in the RAF and WAAF creating an increasing work load.

Missing Section: Work load also increasing as more cases arrived on top of those already open and under investigation.

If nothing else Burges's report convinced his superiors that more resources were needed. By the end of July 1943 P.4 (Cas) stood at seventeen Higher Clerical Officers and 331 Clerks, over eighty of whom were WAAFs. This number helped alleviate the situation, but manning continued to be a problem. As the war continued the numbers of casualties continued to rise, and the battle for more staff dragged on. This led in May 1944 to one of the stranger sets of correspondence to come out of the Branch. One drain on staff time was the need to maintain a reception area for the visitors who came into the Oxford Street offices, either seeking more information or offering it to the Missing Research Section. Five WAAF's were used on a rotation, in order 'to entertain visitors in a manner appropriate to the position of the Air Ministry as custodian of the interest of the next-of-kin of casualties'. Burges finally applied to S.1 for one

WAAF corporal and one ACW to cover this duty, if for no other reason than 'owing to approval which has now been obtained to supply cups of tea for the comfort of visitors'.[428] The terse reply dismissed the idea, stating that 'We cannot agree that there is any necessity to increase the establishment of P.4 (Cas) to cover the duties of receptionist, or for making tea and dealing with the tasks related there to.'[429]

On 19 August 1946 P.4 (Cas) was transferred back to S.7 from the Directorate of Personal Services, and reverted to the name S.7 (Cas). Group Captian Burges was replaced as Head of Branch at the same time by Mr A. Beckess, and resigned from the RAF shortly afterwards. The offices, and all contact details, remained the same.[430]

Tracing Royal Air Force Airmen

The ease of tracing Second World War airmen depends very much on two things: whether the person survived the war, and whether you are related to them.

If you are related, the process is very straightforward. A letter to the RAF Personnel Management Agency will, after proof of identity and a fee being produced, procure you a copy of the individual's record of service. This contains a lot of information, including addresses at the time of enlistment, next of kin, basic physical description, and any details on commendations or disciplinary actions. However, the meat of the record is a list of dates, units and places. Everywhere that someone went will be recorded here, and this creates a comprehensive, if not daunting, document. RAF records are difficult for several reasons, but perhaps highest on the list is that the RAF is a far more fluid organisation than most. Soldiers join a battalion and sailors a ship, and they tend to stay there for years at a time, if not their whole service. Airmen tend to move around a lot, and can be attached to either units or stations. Squadrons generally don't have the age-old traditions and staunch identities of regiments and ships for just this reason. Airmen can be sent wherever men of their trade (airmen, riggers, fitters, clerks, drivers, etc.) are needed. This can lead to some pretty densely packed records, with much more jargon than the other services.

Armed with this mass of abbreviations and numbers, you can seek aid from several sources. Probably the best is the Royal Air Force Museum (RAFM) at Hendon, who have the necessary sources to turn the list into meaningful English. Abbreviations and acronyms can be expanded and explained, and unit locations and duties uncovered. It is unlikely that the details will go into any great depth, but a general picture will be drawn up. For the finer points, you will need to turn to the official records held at The National Archives (TNA) at Kew. These, in particular the Operations Record Books (ORB), are in the form of a daily diary of the unit's or station's activities. The level of information given varies drastically. At best, postings in or out of the unit, accidents and sickness, or minute details of operations and crews will appear; at worst a brief description of the day's events. Even this can be of help. While the service record (with the help of the RAFM) can provide the dates served with, say, a Lancaster squadron, the ORBs can give details on individual raids that unit was involved in. There is also an immense range of books on the RAF or units histories out there that could provide further information to lay on the basic framework as well.

Of course the best way to trace the operational service of a member of aircrew is through their flying log book. These were kept by individuals and are particular to them; even members of the same crew will have different entries. They can also vary greatly in their detail, from bland lists of flights (aircraft, crew, target/purpose, duration) to some which read more like diaries. The bad news is that these were kept by each airman after discharge, and if they are not held by the family anymore the chances of finding them are very slim. For casualties, log books were sent to the Central Depository at Gloucester and returned to the families after the war (the delay so as to avoid revealing any sensitive operational details that they may have contained). In many cases, the addresses for the next of kin were out of date, and by 1960 there was still about 2km (6,400ft) of shelf space being used for unclaimed log books. At this point The National Archives were called in to take a representative sample (plus any famous ones, like Wing Commander Guy Gibson's) of 249, or about 6m (20ft). The rest were burned.

Records of service are only open to next of kin, but there are avenues to try if you are not related. If the individual was an officer you can trace their promotions and trades through the Air Force Lists. These were published monthly from 1918, quarterly from 1945, twice a year from 1963, and finally annually since 1980. Medals can also be easily traced. All citations for all awards appear in the London Gazette, much of which is now available on line. These do not always give the full citation, though, and you really need a rough date to find the award you are looking for. Therefore, you may also like to try either a superb series of books listing the citations for the Distinguished Flying Cross and Distinguished Flying Medal published by Savannah, or try the Air Ministry Bulletin. The latter, available at TNA or RAFM, is indexed by name, and often gives more information on all awards than the Gazette. However, citations do not always exist for medals. There were two types of awards during the war: Immediate awards for a specific action, which usually have a citation, and Non-immediate awards for conspicuous behaviour over an extended period, which usually do not.

It is one of the more ironic facts of service life that the dead are far easier to trace than the living. The central casualty files of the RAF are still closely guarded. A letter to the Air Historical Branch, again with proof of kinship, should gain you some of the details from the old Air Ministry files on the person and their cause of death. These include details obtained by the MRES in their investigations, and to a certain degree the evidence to support their conclusions. However, most MRES records are not accessible by the public. Investigation and exhumation reports do not make very pleasant reading, and are almost certain to cause distress to family members. They are, after all, essentially autopsy reports. Most of the details given in the preceding pages have come from 'sanitised' reports compiled by the Air Ministry and now held at TNA, although these only cover a fraction of the cases talked by the MRS or MRES.

Therefore the best place to start is the Commonwealth War Graves Commission. Although they do not hold records on how or even where a service person was killed (their interest and records begin the instant the body was handed into their care, and not a moment before), the database on their website is still very useful. A name entered will provide a very rough place and date of death, and with luck a unit too. The cause of death can then be discovered through several avenues. If a body is buried in a combat zone, say France or Germany, it is likely to have been through enemy action. More details can be found through a range of books produced by Midland Publishing, which give chronological lists of Bomber, Fighter and Coastal Command losses. Further information can then usually be found through general reference books as to what the operation was, and what it achieved. Some deaths, particularly those in this country, are harder to pin down as being combat losses, accidents, or even illness. Again, ORBs can be consulted, as can the details on the record of service. An airman serving at a Flying Training School, for example, is more likely to have been killed in an accident. If you believe that the cause was an accident involving an aircraft, try the Form 1180 Accident Cards held at the RAFM. You will need a date and preferably a type involved (this can be guessed at judging by the unit they were in). The Accident Card will report in full the conditions and circumstances surrounding an accident, as well as the conclusions of any inquiries.

APPENDIX E

War Crimes and the MRES

It is a fact that a small but significant number of British and Allied aircrew were subject to brutal treatment or even murdered after being shot down over Germany or occupied territories. A modern United States Air Force training manual teaches its readers that 'It is generally inadvisable to eject directly over the area you just bombed.' As frivolous as this may sound, it is true that aircrew were not going to be well received by the people that they have been attacking. A certain amount of evidence can be gathered to show that in at least a few cases German air crew who baled out over England in 1940 were attacked and murdered by the civil population they had been bombing. Concrete evidence can be found that it happened to Allied aircrew over Germany. These were, after all, the hated *Terrorfleiger*, and as the Allied attacks on Germany escalated from 1942 onwards so do the recorded incidents. Many of the perpetrators were later apprehended and put before war crimes tribunals.

Even so statistics are hard to find on this subject; by their nature cases tend to be hidden. After several years underground the body of an airman who had been beaten to death, or shot even, would not differ enough from that of one killed in action or a crash to warrant any suspicion. Missing Research and Enquiry Service search officers were not trained in pathology as we know it today. For perhaps this reason, the officers of the MRES were given strict instructions on this area:

> While the tracing of war criminals is not one of the primary duties of the Missing Research and Enquiry Sections, there is no objection to this activity if pursued as a sideline, provided that it does not interfere with their regular work.
>
> The War Crimes Commission is concerned with the criminals; the Missing Research and Enquiry Service is concerned, inter alia, with their victims. The War Crimes Commission has undertaken to pass on to the Air Ministry or to the Missing Research and Enquiry Section concerned traces of missing officers and airmen which their investigations have brought to

light. As a reciprocal gesture, any suggestion of a war crime which our investigators uncover should be passed to the War Crimes Commission or one of its representatives.[431]

In June 1946 a search team from 19 Section, 4 MREU, discovered the body of a Canadian airman at Opladen. The body had no identifying marks or papers, which was in itself not unusual, but it was also on its own, which this far into Germany was. Questions were asked among the locals and evidence was gathered to suggest this may be one of three RCAF airmen who had been murdered. One of the other men had already been found at Leichlingen, and on the evidence garnered there, four men (three *Volksturm* (German Home Guard) and one regular German army) had been arrested. Three were convicted; by the time the second body was discovered two had been executed and one was serving fifteen years in prison. This meant that the men involved were either unavailable or unwilling to provide the information needed to identify the second Canadian, or to locate the third.[432]

In this case, the circumstances surrounding the remains were the biggest clue that a crime had been committed. It was the unusualness of finding a crew separated and widely dispersed in single graves that aroused suspicions. The same was true of the possibly apocryphal case of the Norwegian Typhoon pilot exhumed near Osnabruck. When the grave was opened the investigating officer found a complete, clean skeleton wearing an Irving flying jacket. Not only was the skeleton far too clean to have been under the ground for only two years, but the lack of damage was inconsistent with a combat loss. Finally, the fact that the body was entirely naked except a flying jacket was unusual to say the least.[433]

Sometimes the evidence came from more direct sources. Flight Lieutenant Ron Myhill worked on the case of a Lancaster pilot who had baled out in daylight in April 1944, landing in the Rhine. As he struggled on to the shore, he was shot in the head by the *Volksturm* corporal commanding the guard on the nearest bridge. In this case, the war crime came to light when no less than eleven local German civilians reported it to the investigating officer. An exhumation was mounted, and the unusual step of employing a pathologist from Dusseldorf University to conduct an autopsy taken. The culprit, also being local, was easy to locate, and Flight Lieutenant Myhill accompanied a British Army officer to his house to arrest him. While they waited for the man to pull on his boots and jacket they asked him about the five photographs lined up on the mantelpiece; each was of a son killed during the war. Once he was ready, the arresting officers took him to Nuremburg prison, where he later hanged himself.[434]

It must be remembered that these were not simply legal cases to be dealt with as academic curiosities in isolation. Every airman who was murdered was another man who, despite beating the odds by surviving being shot down, would be cheated of the chance of going home. It would be another family left bereft. To its credit, the Air Ministry maintained the highest levels of compassion and sensitivity to the families. Perhaps the most extreme example illustrates this best. In March 1947 a tip off was received from an anonymous source that an airman was buried in the woods in the area of Kreis Melle. This man had been shot by a guard on the Long March of the spring of 1945, when the Germans moved their prisoners of war west to escape the advancing Soviet forces. The victim had managed to make it to a nearby house. Here he had handed the occupant a note with his name and address, stating (according to the report):

> Tell her, that I die for the country and that I am happy to do so and that in all my thoughts, I have always been with her. Send her this last greeting and tell her still not to forget me entirely.

The note was passed to the Air Ministry, but no matches were found with their personnel records. However, the MRS investigated and found that the husband of the lady at that address was a member of the RAF and was missing. Unfortunately it did not stop there. Further investigation led to the discovery that he had signed up under an assumed name, and that he actually had two wives. This man had been married for the first time in the mid-1930s. He had abandoned this family, with a four month old daughter, and not been heard of again. He had later met and married a second woman, and again had a daughter. They had been together for three years before he committed an unspecified offence and was arrested. After serving 18 months hard labour, his second family had kicked him out with instructions to make something of himself. Apparently, he had done so by joining the Royal Air Force.

This left the Air Ministry with a dilemma, as the man had two families. Questions were raised about which should be informed as next of kin, and who should be the recipient of any allowances and personal effects. The debate continued for several months until in June No. 4 MREU were ordered to help the War Crimes Commission as much as possible, and informed that:

> We are particularly anxious, because of domestic circumstances conveyed to us in confidence, that all possible efforts should be made to find out the location of this grave and the service details of the occupant.[435]

According to WAAFs who worked at the Air Ministry, cases of bigamy, or more usually having several girlfriends or fiancées, were a fairly common occurrence, and each would lead to questions over who has the most legitimate claim on any effects. In real terms, all that these cases led to were twice the grief at the airman's loss.

In May 1947 Flight Lieutenant T. Bickerton, 16 Section 3 MREU, investigated another case of a prisoner shot by a *Luftwaffe* guard in March 1945, supposedly for looting. The incident had also happened during the Long March. Faced with incredibly harsh winter conditions and an almost complete lack of supplies, disorder and even looting became inevitable. On closer investigation, documents were found on the remains naming them as Cameron Ross, a South African. In strict accordance with his instructions, Bicketon passed his report up the line to the Air Ministry, who handed the case to the Judge Advocate General of the British Army of the Rhine with a note saying that they had no record of any airman of this name. In the event, he turned out to be a soldier of the Union Defence Force, and the War Crimes Commission investigated accordingly.[436]

A more relevant case to the core duties of the MRES appeared in November 1948 when a team from 4 MREU called at the cemetery outside what had been *Stalag Luft III*, near Sagan in Poland. The inmates had primarily been RAF aircrew, and many of those who had died in captivity were buried there. More famously, a monument in the cemetery held fifty urns containing the ashes of the officers murdered by the Germans after the mass break out in March 1944. Each murdered man had been cremated by the Germans and the urns inscribed with the name, and date and place of death. Immediately after the war a team under the ex-Scotland Yard detective Wing Commander Bowes of the RAF Special Investigations Branch hunted down and arrested eighteen Germans suspected of being involved in the murders. The inscriptions on the urns were a vital piece of evidence in the enquiry, but were only supplied to the investigators second hand from notes made by the prisoners who had built the memorial and interred the urns a year previously. The eighteen were put on trial in July 1947; all were convicted and fourteen executed for their crimes in February 1948. It was not until the affair was long over that the MRES arrived to collect the urns themselves: by the various remits issued, the search teams needed only to concern themselves with the retrieval of remains and not the pursuit of war criminals. By this late date, though, some of the urns were found to be either damaged or missing altogether.[437]

MRES Unit Badge

T he armed forces have always maintained a strong sense of humour. Ever since, as they say, Pontius was a pilot and Mortis was his rigger, this has been the natural way to cope with a life full of hardships and sudden, violent death. Usually, the humour is dark and heavily fatalistic. This was perhaps even more the case with the MRES. Occasional black humour, not always appropriate, comes through in investigation reports, and several sets of the more ridiculous or humorous were compiled and probably circulated in Nos 3 and 4 MREU at least.[438] Probably the most obvious manifestation of this humour is the unofficial unit crest.

Some parts of the crest are self-explanatory: the black mourning cloth draped over the top; the heraldic helmet of the cavalry of the clouds next to the detective's rubber glove and magnifying glass, and; the mock-Latin motto. On the shield itself, the top left refers to both the gruesome nature of the work, plus the multi-national character of the Service, with British, Australian, New Zealand and Canadian staff working together. Top right is slightly more obscure, but Squadron Leader Bill Lott explains:

[In previous correspondence I referred] to 'characters swanning around'. This was a term in general use to describe members of the Occupation Forces using official transport (which was strictly controlled) for expeditions that would not stand up to official scrutiny as to work-related purpose ... The haphazard movement of swans on a lake may have inspired the analogy.

My personal major 'swan' was to drive some 200 miles south to Stuttgart, ostensibly to visit a nearby military cemetery, but actually to renew contact with the German forester who captured me in August 1944 when I was trying to escape into Switzerland after having been shot down on my 23rd night operation. But that's another story!

The panel illustrates a Service vehicle setting off almost certainly to an event where the wine would flow.[439]

The bottom left section is again a little more obscure, but again Squadron Leader Lott can shed some light:

The Cigarettes and Coffee segment. As I am sure you will have gathered, in post-war Germany, normal currency was virtually useless and the Occupation Forces used a special currency called BAFs – British Armed Forces vouchers. Cigarettes and coffee were the real currency in daily use for 'transactions' involving Forces personnel and Germans at any level. This was not unknown to Higher Authority and MRES units were issued with free allocations of cigarettes in tins of fifty which we used where necessary in our investigations and interrogations. These, and coffee which we often imported through the Army Postal Service in parcels marked 'Personal Effects' were indispensable as 'memory-revivers and tongue-looseners' during interviews with Germans of whatever status when probing for information about crash sites, burials, prisoner-taking and disposal, witnesses and the possible whereabouts of items taken from crash sites as trophies and by whom. 'Smuggling' was not considered an appropriate term for our acquisition of these commodities. I recall one incident when one of our number called at the local Army Post Office to collect a parcel of 'personal effects' addressed to him and was presented by a blank-faced Army postman with a cardboard box from one corner of which poured a stream of coffee beans! Nothing unpleasant ensued!

We certainly did what we could to ensure that the German civilian staff who worked for and with us were adequately catered for.[440]

The final segment is much easier to explain, commemorating the close co-operation enjoyed with the Army Graves Concentration Units, and the somewhat unpleasant exhumation tasks they performed.

The final aspect is the battle honours, listing just a handful of the places scoured by the Missing Research and Enquiry Service in their quest to bring their comrades home.

Select Bibliography

The National Archives:

AIR2/2000 Air Ministry Branch S.7: Reorganisation

AIR2/3549 Casualties: Question of issue of notices to press in time of war

AIR2/6330 Missing Research Section P.4 (Casualties) Branch

AIR2/6469 P.4 (Casualties) Branch: research Section, missing

AIR2/6474 Report on RAF and Dominions Air Forces Missing Research and Enquiry Service (MRES)

AIR2/6476 P.4 (Casualties) Branch: Reorganisation to absorb airman casualty work

AIR2/6959 RAF liaison with Graves Service

AIR2/7056 Missing Research and Enquiry Service: Russian Zone of Germany

AIR2/7088 War Crimes information received from Judge Advocate General on unidentified casualties

AIR2/9602 Far East casualties, death presumption: Policy

AIR2/9816 New Year's Honours List 1948

AIR2/9910 Missing Research and Enquiry Service: Long term policy

AIR2/10121 Court of Inquiry: Killing of Fifty RAF officers from *Stalag Luft III*

AIR2/10148 German Board for Registration of War Casualties

AIR2/10199 Missing Research: South East Asia

AIR2/10345 RAF Graves Service

AIR2/10346 RAF Graves Service

AIR20/6211 Casualty statistics by commands, including R.A.F., Dominion and Allied personnel, 3 September 1939 – 14 August 1945

AIR20/9050 Casualties: RAF Missing Research and Enquiry Service

AIR20/9305 Report on RAF and Dominions Air Forces Missing Research and Enquiry Service (MRES)

AIR29/1008 Operations Record Books: No. 49 Maintenance Unit

AIR29/1598 Missing Research and Enquiry Service: Operations Record Books

AIR55/53 No. 1 Missing Research and Enquiry Unit: Operational areas and location statements

AIR55/54 No. 1 Missing Research and Enquiry Unit

AIR55/55 No. 1 Missing Research and Enquiry Unit: Memorial services and inauguration ceremonies

AIR55/56 Graves registration policy

AIR55/57 No. 1 Missing Research and Enquiry Unit: H.Q. Missing Research and Enquiry Service Casualty Branch Instruction and Missing Research Memoranda

AIR55/58 HQ (Western Europe) Missing Research and Enquiry Service (MRES): Location statements

AIR55/59 HQ (Western Europe) Missing Research and Enquiry Service (MRES): Civilian labour

AIR55/60 HQ (Western Europe) Missing Research and Enquiry Service (MRES): MRES policy: disbandment of No. 4 MREU

AIR55/61 HQ (Western Europe) Missing Research and Enquiry Service (MRES): Establishments (framing and filling)

AIR55/62 HQ (Western Europe) Missing Research and Enquiry Service (MRES): Liaison with Deputy Director Graves Registration and Enquiries and American Graves Registration Command

AIR55/63 HQ (Western Europe) Missing Research and Enquiry Service (MRES): Operational and domestic returns

AIR55/64 Guide to Section Administration: No. 3 MREU

AIR55/65 Report on Royal Air Force and Dominions Air Forces Missing Research and Enquiry Service 1944–1949 by Gp. Capt. E. F. Hawkins, D.S.O. Air Headquarters B.A.F.O.

AIR55/66 No. 5 MREU: Operations policy

AIR55/67 HQ MED/ME: Minutes of conferences

AIR55/68 H.Q. MED/ME M.R.E.S.: reports on staff visits

AIR55/69 Operations policy and administration: No. 2 Searcher Party HQ (Balkans)

AIR55/70 Operations policy and administration: No. 3 Searcher Party HQ (Greece and Aegean Islands)

AIR55/71 Operations policy and administration: No. 3 Searcher Party HQ (Greece and Aegean Islands)

AIR55/72 Operations policy and administration: No. 3 Searcher Party HQ (Greece and Aegean Islands)

AIR55/73 Operations policy and administration: South Balkans

AIR55/74 Operations policy and administration: South Balkans

AIR55/75 MRES policy and administration

AIR55/76 No. 1 MREU: MRES policy

AIR55/77 No. 1 MREU: Memorial Services and Inauguration Ceremonies

AIR55/78 No. 1 MREU: Locations, postal and telegraphic addresses of MREUS

AIR55/79 HQ MRES MED/ME: Searcher Party instructions

AIR55/80 HQ MRES MED/ME: Centralisation of investigation into fate of missing casualties: reports and memoranda

AIR6/72 Air Council: Meetings 13–24 1941

AIR6/75 Air Council: Meetings 1944–1945

AIR6/77 AIR Council: Conclusions of meetings 1–17 1948

WO203/6059 Report on the graves service in SEAC and India by Deputy Director of Graves Registration ALFSEA

Royal Air Force Museum:

AC1997/45 WO Charles Walter Gentry Collection

B3294 Sqdn Ldr Rideal photograph album

B3295 Progress report on the work of twenty Missing Research and Enquiry Section (Ruhr Area), 1949

B3613 The biggest detective job in the world, Cpl Douglas Hague

DC74/39 Documents relating to Missing Research and Enquiry Service, 1945–1955 (includes Missing Research Memorandum)

X001-3527 Plt Off A.G.G. Machin

X002-9269 Flt Lt Harry Wilson Collection

X004-2350 WO James Kingham interview

X003-2433 Sqdn Ldr William Lott Collection

X003-8818 Lt Aubrey Matthews Collection

X002-9274 Sgt Henry Jones Collection

X004-1415 Fg Off George Williams Collection

X004-1438 Memoir of Flt Lt Roger St. Vincent

X004-2334 Sgt David Harrap interview

X004-2335 Flt Lt Ron Myhill interview

X004-2336 Flt Lt Ron Myhill Collection

X004-2337 Wg Cdr Moorcroft interview

X004-2346 Cpl Douglas Hague Collection

X004-2347 Cpl Douglas Hague interview

X004-2378 LACW Iris Catlin interview

X004-2379 LACW Lillian Taylor interview

X004-2400 Flt Lt Noel Archer Collection

X004-2414 Report by Fg Off A. Green on No. 62 Graves Concentration Unit's mission into west and south-west China for the purpose of recovering British war dead

X004-2433 Sqdn Ldr William Lott Collection

AC92/1/9 Air Ministry Report on Royal Air Force and Dominions Air Forces Missing Research and Enquiry Service, 1944–1949

Air Headquarters Royal Air Force Netherlands East Indies Review 1946 January-September issues

Air Publication 1921 'Notes on Casualty Procedure in War', 1941

R012515 The Runnymede Memorial to Airmen who have no known grave, Imperial War Graves Commission 1953

Locations of units lists

Summary of Aircraft Recovered by the RNETHAF since 1960, Netherland Ministry of Defence 1986

Air Ministry Orders

Air Force Lists

S.D. 155 Secret Organisational Memoranda 1944–1950

Air Historical Branch:

Air Historical Branch, (1954) The Second World War 1939–1945 Royal Air Force Maintenance, Air Ministry, London

Air Ministry War Books

Air Historical Branch, (1945) The Expansion of the Royal Air Force 1934–1939, Air Ministry, London

Air Ministry Office Memorandum T154/46: Casualty Branch

Missing Research and Enquiry Service training notes

Report by Fg Off A. Green on No. 62 Graves Concentration Unit's mission into west and south-west China for the purpose of recovering British war dead

Imperial War Museum:
IWM 015248 Flt Lt Colin Mitchell
IWM 017729 Flt Lt Kelbrick
IWM 215 (3115) Flt Lt Colin Mitchell

Australian War Memorial
AWM MSS 689-691. Research for Missing Personnel in Korea, Sqdn Ldr E W New
and Sgt T S Henderson MBE, December 1950-January 1951

Published books:
Arnold, K, (2003) *Green Two: Sgt Dennis Noble*, Southern Counties Aviation
Publications, Eastbourne.
Bowden, B, (1999) *Black Hawk Down*, Corgi, London.
Chorley, W, (1992–2003) *Royal Air Force Bomber Command Losses of the Second
World War* (eight volumes), Midland Publishing, Hinckley
Eames, J, (1999) *The Searchers and their endless quest for lost aircrew in the Southwest
Pacific*, University of Queensland Press, Queensland
Eldridge, Maj. A, and Babbs, Padre, (1995) *First reconnaissance of the Burma-Siam
Railway*, James Hikton, Lytham
Falconer, J, (1995) *Stirling Wings: The Short Stirling goes to war*, Alan Sutton
Publishing, Stroud
Franks, N, (1985) *The Air Battle for Imphal*, William Kimber & Co. Limited, London
Franks, N, (1997–2000) *Royal Air Force Fighter Command Losses of the Second World
War* (three volumes), Midland Publishing, Hinckley
Fyfe, J, (1993) *The great ingratitude: Bomber Command in World War II*, G.C. Book
Publishers Gale & Polden, London
Gray, J, (2000) *Fire by night: The dramatic story of one pathfinder crew and Black
Thursday, 16/17 December 1943*, Grub Street, London
Hanson, N, (2005) *The Unknown Soldier: The story of the Missing of the Great War*,
Doubleday, London
Jackson, P, (2006) *Royal Air Force Uetersen: The story of an unusual station*, privately
published
Jackson, R, (1988) *The Berlin Airlift*, Patrick Stephens Limited, Wellingborough
Longworth, P, (1985) *The Unending Vigil*, Leo Cooper, London
Lyman, R, (2004) *Slim: Master of war*, Constable and Robinson, London
Marrett, G, (2003) *Cheating death: combat air rescues in Vietnam and Laos*, Leo
Cooper, London
McLachlan, I, (1994) *Night of the Intruders*, Patrick Stephens Limited, Welling-
borough
McNeill, R, (2003) *Royal Air Force Coastal Command losses of the Second World War
Vol 1: Aircraft and crew losses 1939–1941*, Midland Publishing, Hinkley
Middlebrook, M, and Everitt, C, (1985) *The Bomber Command war diaries: An
operational reference book 1939–1945*, Viking, London
Middlebrook, M, (1973) *The Nuremberg raid: 30–31 March 1944*, Allen Lane,
London
Middlebrook, M, (1980) *The Battle of Hamburg: Allied bomber forces against a German
city in 1943*, Allen Lane, London

Middlebrook, M, (1982) *The Peenemunde raid: The night of 17–18 August 1943*, Allen Lane, London

Middlebrook, M, (1988) *The Berlin Raids: RAF Bomber Command Winter 1943–44*, Viking, London

Moulson, T, (1964) *The Flying Sword: The story of 601 Squadron*, Macdonald, London.

Probert, Air Cdre H, (1995) *The Forgotten Air Force: The Royal Air Force in the war against Japan 1941–1945*, Brassey's (UK) Limited, London

Ramsey, W, (Ed.) (1982) *The Battle of Britain then and now*, Battle of Britain Prints International Limited, London

Ross, D, Blanche, B, and William, S, (2003) *'The Greatest Squadron of them all': The definitive history of 603 (Cit of Edinburgh) Squadron, RAUXAF. Volume One: Formation to the end of 1940*, Grub Street, London.

Runcie, R, (1988) *The God of Battles and the Fight for Faith* Gallipoli Memorial Lecture, Gallipoli Association

Ryle, P, (1979) *Missing in action: May-September 1944*, W. H. Allen, London

Sarker, D, (1998) *Missing in Action: Resting in Peace?*, Ramrod Publications, Worcester.

Swift, E, (2003) *Where they lay: The search for those who fell in battle and were left behind*, Bantam Books, London

Webster, Sir C, and Franklin, N, (1961) *The strategic air offensive against Germany 1939–45* (four volumes), HMSO, London

Published periodicals:

Airforce News, RAAF, June 2001.

Anon, *The Lady Be Good*, After the Battle No. 25.

Greenslade, A, *Known to God, unknown to man*, After the Battle No. 62.

Hansard The Commons Debates 1942, 1945 & 1946

Palestine Post, 1 August 1947

RAF Review February 1950

Rollings, *Dulag Luft*, After the Battle 106, 1999.

Saint-Vincent, Flt Lt R, *Missing in Action*, Airforce magazine, Fall 2005.

The People, 28 November 1948

Wood and Stanley, *Recovery and identification of World War II dead: American Graves Registration activities in Europe*, Journal of Forensic Sciences 34 (6)

Notes

Introduction

1. RAFM B3613 The biggest detective job in the world.
2. Webster and Frankland *Strategic air offensive* Volume IV Appendix 41.

Chapter One

3. Royal Air Force Museum (RAFM) RAFM X003-8818/005 Lieutenant Aubrey Matthews, 22 April 1917.
4. First coined by Arthur Mee in his King's England series of books in the 1930s. He states the number as thirty-two, but some estimates are a little higher.
5. AIR2/9910 Missing Research activities Oct–Dec 1950.
6. AWM MSS 689-691 Research for Missing Personnel in Korea, Squadron Ldr E. W. New and Sgt T. S. Henderson MBE, December 1950 – January 1951.
7. Palestine Post, 1 August 1947.
8. Marrett *Cheating death*.
9. Bowden *Black Hawk Down*.

Chapter Two

10. The most complete, if a little incoherent, account of this rise in interest and legal/ethical wrangling, is in: Sarker *Missing in Action: Resting in Peace?*
11. Sarker *Missing in action*, p. 86.
12. Air Historical Branch Expansion, p. 36.
13. Expansion Progress Meeting 137, 27 September 1938, pp. 9–10. Quoted in AHB Expansion, p. 65.
14. Air Historical Branch Maintenance, pp. 25–26.
15. AHB Maintenance, p. 11.
16. AIR29/1008 49 MU Operations Record Book.
17. Arnold *Green Two*.
18. Moulson *The Flying Sword*.
19. Ross, Blanche, & William *The Greatest Squadron of them all*, p. 214.
20. Sarker. *Missing in Action*, p. 18.
21. AHB Maintenance, p. 399.
22. AHB Maintenance, pp. 49–50.

23. AHB Maintenance, p. 73.
24. AHB Maintenance, p. 412.
25. AHB Maintenance, p. 94.
26. AHB Maintenance, 94.
27. Air Publication 1922 Notes on casualty procedure in war, 1941.
28. McLachlan *Night of the Intruders*, p. 181.
29. Information supplied by Commonwealth War Graves Commission.

Chapter Three

30. AHB Air Ministry War Book.
31. RAFM AC92/1/9 Part 1 Paragraphs 1–6.
32. Ryle *Missing in action*, p. 25.
33. Ryle *Missing in action*, p. 166.
34. AIR2/6476. Minute Sheet, Minute 55, 29 June 1943.
35. RAFM X003-9274.
36. RAFM X003-9274.
37. RAFM AC1997/45/13.
38. RAFM AC1997/45/14.
39. RAFM AC1997/45/15.
40. AIR2/6476. Referred to in Minute 2, 9 September 1942.
41. Hansard. House of Commons, 11 September 1942.
42. RAFM AC1997/45/12.
43. RAFM AC1997/45/14.
44. RAFM AC1997/45/23.
45. RAFM X001-3527.
46. RAFM B3613.
47. The People, 28 November 1948.
48. At that time Doctor to the Royal Household, and a major influence on the founding of the National Health Service.
49. RAFM AC92/1/9. Hawkins Report, Section VI Case 11.
50. X004-2378 LACW Iris Walter.
51. X004-2379 LACW Lillian Taylor.
52. X004-2378 LACW Iris Catlin.
53. X004-2379 LACW Lillian Taylor.

Chapter Four

54. AIR2/6330 Minute Sheet, Minute 1, 31 October 1941.
55. AIR2/6330 Minute Sheet, Minute 2, 1 November 1941.
56. AIR2/6330 Minute Sheet, Minute 3, 3 November 1941.
57. AIR2/6330 Minute Sheet, Minute 4, 17 November 1941.
58. AIR2/6330 Minute Sheet, Minute 5, 18 November 1941.
59. AIR2/6330 Minute Sheet, Minutes 6–9, 19 November 1941 – 23 December 1941.
60. AIR2/6330 Minute Sheet, Minute 15, 3 September 1942.
61. AIR2/6330 Minute Sheet, Minutes 30 and 34, 1 April 1944 and 9 October 1944.

62. AIR2/6476 Loose minute from Burges 10/5/45.
63. AIR2/6330/10d.
64. AIR2/6330/10a.
65. AIR2/6330/10b.
66. AIR2/6330. Report No. 2, Case I.
67. AIR2/6330/24a. Case VII.
68. AIR2/6469/5a.
69. AIR2/6469/4a.
70. AIR2/6469/3a.
71. AIR2/6469/8a. 9 September 1942.
72. AIR2/6330. Report No. 2, Case II.
73. AIR2/6330/29a. Case I.
74. AIR2/6330/33a. Case I.
75. AIR2/6330/29a. Case V.
76. RAFM AC92/1/9 Section 1 paragraph 9.
77. AIR2/6330/33a. Case V.
78. AIR2/6330. Report No. 2, Case III.
79. AIR2/6330. Report No. 2, Case IV.
80. AIR2/6330/33a. Case II.
81. AIR2/6330. Report No. 2, Case V.
82. AIR2/6330/24a. Case III.
83. AIR2/6469/39a. Sinkinson to HQ RAF ME, 2 Feb 1943.
84. AIR2/6330/33a. Case VI.
85. AIR2/6330. Report No. 2, Case VI.
86. RAFM X004-1415.
87. RAFM AC92/1/9 Part 2 Section B.
88. See OBE citation, AIR2/9816.
89. RAFM AC92/1/9 Part 2 Section B.
90. RAFM AC92/1/9 Part 2 Section B.
91. AIR2/9816.
92. RAFM AC92/1/9 Part 2 Section B.

Chapter Five

93. AIR20/9050/8.
94. AIR20/9050/3.
95. RAFM AC92/1/9.
96. Quite simply, through the last year of the war the RAF training schools around the world turned out more trained aircrew than the RAF could employ in their active squadrons.
97. AIR20/9050/4.
98. AIR20/9050/7.
99. AIR20/9050/8.
100. RAFM AC92/9/1.
101. RAFM AC92/9/1.
102. RAFM AC92/9/1.
103. RAFM AC92/9/1.

104. RAFM SD155/1945/2055 and SD155/1947/575.

105. RAFM SD155/1947/518.

106. AIR20/9050.

107. AIR20/9050/42a Case VI.

108. AIR 20/9050/42a Case VII.

109. Rollings 'Dulag Luft'.

110. AIR20/9050/38a Case VI.

111. AIR20/9050/38a Case VII.

112. AIR20/9050/39a Case VIII.

Chapter Six

113. Personal correspondence with Sqdn Ldr Lott.

114. RAFM X004-2336/007.

115. RAFM X004-2337.

116. IWM Misc 215 (3115).

117. RAFM X004-1438.

118. RAFM X004-2335.

119. RAFM X002-9296/001.

120. IWM 15248 Reel 2.

121. RAFM X004-1438.

122. AIR20/9050.

123. MRES training notes from Air Historical Branch.

124. AIR29/1598 October 1946.

125. RAFM X004-2347 Cpl Douglas Hague.

126. AIR9/9050/27 1 August 1946. Air Marshal Sir Philip Wiggleswade to Air Member for Personnel.

127. Hansard *The Commons Debates*. 14 November 1945, 20 February 1946, 20 March 1946, 24 July 1946, 2 August 1946.

128. AIR9/9050/26.

129. SD155/1947/846.

130. SD155/1947/1042.

131. AIR2/9050/42. Memo, 21 July 1947.

132. AIR2/9050 Note from ACM Sir John Slessor, 28 June 1947.

133. AIR2/9050 Letter to ACM Sir John Slessor from HQ RCAF 7 February 1947.

134. In conversation with Sqdn Ldr Thompson.

135. In correspondence with Sqdn Ldr Lott.

136. IWM 015248 Reel 4: Flt Lt Colin Mitchell.

137. RAFM X004-2347 Cpl Douglas Hague.

138. Missing Research Memorandum (MRM) 12 19 November 1945.

139. X004-2400 Jacob case.

140. See Myhill, Mitchell, etc.

141. AIR2/10199.

142. RAFM X004-2400 Pirie file.

143. RAM X004-2400.

144. MRM 10a 14th March 1946 and MRM 25.

145. MRM 1 20 July 1945.

146. MRM 25.
147. MRES Standing Orders paragraph 5.
148. IWM 015248 Reel 4: Flt Lt Colin Mitchell.
149. In correspondence with Flt Lt R. St. Vincent.
150. Flt Lt R. St. Vincent in *Missing in Action*, p. 26.
151. Flt Lt R. St. Vincent in *Missing in Action*, p. 27.
152. Jackson, P (2006) 'Royal Air Force Uetersen', p. 81.
153. Wood and Stanley 'Recovery and identification of World War II dead'.
154. RAFM DC74/39/13, case X734.
155. RAFM DC74/39/13, case G878.
156. RAFM X002-9269/009 Flt Lt Harry Wilson.
157. RAFM AC92/1/9 Section 5 Case 6.
158. For example, see RAFM DC74/39/4 G.7.
159. Flt Lt R. St. Vincent in 'Missing in Action', p. 28.
160. Flt Lt R. St. Vincent in 'Missing in Action', p. 28.

Chapter Seven

161. RAFM DC74/39/3 N.3.
162. RAFM AC92/1/9 Part 6 Case 3.
163. RAFM X004-2400 Archer Collection.
164. RAFM X004-2400 Archer Collection.
165. RAFM X004-2400 Archer Collection, Coolbrandt file.
166. RAFM-2400 Archer Collection, Marchal and Porchon file.
167. RAFM X004-2400 Archer Collection.
168. SD155/1947/846.
169. RAFM X004-2400 Archer Collection, Ruber and Ball file.
170. RAFM X004-2400 Archer Collection, XF 1753 file.
171. RAFM X004-2400 Archer Collection, Healy file.
172. RAFM X004-2400 Archer Collection, Priestley file.
173. RAFM X004-2400 Archer Collection, Mouchotte file.
174. RAFM X004-2400 Archer Collection, letter from Group Captain H. Southey, OC RAF Delegation, Belgium, 29 October 1948.
175. RAFM X004-2337 Wg Cdr Moorcroft.
176. RAFM AC92/1/9 Part 6 Case 10.
177. RAFM X004-2337 Wg Cdr Moorcroft.
178. RAFM X004-2337 Wg Cdr Moorcroft.
179. Flt Lt R Saint-Vincent, *Missing in Action*.
180. Flt Lt R Saint-Vincent, *Missing in Action*.
181. Flt Lt R Saint-Vincent, *Missing in Action*.
182. Flt Lt R Saint-Vincent, *Missing in Action*.
183. Falconer *Stirling Wings*, Chapter Fourteen.
184. Obituary, Daily Telegraph, 15 February 2002.
185. RAFM DC74/39/10 The Formation and Activities of Missing Research and Enquiry Service In Norway.
186. RAFM DC74/39/3 N.1.
187. RAFM DC74/39/3 N.3.

188. RAFM DC74/39/3 N.2, and Chorley *Bomber Command Losses*, Vol. 3, p. 63.
189. RAFM DC74/39/3 N.1.
190. *Ost Preussen heimatlos*: East Prussian and homeless; presumably a reference to the Russian occupation of that area.
191. RAFM B3294 Short Summary of Operations Polesearch Northern Norway 1946.

Chapter Eight

192. AIR55/70/56.
193. MRM 4, 9 August 1945.
194. AIR55/80/ 9a: Report on visit to HQ RAF MED/ME Cairo on staff matters, by Wg Cdr V. G. H. Gee, December 1945.
195. AIR55/80/10a.
196. MRM 4a, 5 March 194.
197. Appendix to MRM 4a.
198. AIR55/80/11a.
199. AIR2/7088/113. May 1948. As no concluding evidence can be found, these men were most likely Americans.
200. AIR55/66/7a.
201. AIR 55/66/70.
202. AIR55/72/28.
203. AIR55/70/9a.
204. AIR55/70/23a.
205. AIR55/70/12a.
206. AIR55/70/40.
207. AIR55/70/36.
208. AIR55/70/4b.
209. AIR55/72/237.
210. AIR55/79/2a.
211. AIR55/79/1a.
212. AIR55/67/3.
213. AIR55/69/43.
214. AIR55/79/1a.
215. AIR55/79/3a.
216. AIR55/66/34.
217. Airgraphs are types of letters that saved on transport space. Photographs were taken of letters and the negatives were sent to the relevant overseas HQ. Here they were developed and sent to the addressee. Negatives were much smaller and easier to transport than letters.
218. AIR2/6330 Part IX.
219. AIR55/67/2.
220. AIR55/69/43.
221. AIR55/67/2.
222. AIR55/67/2.
223. AIR55/75/9.
224. AIR55/67/2.

225. AIR55/67/2.
226. AIR55/67/2.
227. AIR55/67/2.
228. AIR55/75/8 & 20.
229. See Location of Units, RAFM.
230. AIR55/66/69.
231. AIR55/70/36.
232. AIR55/70/55.
233. AIR55/70/55.
234. AIR55/70/56.
235. AIR55/70/71.
236. AIR55/70/72.
237. AIR55/70/47.
238. AIR55/70/47.
239. AIR55/70/72.
240. AIR55/70/82.
241. AIR55/70/72.
242. AIR55/70/104.
243. AIR55/70/121a.
244. AIR55/72/259.
245. AIR55/66/69.
246. AIR55/72/259.
247. Information from CWGC.
248. AIR55/66/69.
249. AIR55/66/69.
250. AIR20/9050 12 July 1948 'No. 5 MREU – Disbandment'.
251. RAF Review February 1950, p. 10.
252. AIR55/72/371.
253. AIR55/72/372.
254. AIR55/72/239.
255. AIR55/69/15a, /66a, /83 & /89.
256. AIR55/69/66a.
257. AIR55/69/81 & /102.
258. AIR55/69/66a.
259. AIR55/69/43.
260. AIR55/73/68.
261. AIR55/74/48.
262. AIR55/73/96.
263. AIR55/74/48.
264. AIR55/74/48.
265. AIR55/74/48.
266. AIR55/73/96.
267. AIR55/74/43.
268. AIR55/74/43.
269. AIR55/74/43.
270. AIR55/74/43.
271. AIR55/66/63.
272. AIR55/74/48.

273. SD155/1948/564.
274. AIR20/9050 12 July 1948 'No. 5 MREU – Disbandment'.

Chapter Nine

275. RAFM B3295.
276. RAFM DC74/39/13 cases G.1713, G.316 and X.729.
277. RAFM DC74/39/13 case G.698.
278. Private correspondence with Sqdn Ldr W. Lott.
279. RAFM DC74/39/4 G.3-5.
280. RAFM AC92/1/9 Part 6 Case 4.
281. RAFM X004-2335 Flt Lt Myhill.
282. IWM 215 (3115) Flt Lt Colin Mitchell.
283. IWM 015248 Reel 4 Flt Lt Colin Mitchell.
284. Middlebrook *Bomber Command War Diaries*, pp. 601–602.
285. IWM 215 (3115) Flt Lt Colin Mitchell, case G.221.
286. IWM 017729 Reel 5 Flt Lt Kelbrick.
287. RAFM X004-2337 Wg Cdr Moorcroft.
288. RAFM X004-2347 Cpl Douglas Hague.
289. IWM 215 (3115) Flt Lt Colin Mitchell.
290. IWM 015248 Flt Lt Colin Mitchell.
291. Private correspondence with Sqdn Ldr W. Lott.
292. Private correspondence with Sqdn Ldr W. Lott.
293. AIR55/59/34.
294. Jackson *Berlin Airlift*, p. 24.
295. RAFM X002-9269 Flt Lt Harry Wilson.
296. RAFM X004-2335 Flt Lt Ron Myhill.
297. RAFM X004-2335 Flt Lt Ron Myhill.
298. From BBC People's War website.
299. RAFM X002-9269 Flt Lt Harry Wilson.
300. RAFM X004-2335 Flt Lt Ron Myhill.
301. AIR29/1598.
302. AIR29/1598.
303. RAFM X002-9269 Flt Lt Harry Wilson.
304. RAFM B3294.
305. RAFM AC92/9/1.
306. AIR20/9050 AMPL 936.
307. RAFM B3294.
308. RAFM DC74/39/14.
309. RAFM X004-2433 Sqdn Ldr Bill Lott.
310. RAFM X004-2433 Sqdn Ldr Bill Lott.
311. AIR2/6330/42a.

Chapter Ten

312. AIR2/10199/72c/59 Appendix 3: No. 3 RAF Search Team.
313. Eames *Searchers*, p. 64 & 82.
314. Eldridge and Babbs *First reconnaissance*, p. 5.

315. Private correspondence with Matt Poole.
316. See Eldridge and Babbs *First reconnaissance*.
317. AIR2/10199/23a Tracing of Missing Personnel – unlocated prisoners of war etc 27 November 1945.
318. AIR2/10199/23a and AIR2/10199 Enc 26b Missing Research Memoranda: Search organisation – South East Asia 18 January 1946.
319. RAFM X004-2334 Sgt David Harrap.
320. AIR2/10199/72b Report of Missing Research under AHQ Burma January 1946 – May 1947.
321. AIR2/10199/72c/59 Appendix 3: No. 3 RAF Search Team.
322. AIR2/10199/72c/58 Appendix 2: No. 2 RAF Search Team.
323. Lyman *Slim*, p. 142.
324. AIR2/10199/72c/58 Appendix 2: No. 2 RAF Search Team.
325. AIR2/10199/72b/52.
326. RAFM X004-2350.
327. RAFM X004-2350.
328. AIR2/10199/72b/50.
329. AIR2/10199/72b/51.
330. Lyman 'Slim', p.142.
331. AIR2/10199/72b/51 & 52.
332. AIR2/10199/72b/52.
333. AIR2/10199/59a/90 Search team expenses – Policy 31 December 1946.
334. RAFM X004-2334.
335. AIR2/10199/72b/53.
336. RAFM X004-2334 Sgt David Harrap.
337. RAFM X004-2334 Sgt David Harrap.
338. RAFM X004-2334 Sgt David Harrap.
339. RAFM X004-2334 Sgt David Harrap.
340. Sgt David Harrap, via correspondence with Matt Poole.
341. RAFM X004-2334 Sgt David Harrap.
342. RAFM X004-2334 Sgt David Harrap.
343. RAFM X004-2334 Sgt David Harrap.
344. RAFM X004-2334 Sgt David Harrap.
345. RAFM X004-2334 Sgt David Harrap.
346. AIR2/10199/72c/60-61 Appendix 4: No. 5 RAF Search Team.
347. AIR2/10199/70a/66 Search Teams Progress Report 8 April 1947.
348. AIR2/10199/72c/62 Appendix 5: No. 6 RAF Search Team.
349. Franks *Air battle of Imphal*, pp. 31–32.
350. AIR2/10199/72c/62 Appendix 6: No. 7 RAF Search Team.
351. Sgt David Harrap, via correspondence with Matt Poole.
352. AIR2/10199/94a/22 1 January 1948.
353. AIR2/10199/76a Flt Lt Stares (for ACinC ACFE) to USoS 26 June 1947.
354. Eames *Searchers* Chapter 8.
355. RAFM Air Headquarters Royal Air Force Netherlands East Indies Review 1946 January-September issues.
356. AIR2/10199/78a/40 Missing Research in Malaya 14 July 1947.
357. AIR24/1758 Air Command Far East Monthly Intelligence Summary, January 1948, quoted in Probert *The Forgotten Air Force*, p. 300.

358. Figures quoted by Probert *Forgotten Air Force*, p. 300.
359. Eames *Searchers*, p. 86.
360. Eames *Searchers*, p. 77.
361. Eames *Searchers*, p. 123.

Chapter Eleven

362. AIR2/10345/85a.
363. AIR55/54 HQ GRU Directorate WE, 10 March 1947 Point 4.
364. Longworth. *Unending vigil*, p 189.
365. Longworth. *Unending vigil*, Ch 8.
366. AIR2/10345 RAF Graves Service report, 30 January 1950.
367. AIR55/57/10.
368. AIR2/10345/18a Minutes of meeting held at RAF Graves Service Rheinberg on 13 October 1949.
369. AIR2/10345/49a 3 MRGS RAF Graves Service, Rheinberg.
370. AIR2/10345 Report on Royal Air Force Graves Service Rheinberg.
371. AIR2/10345/82 Royal Air Force Graves Service.
372. AIR2/10345/87a Leave.
373. AIR2/10345/85a Royal Air Force Graves Service.
374. RAFM X004-2400 Archer Collection.
375. AIR2/10346/171a RAF Graves Service – Final Report.
376. AIR2/10346/171a RAF Graves Service – Final Report Appendix A.
377. AIR2/9050.
378. AIR2/10148/157 IWGC to S.14 (Cas) 14 February 1952.
379. AIR2/7056 Minute sheet.
380. AIR2/10148/118.
381. AIR2/10346/171a RAF Graves Service – Final Report.
382. AIR2/10148/126a Berlin Detachment Monthly Report May 1951.
383. AIR2/10148/131a Berlin Detachment Monthly Report July 1951.
384. AIR2/10148/155a.
385. AIR2/10148/157 IWGC to S.14 (Cas) 14 February 1952 and AIR2/10148/155a.

Chapter Twelve

386. Summary of Aircraft Recovered by the RNETHAF since 1960, Netherland Ministry of Defence 1986.
387. Eames *Searchers*, Ch 12.
388. Eames *Searchers*, Ch 15.
389. Eames *Searchers*, pp. 211–212.
390. Airforce News, RAAF, June 2001.
391. Australian Ministry of Defence.
392. Greenslade *Known to God, unknown to man*.
393. *The Lady Be Good*, After the Battle.
394. Swift *Where they lay*.
395. AIR6/75.

396. AIR6/75.
397. AIR6/77.
398. RAFM R012515 *The Runnymede Memorial*.
399. Runcie *The God of Battles and the Fight for Faith*, p. 4.
400. Runcie *The God of Battles and the Fight for Faith*, p. 12.

Appendix A

401. AIR20/9050/7.
402. AIR20/9050/8.
403. AIR20/9050/26. Air Minister for Personnel to Under Secretary of State for Air, 1 August 1946.
404. AIR20/9050/4. Air Minister for Personnel MRES sub-committee 2 August 1945.
405. Polish, Czech, French, Norwegian, Belgian, etc.
406. AIR 2/9602. P.4 (Cas) report: Far East, 20 February 1946.
407. AIR20/9050. Letter Sqdn Ldr Sinkinson to Air Minister for Personnel, 2 October 1947.
408. AIR20/9050. Report on the MRES in North-West Europe, February 1948.
409. AIR2/9910. Missing Research activities Oct-Dec 1950 report, by S.14 (Cas), 3 January 1951.
410. AIR2/9910 Missing Research activities Oct-Dec 1950 report, by S.14 (Cas), 3 January 1951.

Appendix B

411. AC9/29/1, Pt. III.

Appendix C

412. AIR2/2000. Proposed reorganisation of S.7.
413. RAFM AC92/1/9 Part 1 Paragraphs 1–6.
414. Unless otherwise stated, details are drawn from Air Publication 1921 *Notes on Casualty Procedure in War*, 1941.
415. AP 1921. Section II paragraph 15.
416. AIR2/6476. Minute Sheet. Minute 23, 11 December 1942.
417. AIR2/6476. Referred to in Minute 2, 9 September 1942.
418. Hansard. House of Commons, 11 September 1942.
419. AIR2/9602. Minute Sheet. Minute 5, 30 September 1942.
420. AIR2/6476. Minute Sheet. Minutes 7 (17 September 1942) and 10 (26 September 1942).
421. AIR2/6476. Minute Sheet, Minute 20.
422. AIR2/6476. Minute Sheet, Minute 22.
423. AIR2/6476. Minute Sheet, Minutes 23–30, 5 March – 2 April 1943.
424. AIR2/6476. Minute Sheet, Minute 55, 29 June 1943.
425. AIR2/6476. Minute Sheet. Minute 58, 7 July 1943.
426. Middlebrook & Everitt *Bomber Command War Diaries*, p. 644.

427. X004-2378 LACW Iris Walter.

428. AIR2/6476. Minute Sheet, Minute 78, 4 May 1944.

429. AIR2/6476. Minute Sheet, Minute 81, 5 June 1944.

430. Air Ministry Office Memorandum T154/46: Casualty Branch.

Appendix E

431. Missing Research Memorandum No. 5: War Crimes, 6 August 1945.

432. AIR2/7088/31.

433. Fyfe *The great ingratitude*, pp. 350–351.

434. RAFM X004-2335 and X004-2336/006.

435. AIR2/7088/56.

436. AIR2/7088/61.

437. RAFM DC74/39/14 Report from Poland by Squadron Ldr E. C. Rideal.

Appendix F

438. RAFM DC74/39/3 & /4.

439. RAFM X004-2433.

440. RAFM X003-2433.

Index